THE PEOPLE
OF
WILSON COUNTY
TENNESSEE
1800 — 1899

By

Thomas E. Partlow

Southern Historical Press, Inc.
Greenville, South Carolina

Please Direct All Correspondence and Book Orders to:

Southern Historical Press, Inc.
PO Box 1267
375 West Broad Street
Greenville, S.C. 29602

ISBN # 0-89308-308-9

Printed in the United States of America

THIS BOOK

IS

RESPECTFULLY DEDICATED

TO MY GRANDPARENTS

Mitchell W. Johnson
Nora Dovie Ligon

and

William Allen Partlow
Rosa Lee Johns

PREFACE

This book offers a rare glimpse into the lives of those people who lived in Wilson County during the 1800's. It is often much easier to find the names of ancestors than it is to learn what they were like. Hopefully, this book does both.

Oftentimes, individuals prefer not to know the more human frailties of their ancestors. This book is not recommended for such people. There has been no attempt made to conceal the truth as revealed in the records.

The court records are found in the basement of the Wilson County Courthouse at Lebanon. They consist of books and pieces of books. Some are in such a bad state of repair that they are not available for daily use.

The other material is to be found in various places. For example, the church records and obituaries are in private hands. The newspaper articles are on microfilm at the Wilson County Public Library.

It is to be hoped that other such material will become available with the passage of time.

Thomas E. Partlow
March, 1982

CONCERNING THE FORMATION OF
TENNESSEE COUNTIES

The Carolinas were settled in the seventeenth century as a proprietary colony with a sea to sea charter. While Tennessee was the western part of what later came to be known as North Carolina, six counties were created. Washington (1777), the first to be created from the western areas of Burke and Wilkes counties (North Carolina), encompassed the entire area and was later to be named Tennessee. Washington enjoyed the distinction of being the only county until 1779 when Sullivan County was created. The remaining counties to be created while Tennessee was yet a part of North Carolina were: Greene (1783), Davidson (1783), Hawkins (1786), and Sumner (1786).

The Territory of the United States of America South of the River Ohio was organized in 1790, and while in this condition, four counties were created: Jefferson (1792), Knox (1792), Sevier (1794), and Blount (1795). A total of ten counties were in existence by the time Tennessee was admitted to the Union in 1796. Between the admission of Tennessee as the sixteenth state and the end of the century, eight more counties were added, making a total of 18 by 1800. Counties added during this early period of statehood were: Carter (1796), Grainger (1796), Montgomery (1796), Robertson (1796), Cocke (1797), Smith (1799), Williamson (1799), and Wilson (1799).

By the end of the first decade 20 new counties were created, making a total of 38 by 1810. This number was increased to 47 during the next decade. By 1830 there were 62 counties in Tennessee, which were supplemented with 10 additional counties by 1839, for a total of 72. Twelve additional counties were added before 1860, for a total of 84. The remaining counties were created in the decade of the 1870's when 12 additional counties were created, making a total of 96 counties, the maximum number. This number remained through 1919, when James County - created in 1871 - was dissolved and absorbed in January 1920 by Hamilton County.

TABLE OF CONTENTS

COURT RECORDS
    County Court Minutes 1802-1807......................1
    County Court Minutes 1809-1819.....................2
    County Court Judgments 1809-1819...................3-4
    County Court Minutes 1833-1836.....................5-10
    County Court Minutes 1836-1844.....................11
    County Court Minutes 1848-1852.....................12
    County Court Minutes 1852-1856.....................13
    County Court Minutes 1856-1858.....................14
    County Court Minutes 1859-1864.....................15
    County Court Minutes 1865-1867.....................16
    County Court Minutes 1867-1870.....................17-18
    County Court Minutes 1870-1872.....................19
    County Court Minutes 1872-1875.....................20
    Quarterly Court Minutes 1816-1819..................21-24
    Quarterly Court Minutes 1822-1824..................25-28
    Quarterly Court Minutes 1826-1828..................29-33
    Quarterly Court Minutes 1846-1848..................34-36
    Wills & Inventories 1866-1871......................37-60
    Wills & Inventories 1871-1878......................61-78

CHURCHES
    Church Deeds.......................................79-92
    Sugg's Creek Church Book...........................93-98
    Barton's Creek Baptist Church......................99
    Minutes Of Big Spring Church.......................100-104

LEBANON DEMOCRAT EXCERPTS...............................105-112

OATHS OF LOYALTY..113-121

OBITUARIES...122-125

NAME INDEX...126-158

COUNTY COURT MINUTES 1802-1807

Obediah Spradlin is fined $1.50 and costs for profane swearing. Recorded December Term 1803. (P. 2)

Nathaniel A. McNairy produced his license as an attorney. Recorded March Term 1804. (P. 26)

John Taylor charged Obediah Spradlin with assault and battery. Spradlin fined one cent and costs. Recorded March Term 1804. (P. 32)

John Herrod and Barnard Tatom indicted by the Grand Jury. Recorded March Term 1804. (P. 34)

Frederick Wilson indicted by the Grand Jury. Recorded March Term 1804. (P. 35)

James Carter indicted for assault and battery and also for trespassing. Recorded June Term 1804. (P. 40)

Burwell Perry indicted by the Grand Jury. Fined three dollars and costs. He is in the custody of the Sheriff. Recorded June Term 1804. (P. 45)

Jackson Brown charged Obediah Spradlin with assault and battery. Spradlin fined three dollars and costs. Recorded June Term 1804. (P. 49)

Zebulon Baird indicted on a certain matter of controversy. Bond set at one hundred dollars. Recorded September Term 1804. (P. 93)

Jackson Brown charged Obediah Spradlin with slander. Guilty. Recorded September Term 1804. (Pp. 95,107)

John Stamps charged Obediah Spradlin with assault and battery. Guilty. Damage to the defendant is set at twenty-five dollars. Recorded December Term 1804. (P. 104)

Thomas Clark charged Reuben Bradbury with assault and battery. Guilty. Recorded March Term 1805. (P. 114)

John Drennan indicted by the State. Guilty. Defendant is fined twenty-five cents and costs. Recorded September Term 1805. (P. 170)

Robert Hamilton indicted by the Grand Jury. He submitted himself to the mercy of the court. Recorded September Term 1805. (P. 171)

Martha Wilson, wife of Joseph Wilson, appointed to a joint guardianship with James Wilson for the purpose of securing the personal property of Joseph Wilson who is in a state of lunacy. Recorded September Term 1805. (P. 171)

Thomas Smith indicted by the State. Guilty. Recorded September Term 1806. (P. 260)

Elijah Ray indicted by the State. Not guilty. Recorded December Term 1806. (P. 271)

Thomas George found guilty of bastardy. Recorded March Term 1806. (P. 286)

1

John Bonner found guilty of assault and battery. Recorded June Term 1815. (P. 93)

James Shaw and wife indicted by the Grand Jury on a charge of assault and battery. Recorded June Term 1815. (P. 95)

COUNTY COURT JUDGMENTS 1809-1819

Be it remembered that on the fourth Monday in December 1808 Seth P. Pool was attached to answer David McMurry of a plea that he render to him $412 which to him he owed. So ordered. Recorded March Term 1809. (Pp. 1-3)

John Bonner found guilty of the charge of assault and battery against Seth P. Pool. Said defendant fined one cent. Recorded June Term 1815. (P. 93)

Humphrey Chapple entered a plea of guilty to the charge of assault and battery. He placed himself on the mercy of the court. Fined twenty dollars. Recorded June Term 1815. (Pp. 93-94)

Shadrack Gregg found not guilty of the charge made against him. Recorded June Term 1815. (Pp. 94-95)

James Shaw and wife found guilty of the charge of assault and battery. Fined fifty dollars and committed to jail until the same is paid. Recorded June Term 1815. (Pp. 95-96)

Isaac Hilliard and wife charged Wyatt Bettes with trespass. Guilty. Recorded June Term 1815. (P. 100)

Whereas Nancy Bass has charged Jane Crayton, a daughter of Richard Wammack, with having a bastard child and not being able to support the said charge, we do award and say that Dreddin Bass shall pay all costs in anywise relating to or concerning the said premises. Recorded 13 September 1815. (Pp. 101-102)

Dawson Hancock charged Humphrey Chapple with assault and battery. Recorded 7 September 1815. (P. 110)

William Halliman and wife charged James Shaw and wife with assault and battery. Fined five dollars. Recorded 7 September 1815. (P. 110)

William Edwards charged Samuel Alsup with trespass and false imprisonment. Plaintiff prayed that said suit be dismissed. Recorded 1815. (Pp. 111,127)

Humphrey Chapple charged John Smart with assault and battery. Recorded December Term 1815. (P. 143)

John Smart charged Humphrey Chapple with assault and battery. Recorded December Term 1815. (P. 143)

Armstead Lain found guilty of the charge made by James Henderson. Lain ordered to pay the plaintiff one cent. Recorded June Term 1816. (P. 145)

Adam Mires charged Thomas C. Davis with assault and battery. Case dismissed. Recorded June Term 1816. (P. 146)

Thomas J. Read and Gilbert G. Washington charged Baker Rather and wife, Sarah G. Rather, with failure to pay $61.75 for goods, wares, and merchandise which the said Sarah G. Rather purchased prior to their marriage. During the proceedings, the said Sarah G. Rather died.

3

Case then dismissed against said Baker Rather.   Recorded
June Term 1816.   (Pp. 147-149)

John Bonner charged Joseph Irby with giving him a
worthless note as payment for a flat bottom boat.   Plaintiff awarded $107.25 in damages.   Recorded May Term 1819.
(Pp. 197-201)

Adam Cowger indicted for an affray. Recorded March Term 1833. (P. 13)

Jacob Harpole indicted by the Grand Jury. He entered a plea of guilty and threw himself on the mercy of the court. Recorded 25 December 1833. (P. 19)

Parks Goodall indicted for an affray. Recorded 25 December 1833. (P. 19)

The Grand Jury brought in bills of indictment against Henry H. Morris for trading with a negro, Pryor Crittenden for assault and battery, and against John Nickens and Archibald Nickens for an affray. Dawson Hancock, foreman. Recorded 25 December 1833. (P. 20)

William W. Ferrell found not guilty of the charge of affraying. Recorded 25 December 1833. (Pp. 20,22)

John Pryor indicted for assault and battery. Recorded 26 December 1833. (P. 22)

Larkin Allen indicted for an affray. Recorded 26 December 1833. (P. 23)

Robert Williams entered a plea of guilty to the charge of gaming. He threw himself on the mercy of the court. Recorded 26 December 1833. (P. 23)

Thomas Brown found guilty of gaming. Recorded 26 December 1833. (P. 23)

William Harrington indicted on a charge of affraying. Recorded 26 December 1833. (P. 23)

Levi Lancaster found guilty of affraying. Recorded 26 December 1833. (P. 24)

David Martin entered a plea of guilty to affraying. He threw himself on the mercy of the court. Recorded 26 December 1833. (P. 24)

Allison Woollard indicted for an affray. Allen Jones served as security. Recorded 26 December 1836. (P. 25)

William Hodge, Jonathan Eatherly, William B. Vivrett, John B. Vivrett, Jeremiah Williams, Thomas P. Hill, Jesse Cook, Benjamin Tarver, John R. Eatherly, and Elijah Williams indicted by the Grand Jury. Recorded 27 December 1833. (Pp. 28-30)

John B. Puckett indicted for assault and battery. Recorded 27 December 1833. (P. 31)

William Tomblin found guilty of assault and battery. Recorded 28 December 1833. (P. 33)

Rebecca Medlin charged with bastardy. She refused to name the father of her bastard child. Recorded 24 March 1834. (P. 61)

COUNTY COURT MINUTES 1833-1836

Jane Brashears charged with "nuisance." Recorded 26 March 1834. (P. 72)

State of Tennessee vs. George D. Cummings. False imprisonment. Case continued. Recorded 26 March 1834. (P. 72)

Thomas K. Palmer indicted on a charge of gaming. Recorded 26 March 1834. (P. 72)

George Lash indicted on a charge of gaming. Recorded 26 March 1834. (P. 73)

Braxton Hill indicted on the charge of assault and battery. Recorded 26 March 1834. (P. 74)

William Spradley indicted on a charge of assault and battery. Recorded 26 March 1834. (P. 75)

James R. Johnson indicted on a charge of affraying. Recorded 26 March 1834. (P. 75)

A bill of indictment for usury was brought into court by the Grand Jury against Jonathan Shores, and assault and battery against Andrew Nickens. Recorded 26 March 1834. (P. 78)

Giles H. Glenn indicted for an affray. Recorded 28 March 1834. (P. 85)

Philip Shores and John Mooney indicted for affraying. Recorded 24 June 1834. (Pp. 107-108)

Newbern P. Stone charged by Martha Estes of having begotten upon her body a bastard child of which she has been delivered. Found guilty. Recorded 24 June 1834. (P. 107)

The Grand Jury indicted Arnold Burke for assault and battery, and Nelson Alsup and Jonas Brown for affraying. Recorded 25 June 1834. (P. 109)

James Ozment charged with bastardy by Nancy Bell. The charge has been adjusted between the two. Recorded 25 June 1834. (P. 110)

Reuben Johnson charged with gaming. Recorded 26 June 1834. (P. 118)

Grant Allen came into court and made statement of the ages, heirs, and children of John Brevard, Sr., late of Smith County, as taken from the family register of said John Brevard, Sr. The children are:
Jane M. Brevard (daughter) was born 25 January 1789.
Cyrus W. Brevard (son) was born 11 October 1792.
Alfred A. Brevard (son) was born 10 January 1796.
Clarissa H. Brevard (daughter) was born 26 February 1798.
Cynthia D. Brevard (daughter) was born 4 September 1800.
Hannah L. Brevard (daughter) was born 29 October 1802.
John C. Brevard (son) was born 9 June 1805.
Nancy Brevard (daughter) was born 17 September 1808.

Polly Brevard, another daughter, married Benjamin Benton. She is now dead, but left four sons viz. Lewis, Hugh, Jackson, and Franklin Benton.

William Brevard and Hugh Brevard are also dead. They were without issue.

William L. Alexander, about 59 years of age, made oath that he lived but a few miles from the said John Brevard, Sr. before his death. He has heard his father, William Alexander, who was also in the Service in the Revolution, and several old men say that the said John Brevard was a Lieutenant in the Regular Army during the Revolutionary War. Recorded 26 June 1834. (Pp. 119-120)

The Grand Jury brought into court a bill of indictment against John C. Tippitt, Samuel Brown, Thomas Brown, and Alfred Woollard marked with the name William Goodall, prosecutor for an affray. Endorsed a true bill. Recorded 23 September 1834. (P. 133)

Rial C. Jennings swore that he is not the father of Mary Johnson's bastard child. Jennings to stand trial. Recorded 24 September 1834. (P. 140)

Robert Rogers, Gabriel Beasley, and James Partin all charged with an affray. Recorded 24 September 1834. (P. 142)

Elizabeth McHenry, widow of Jesse McHenry deceased; William J. Goodwin and his wife, Mary; John McHenry; and Joseph B. Wynn, the guardian for the minor heirs state that Jesse McHenry died intestate in 1833. Recorded 24 September 1834. (P. 144)

James McAdow found guilty of the indictment made against him. Recorded 24 December 1834. (P. 167)

Alfred Woollard and Thomas Harris indicted for an affray. Recorded 24 December 1834. (P. 168)

John Jones and John O'Bryan indicted on a gaming charge. Recorded 24 December 1834. (P. 168)

Rufus L. Watson charged with assault and battery. Recorded 24 December 1834. (P. 168)

Reuben Johnson and James R. Johnson indicted for gaming. Recorded 24 December 1834. (P. 168)

James H. Johnson indicted on a charge of tipling. Henry F. Johnson was his security. (P. 169)

Edward P. Falconer, Peter Reson, James G. Roulston, Samuel Brown, William Sypert, and Robert C. Davis all indicted by the Grand Jury for tipling. Recorded 24 December 1834. (P. 169)

Berry Price charged with an affray. Recorded 24 December 1834. (P. 171)

William Carter found guilty of being the father of

Elizabeth Lyon's bastard child. Recorded 24 December 1834. (P. 172)

William H. Maxwell and Nelson Hancock indicted for assault and battery. Recorded 24 March 1835. (P. 191)

Robert Hughs charged with an affray. Recorded 26 March 1835. (P. 204)

Josiah Archer charged with gaming. Recorded 24 June 1835. (P. 233)

Newbern P. Stone charged with an affray. Recorded 24 June 1835. (P. 234)

William Tumblin and Jeremiah Johnson charged with gaming. Recorded 24 June 1835. (P. 235)

A. M. Leatherwood, William Johnson, Reuben Johnson, Etheldred Brantley, Whitehead Woodliff were all charged by the Grand Jury with gaming. Recorded 24 June 1835. (P. 236)

Levi Lancaster, Robert Fullerton, and Samuel Rigan charged with gaming. Recorded 24 June 1835. (P. 237)

Nelson Hancock entered a plea of guilty to the charge of assault and battery. He threw himself on the mercy of the court. Recorded 24 June 1835. (P. 237)

John Muirhead and Robert M. Burton charged with an affray. Recorded 24 June 1835. (P. 238)

Caleb Howell charged by the Grand Jury with malicious mischief. Recorded 24 June 1835. (P. 238)

Joseph S. Gibson found guilty of the charge of being the father of Elizabeth Lain's bastard child. Recorded 25 June 1835. (P. 241)

Alfred Walker found guilty of being the father of Elizabeth West's bastard child. Recorded 25 June 1835. (P. 242)

The Grand Jury returned indictments against William M. Maxwell for assault and battery; Benjamin B. Cooper for tipling; and John Hudson for an affray. Recorded 25 June 1835. (P. 243)

The Grand Jury returned indictments against John Jones for assault and battery; Woodford Organ for assaulting a constable; and William H. Peace and Seth Thornton for assault and battery. Recorded 29 September 1835. (P. 264)

James Epps and James Scott charged with assault and battery. Recorded 30 September 1835. (P. 276)

Charles Catherall charged with assault and battery. Recorded 30 September 1835. (P. 277)

The Grand Jury returned indictments for an affray against Wilson Hodge and assault and battery against

Calvin Spradley. Recorded 1 October 1835. (P. 278)

Bernard Richardson was charged with trespassing. A ten day notice to be given if in Tennessee. A fifteen day notice if in Alabama. Recorded 1 October 1835. (P. 278)

Robert H. Ricketts charged with assault and battery. Recorded 1 October 1835. (P. 281)

Micha Webb charged with keeping a bawdy house. Says that she is not guilty. Recorded 1 October 1835. (P. 281)

Mark Brinkley charged with gaming. Recorded 2 October 1835. (P. 284)

James Fuston charged with gaming. Recorded 2 October 1835. (P. 287)

William Steel vs. Samuel Johnson. Directed that testimony be taken from William Bradshaw and William Clendening in North Carolina. Recorded 3 October 1835. (P. 290)

Madison Organ charged with assault and battery. Recorded 3 October 1835. (P. 291)

Burrel G. Nettles and Dennis Hegarty charged with assault and battery. Recorded 3 October 1835. (Pp. 291-292)

Joseph Temples charged with assault and battery. Recorded 3 October 1835. (P. 294)

Henry Heath vs. William Campbell. Charged with trespassing. Recorded 31 December 1835. (P. 340)

David Rotramel charged Larry Vivrett with trespassing. Recorded 31 December 1835. (P. 340)

Alex Bligh charged with gaming. Recorded 31 December 1835. (P. 341)

Mayfield Johnson charged with assault and battery on the person of E. P. Falconer. Recorded 31 December 1835. (P. 343)

Robert Manning charged with an affray. Recorded 31 December 1835. (P. 349)

John Stewart charged with an affray. Recorded 1 January 1836. (P. 353)

David B. Smith charged with assault and battery. Recorded January 1836. (P. 354)

Jesse J. Finley applied for a certificate to practice law. Recorded January 1836. (P. 355)

John Perkins charged with assault and battery. Recorded 4 January 1836. (P. 358)

Patience Hunt fined $3.12½ for refusing to declare

the name of the father of her bastard child. Recorded
28 March 1836. (P. 379)

Malinda Parsons fined $3.12½ for refusing to declare the name of the father of her bastard child. Recorded January Term 1837. (P. 22)

Ann Warren fined $3.12½ for refusing to declare the name of the father of her bastard child. Recorded January Term 1837. (P. 22)

Martha Williamson fined $3.12½ for refusing to declare the name of the father of her bastard child. Sarah Williamson and William Williamson were her securities. Recorded January Term 1837. (P. 22)

Nancy Keeton fined $3.12½ for refusing to declare the name of the father of her bastard child. Carol Lewis and William W. Adams were her securities. Recorded January Term 1837. (P. 22)

Lindley Warren charged Pleasant Chumney with being the father of her bastard child. Recorded October Term 1837. (P. 79)

Sarah B. Cole paid her fine of $3.12½ and entered into bond to indemnify the county from her child becoming a county charge. Recorded 6 August 1838. (P. 137)

Crawford M. Craig found guilty of being the father of Partheny Mitchell's bastard child. He is in the custody of the Sheriff until security is given that the child will not become a county charge. Recorded February Term 1839. (P. 191)

James Sanford found guilty of being the father of the bastard child of Martha Martin. He is to pay the grandmother of said child (the mother now being dead) forty dollars for the first year. Recorded February Term 1839. (P. 191)

Mary Goodman fined $3.12½ for refusing to declare the name of the father of her bastard child. Recorded June Term 1839. (P. 219)

Gilla Smith fined $3.12½ for refusing to declare the name of the father of her bastard child. Recorded November Term 1840. (P. 356)

Matilda Craddock fined $3.12½ for refusing to declare the name of the father of her bastard child. Recorded January Term 1841. (P. 374)

It appearing to the satisfaction of the Court that Judgment had heretofore been entered against Wiley W. Bell as the security of Crawford M. Craig to appear before the County Court after said Craig was committed to the jail on a charge and conviction of bastardy. Recorded February Term 1841. (P. 375)

Elizabeth Thrower fined $3.12½ for refusing to declare the name of the father of her bastard child. Recorded 4 September 1848. (P. 6)

Martha Couch charged Robert Rogers with being the father of her bastard child. Papers were issued to the Sheriff of Dekalb County. Recorded 4 December 1848. (P. 29)

Wade Baker charged by Isabella Pride with being the father of her bastard child. He cannot be found in this county. Papers issued to the Sheriff of Davidson County. Recorded 4 March 1850. (Pp. 135,162)

Wade Baker charged by Isabella Rice with being the father of her bastard child. The mother of the said child has since died, and the child has been placed in the hands of Mrs. Nancy Boze, a sister of the mother. Said Wade Baker has made arrangements with the said Mrs. Boze to keep the child. Recorded 1 April 1850. (P. 178)

Elizabeth McNicol charged H. B. Mooningham with being the father of her bastard child. The defendant was found not guilty. Recorded 3 September 1850. (Pp. 230, 246)

Emily Baker charged John McNickols with being the father of her bastard child. Recorded September 1850. (P. 237)

James Shears came into open court and brought with him the body of James Harrison who was charged with bastardy. Recorded 2 September 1850. (P. 243)

John Williamson ordered taken into custody on a charge of bastardy. Recorded 7 October 1850. (P. 254)

Ira McFarland acquitted of the charge of stabbing Wilee Roland on 28 September 1854. Recorded 2 October 1854. (P. 336)

Amzi Bass found not guilty of being the father of Elizabeth Bass' bastard child. Recorded 5 May 1857. (P. 194)

Thomas W. Bodine petitioned for a jury to examine the sanity of mind of his sister, Nancy Bodine. Recorded 7 June 1858. (P. 351)

James A. Bridges denied the charge of bastardy made against him by Sarah Jane Wright. Case continued. Recorded March Term 1860. (P. 228)

William Thompson charged with bastardy. The defendant lives in Bedford County. Recorded 3 April 1860. (P. 271)

James A. Bridges found guilty of the charge of bastardy. The defendant will appeal. Recorded 3 July 1860. (P. 316)

William Thompson admitted that he is the father of the bastard child of Sarah A. Fisher. Recorded 4 June 1860. (P. 297)

Benjamin F. Shuston found guilty of the charge of bastardy. Recorded 2 October 1860. (P. 352)

William Corley found guilty of the charge of being the father of the bastard child of Nancy Jackson. Recorded 1 January 1862. (P. 542)

William H. Carter charged with bastardy. Case to be continued. Recorded 2 February 1863. (P. 591)

Defendant William Corley paid the sum of forty dollars for the support of the bastard child of which he is the reputed father. Nancy Ann Jackson, the mother of this child, has supported and taken care of it since its birth. Recorded 3 July 1866. (P. 325)

Defendant Ned Martin entered a plea of guilty to the charge of bastardy brought against him by Harriet Burros. Recorded 1867. (P. 130)

Richard Tippett entered a plea of guilty to the charge of having fathered the bastard child of Oragon Bass. The child was born 31 August 1867. Recorded 4 November 1867. (P. 149)

Beverly Willard denied being the father of Caldonia Settle's bastard child. There was no one present to prosecute him. Recorded 3 November 1867. (P. 151)

John Stuart failed to appear to answer charges by Susan Juniper that he fathered her bastard child. The child was born in 1867. Judgment by default entered against the said Stuart. Recorded 1868. (P. 151)

Frances P. Wammack acquited of the charge of bastardy brought against him by Martha Wammack. The prosecutor failed to appear in court. Recorded December Term 1867. (P. 167)

Upon application of Dicey Magness, the mother of the bastard child, the case against Henry Goodbar was dismissed. Recorded 5 January 1868. (P. 183)

Henry Myers entered a plea of guilty to the charge of having fathered the bastard child of Margaret Rucks. The child was born in 1867. Recorded January Term 1868. (P. 184)

Thomas Page entered a plea of guilty to the charge of having fathered the bastard child of Margaret Rucks. The child was born in 1867. Recorded January Term 1868. (P. 184)

Wesley Odum charged with having fathered the bastard child of which Lucinda Underwood gave birth on 23 August 1867. Recorded January Term 1868. (P. 184)

John Turner fined forty dollars for having fathered a bastard child. Jo Bass, the grandfather of the bastard child, has had the care and support of the said child since its birth. Recorded January 1868. (P. 197)

Polk Evans entered a plea of guilty to the charge of having fathered a bastard child. The child was born in 1868. Recorded 5 May 1868. (P. 251)

Jefferson Link found guilty of being the father of Unity Basket's bastard child. The child was born 24 April 1867. Recorded 1868. (P. 263)

Defendant Abraham Bedford (colored) found not guilty of having fathered the bastard child of Jane Hicksey Peace. Recorded 10 May 1869. (P. 444)

James Martin entered a plea of guilty to having fathered the bastard child of Sarah Smith (colored). Recorded 6 July 1869. (P. 461)

Lenny Carter jailed for being the father of the bastard child of which Caldonia Settle is now pregnant. Recorded 6 July 1869. (P. 461)

COUNTY COURT MINUTES 1870-1872

Page Reece entered a plea of guilty to the charge of being the father of the bastard children begotten on the body of Jennett Bailey, a colored woman. Recorded September Term 1870. (P. 114)

The Court is pleased to advise that Cain Davis is not guilty of being the father of Lou Parker's bastard child. Recorded July Term 1871. (P. 325)

Benjamin Grandstaff is not the father of the bastard child of Hester J. Warmack. Recorded August Term 1872. (P. 508)

There is no proof to sustain the charge of bastardy brought against Wesley Miller as alleged in the affidavit of Eliza Harris. Case dismissed. Recorded September Term 1872. (P. 536)

John E. Bell confessed that he is the father of the bastard child of Bird Eatherly. Recorded October Term 1872. (P. 565)

COUNTY COURT MINUTES 1872-1875

John E. Bell found guilty of the charge of being the father of Tabitha Bosel Eatherly's bastard child. Recorded December Term 1872. (Pp. 1-2)

T. W. Armstrong denied the charge of bastardy that was brought against him by Nancy J. Moody. The court found the said Armstrong guilty. Recorded March Term 1874. (Pp. 191,213)

Columbus Williams found guilty of the charge of bastardy. Recorded April Term 1874. (P. 234)

Jane Alexander, the prosecutrix, failed to appear to prosecute J. C. Sanders. (P. 445)

Diretha A. Weatherly charged Robert L. Mount with being the father of her two bastard children. The eldest was born 18 June 1872; the young was born 17 October 1874. She received $180 from the defendant. Recorded June Term 1875. (P. 472)

Washington Gambill swore that the woman who named him the father of her child is married and undivorced. Case dismissed. Recorded July Term 1875. (P. 487)

QUARTERLY COURT MINUTES 1816-1819

Babbitt indicted for murder. Recorded December Term 1816. (P. 54)

David Dawson entered a plea of guilty to larceny. Found not guilty. Recorded December Term 1816. (P. 64)

Thomas Turnham found guilty of an affray. Recorded December Term 1816. (P. 66)

Humphrey Chappell found guilty of assault and battery. Deposition to be taken of Henry and John Smith in Madison County. Recorded December Term 1816. (P. 67)

John W. Lumpkin charged with an affray. Found guilty. Recorded December Term 1816. (P. 67)

Humphrey Chappell charged John Smart with assault and battery. Found not guilty. Recorded June Term 1817. (P. 79)

James Willard charged by Jane Miligan with being the father of her bastard child. Guilty. Recorded March Term 1817. (P. 71)

Eli Ozment charged with being the reputed father of a bastard child born of the body of Darkus Ozment. Recorded March Term 1817. (P. 91)

William Green allowed eight dollars for keeping Elizabeth Marlon, orphan of Nancy Marlon. Recorded March Term 1817. (P. 91)

Hugh Black entered a plea of not guilty to a charge of assault and battery. The defendant was found guilty. Recorded March Term 1817. (P. 92)

John Smart charged Humphrey Chappell with assault and battery. The defendant was found guilty. Recorded March Term 1817. (P. 97)

Humphrey Chappell entered a plea of guilty to assault and battery. Recorded March Term 1817. (P. 98)

An account of the sale of the property of George Dillard. Recorded June Term 1817. (P. 105)

Brinkley Bridges and James Tipton found guilty of an affray. Recorded June Term 1817. (P. 101)

Willis Ray and William Young entered pleas of guilty to assault and battery. They submitted themselves to the mercy of the court. Recorded June Term 1817. (P. 101)

John Leech entered a plea of guilty to the charge of bastardy brought against him by Jannett Bogle. Recorded June Term 1817. (P. 124)

William Dillard fined $3.50½ for bastardy. Recorded 1817. (P. 125)

Edward Dillard charged with bastardy. He failed to appear in court. Recorded June Term 1817. (P. 125)

William Dillard forfeited his bond for failing to

bring Edward Dillard into Court. Recorded June Term 1817. (P. 125)

Thomas Grisham charged with assault and battery. Not guilty. Recorded June Term 1817. (P. 126)

Isaac Kennedy found not guilty of a misdemeanor. Recorded June Term 1817. (P. 128)

Humphrey Chappell found guilty of assault and battery. Recorded June Term 1817. (P. 129)

Edward Dillard charged by Matilda Winham with bastardy. She has since left the county. Recorded June Term 1817. (P. 131)

David Enoch charged Carter Crutcher with trespassing. Not guilty. Recorded June Term 1817. (P. 132)

Phebe Philips charged Carter Crutcher with trespassing. Not guilty. Recorded June Term 1817. (P. 134)

Ordered that Martin Hancock be allowed the sum of $12.75 for keeping a crippled negro woman for six months. Recorded September Term 1817. (P. 156)

Isaac Impson and John Trout charged with an affray. They submitted themselves to the mercy of the court. Recorded September Term 1817. (P. 165)

Reuben Stone found guilty of an affray. Recorded September Term 1817. (P. 167)

James Somers found guilty of the charge made against him in the indictment. Recorded September Term 1817. (P. 169)

James Cunningham indicted by the Grand Jury. Recorded December Term 1817. (P. 201)

William Sands indicted by the Grand Jury. Found guilty. Recorded February Term 1818. (P. 231)

John W. Nichols indicted by the Grand Jury. Found guilty. Recorded February Term 1818. (P. 234)

Humphrey Chappell charged with bastardy by Nancy Graves. He entered a plea of guilty. Recorded May Term 1818. (P. 266)

William Conyer indicted by the Grand Jury. Recorded May Term 1818. (P. 271)

James Johnson charged by Elizabeth Tally with assault and battery. The defendant was found not guilty. Recorded May Term 1818. (P. 277)

James Johnson, Gregory Johnson, and Philip Johnson charged with "riot." Found guilty. Recorded May Term 1818. (P. 278)

Allen Rachley charged with petit larceny. He was found not guilty. Recorded May Term 1818. (P. 280)

Allen Rachley found not guilty of mismarking a hog. Recorded May Term 1818. (P. 280)

Lemuel Hickman appointed administrator of the estate of Noah Hickman. Recorded August Term 1818. (P. 292)

Allen Rachley charged Samuel Tittle with trespassing. Recorded August Term 1818. (P. 299)

Ire E. Eason was found guilty as charged. Recorded August Term 1818. (P. 310)

Henry Harvel entered a plea of guilty to the charge made against him. Recorded August Term 1818. (P. 311)

Alexander Provine entered a plea of not guilty to the charge made against him. Recorded August Term 1818. (P. 311)

Cornelius N. Lewis entered a plea of guilty to the charge made against him. He submitted himself to the mercy of the court. Recorded August Term 1818. (P. 313)

Benton Modglin found guilty of the charge of assault and battery. Recorded August Term 1818. (P. 314)

The jury could not agree on the guilt or innocence of Eli E. Eason and Josiah McGehee. Recorded August Term 1818. (P. 315)

On the oath of Sally Mortimer setting forth that she is in dread of some private injury by Joseph Norman and Hannah, his wife. Recorded August Term 1818. (P. 316)

William Chandler found not guilty of the charge made against him. Recorded August Term 1818. (P. 320)

Benjamin Hooker charged by Aquilla Sugg and others with trespassing. He was found guilty. Recorded August Term 1818. (P. 321)

George Hodge charged by Aquilla Sugg and others with trespassing. He was found guilty. Recorded August Term 1818. (P. 321)

Benjamin Piland paid his fine. Recorded August Term 1818. (P. 322)

William Hodge charged with bastardy by Elizabeth Hubbard. He was found guilty. Recorded November Term 1818. (P. 330)

William Baskins charged by Elizabeth Ricketts with bastardy. Recorded November Term 1818. (P. 337)

William W. Johnson found guilty of the charge made against him. Recorded November Term 1818. (P. 352)

Alex Holliman found guilty of the charge of assault and battery. Recorded November Term 1818. (P. 353)

Shadrack Gregg entered a plea of not guilty to the charge of petit larceny. Recorded November Term 1818. (P. 355)

Higdon Harrington found guilty of the charge made against him. Recorded November Term 1818. (P. 355)

Samuel Chamberlain found guilty of the charge of being the father of Susannah Housman's bastard child. Recorded November Term 1818. (P. 356)

Abraham Smith found not guilty of assault and battery. Recorded November Term 1818. (P. 358)

James Shaw found guilty of assault and battery. Recorded November Term 1818. (P. 359)

James Bell found guilty of assault and battery. Recorded February Term 1819. (P. 413)

QUARTERLY COURT MINUTES 1822-1824

Morris Hallum charged with assault and battery. Recorded 27 June 1822. (P. 23)

Samuel T. Hickman charged by Martha Joiner with being the father of her bastard child. He was ordered to pay fifteen dollars a year support. Recorded 27 June 1822. (P. 23)

Isaac Alexander found guilty of the charge of assault and battery. Recorded 27 June 1822. (P. 25)

Allen Bagwell indicted for malicious mischief. Recorded 27 June 1822. (Pp. 27-28)

James Tally and Elizabeth Gates were indicted by the Grand Jury. Recorded 27 June 1822. (P. 28)

John Tippett charged with an affray. He was found guilty and fined seven dollars and a half. Recorded 22 June 1822. (P. 29)

Benajah Cartright charged with an affray. Recorded 22 June 1822. (P. 29)

Solomon Walker charged with assault and battery. Recorded 22 June 1822. (P. 29)

John Bonner indicted by the Grand Jury. He was found guilty and fined ten dollars. Recorded 22 June 1822. (P. 32)

A deed of bargain from Thomas Sperry and Elizabeth Sperry to Hugh Gibson for a half lot in Christianburg, Montgomery County, Virginia. Recorded 28 June 1822. (P. 33)

A deed of bargain from Mark Jackson and Mary M. Jackson to Christopher Daniel for 145 acres in Dinwiddie County, Virginia. Recorded 28 June 1822. (P. 33)

Booth Warren indicted for assault and battery. Recorded 28 June 1822. (P. 34)

Jeremiah Hale indicted for assault and battery. Recorded 21 September 1822. (P. 82)

Sampson Bridges indicted by the Grand Jury. Recorded 21 September 1822. (P. 82)

Eliza Melton charged Henry Woodal with being the father of her bastard child. He asked that the child's name be changed from Samuel Melton to Samuel Woodal. Court costs to be paid by Henry Woodal and George Woodal. Recorded 22 September 1822. (Pp. 82-83)

Benjamin Merrell indicted by the Grand Jury for tipling. Recorded 22 September 1822. (P. 83)

Misha Carral indicted by the Grand Jury for larceny. Recorded 22 September 1822. (P. 84)

Isham Palmer indicted by the Grand Jury. Recorded 22 September 1822. (P. 84)

QUARTERLY COURT MINUTES 1822-1824

Thomas Delay charged with assault and battery. Recorded 22 September 1822. (P. 85)

Henry Thomas charged with an affray. Recorded 22 September 1822. (P. 86)

William Quarles indicted by the Grand Jury. Recorded 22 September 1822. (P. 86)

Samuel Dodd found not guilty of "riot." Recorded 22 September 1822. (P. 89)

George A. Lucas ordered to take charge of the Court House for one year. Recorded 22 September 1822. (P. 89)

John G. Thomas charged with assault and battery. Recorded 24 September 1822. (P. 91)

Samuel W. Sherrell indicted by the Grand Jury. Recorded 28 September 1822. (P. 92)

Jeremiah T. Reeves charged by Mary Standley with being the father of her bastard child. Recorded 28 September 1822. (P. 93)

W. R. D. Phipps indicted by the Grand Jury. Recorded 28 September 1822. (P. 94)

Mishack Carroll found guilty of larceny. He was asked by the Court if he had anything to say for himself. He said nothing. He was ordered taken by the Sheriff to the Public Square and given ten lashes on his bare back. He was then to be imprisoned for one hour. Recorded 28 September 1822. (P. 95)

Edward Clay indicted by the Grand Jury. Recorded 28 September 1822. (P. 96)

John L. White and James Anderson indicted by the Grand Jury for tipling. Recorded September Term 1822. (P. 100)

John Telford entered a plea of guilty to the charge against him. He was fined five dollars. Recorded September 1822. (P. 101)

Samuel H. Porterfield charged William Ricketts with trespassing. Recorded September Term 1822. (P. 110)

Henry Billings indicted by the Grand Jury for "riot." Recorded September Term 1822. (P. 123)

William Nettles indicted by the Grand Jury. Recorded December Term 1822. (P. 158)

George A. Evans allowed ten dollars for the repairs he has done on the Court House. Recorded 25 December 1822. (P. 168)

Thomas Delay and Isham Palmer indicted by the Grand Jury. Recorded 25 December 1822. (P. 171)

Nathaniel Fullerton indicted by the Grand Jury. Not guilty. Recorded 25 December 1822. (P. 174)

26

QUARTERLY COURT MINUTES 1822-1824

Elizabeth Cock, widow of John Cock, given her allotment for one year. Recorded 25 December 1822. (P. 178)

Deed of gift of seventy-one acres from Ezekiel Cloyd to John Cloyd. Recorded March Term 1823. (P. 186)

Edmund B. Drake admitted guilt to the charge of bastardy. Recorded March Term 1823. (P. 214)

James Vowell indicted by the Grand Jury for "riot." Defendant found guilty. Recorded March Term 1823. (P. 215)

Donald McNichols and John Bettes indicted by the Grand Jury. Recorded March Term 1823. (P. 271)

Simpson Wray indicted for assault and battery. Recorded March Term 1823. (P. 271)

Jeremiah M. Hale indicted for assault and battery. Fined ten dollars. Recorded March Term 1822. (P. 272)

Deed of bargain and sale from Jonas Bradley to the Baptist Church for one acre of land. Lewis Chambers and Richard Borum, witnesses. Recorded June Term 1823. (P. 294)

William Dill, a pauper, was allowed forty dollars for one year's support. Recorded September Term 1823. (P. 296)

Ordered by the Court that the Coroner be allowed five dollars for holding an inquest over Polly Williams' death. Recorded September Term 1823. (P. 298)

Samuel Anderson, Abraham Vaughan, Archibald Allen, and Franklin Foster indicted by the Grand Jury. Recorded September Term 1823. (Pp. 327-328)

Thomas Baker charged William Wray and Simpson Wray with trespass. Recorded September Term 1823. (P. 329)

Abraham Gosset appointed administrator of John Gosset deceased. Recorded December Term 1823. (P. 361)

William McHaney and Robert Jennings indicted by the Grand Jury. Recorded December Term 1823. (Pp. 392-393)

Spencer W. Talley charged with assault and battery. Recorded December Term 1823. (P. 394)

Matthew Figures charged with assault and battery. Recorded December Term 1823. (P. 395)

William Hartsfield and wife, Fanny Hartsfield, formerly the wife of Patrick Anderson deceased, sued Francis Anderson, executor of the will of Patrick Anderson, to receive the part belonging to Eliza Jane Anderson her deceased daughter. Recorded December Term 1823. (Pp. 401-402)

Britton Modglin charged Joseph L. Wilson with assault and battery. Recorded 31 March 1824. (P. 4__)

QUARTERLY COURT MINUTES 1822-1824

William Chappell charged Spencer W. Talley with trespass and with assault and battery. Fined 6¼ cents. Recorded June Term 1824. (P. 482)

John Jones, Richard Jones, and Alfred Jones charged with an affray. Recorded July Term 1824. (P. 500)

Ransom H. Byrn, Anthony Winston, William Winston, Joseph Cock, and Arthur Harris charged with assault and battery. Recorded September Term 1824. (Pp. 532-534)

Anthony Winston placed under a peace bond with the condition that he is to keep the peace toward all of the good citizens of this State and particularly toward William Wortham. Recorded September Term 1824. (P. 534)

William Wortham placed under a peace bond with the condition that he is to keep the peace toward all of the good citizens of this State and particularly toward Anthony Winston. Recorded September Term 1824. (P. 535)

Willis Forbis, Leroy Carter, and James Scott indicted for assault and battery. Recorded September Term 1824. (Pp. 535-536)

James Cowen charged with being the reputed father of Martha N. Smith's bastard child. Guilty. Recorded September Term 1824. (Pp. 536-537)

Lathan Patton submitted himself to the charge of assault and battery. He was to be imprisoned for one month and to stand committed until he gave good security to keep the peace toward all the good citizens of this State and particularly toward his wife, Rebecca Patton. Fined one dollar. Recorded 1 October 1824. (P. 541)

Robert Wier charged Robert Dallis with assault and battery. Guilty. Recorded 1 October 1824. (P. 542)

Shadrack Owen charged with assault and battery. Recorded 2 October 1824. (P. 544)

Jesse Phelps vs. Jacob B. Lasater. Charge of false imprisonment. Recorded 26 September 1826. (P. 15)

Legatees of Herrod Seatt given the right to sell his land. Legatees: Timothy, Margaret, Jane, Harrison, Jarratt, Polly, Nancy, and Sally Seatt. Recorded 27 September 1826. (P. 16)

Piety Tisdale vs. Elisha S. Rhodes and Frederick L. Rhodes who are heirs of Thomas Rhodes. Recorded 27 September 1826. (P. 17)

Nathan Williams ordered to keep the peace toward all the good citizens of this State, and particularly toward John Allen. Recorded 29 September 1826. (P. 21)

Sion Bass appointed guardian of Susan Bass, the minor heir of Orren Bass. Recorded December Term 1826. (P. 46)

John Wier allotted $32.62¼ for keeping Pius Simpson a prisoner in jail. Recorded December Term 1826. (P. 47)

Allen Jones charged with being the reputed father of Sally Hearn's bastard child. Recorded 28 December 1826. (P. 60)

"Here is nice work for you. An't it now. Court Clerk and the whole business ought to be broke-----." (P. 85)

Jarratt Cock appointed guardian of Martha Cock. Recorded 26 March 1827. (P. 90)

Samuel Henry and his wife and daughter, Sally, who are paupers allowed fifty dollars. Recorded 26 March 1827. (P. 93)

The petition of Allen Jones stated that he has heretofore been adjudged to be the father of an illegitimate child named John Thomas, begotten on the body of Sally Fullerton, and he believes himself to be the father of the said child. He further states that the child is and has been misused by the said Sally Fullerton. He asks that the child be legitimitized and given the name of John Thomas Jones. So ordered. Recorded 27 March 1827. (Pp. 101-102)

Joseph W. Perriman charged with being the reputed father of Synthia Tims' bastard child. Recorded 29 March 1827. (P. 110)

Eaton Edwards charged with being the reputed father of Polly Sanders' bastard child. Recorded 29 March 1827. (P. 110)

Jesse A. Goodwin ordered to keep the peace toward all the citizens of this State and particularly toward Boswell Goodwin. Recorded 29 March 1827. (P. 111)

Jesse A. Goodwin entered a plea of not guilty to

the charge of assault and battery. Guilty. Recorded 29 March 1827. (Pp. 111-112)

Wilson L. Maddox charged with assault and battery. Recorded 29 March 1827. (P. 113)

John Pemberton charged with an affray. Guilty. Recorded 30 March 1827. (P. 114)

William Carlin, Jr. charged with assault and battery. Recorded 30 March 1827. (P. 117)

Ira E. Eason charged with bastardy on the body of Patsy Corder, a married woman, and her husband is yet alive. It is therefore ordered that the charge be dismissed. The County is ordered to pay the costs. Recorded March Term 1827. (P. 126)

James Modglin entered a plea of not guilty to the charge of gaming. Recorded March Term 1827. (P. 126)

William and Fanny Dyer sued Thomas Harrington for their distributive share. Defendant is not an inhabitant of this State. Recorded March Term 1827. (P. 131)

Samuel H. Laughlin, Attorney General of the Sixth Solicitorial District, not being satisfied with the decision in the case of Ira E. Eason appealed to the Circuit Court. Recorded 4 April 1827. (P. 132)

Thomas Bradley versus John and Rachel Fields, the minor heirs of David Fields. Recorded March Term 1827. (P. 134)

Arthur L. Davis charged Wilson Mattock with an affray. Guilty. Recorded April Term 1827. (P. 136)

Mary Nowlin allowed $25 for the support of two deaf and dumb children. Recorded June Term 1827. (P. 151)

Isaiah Tribble allowed one hundred dollars for keeping John Garrison and Elizabeth Garrison and her children, paupers. Recorded June Term 1827. (P. 152)

John Patton charged John F. Patterson with trespass. Recorded 27 June 1827. (P. 157)

Elizabeth Dunn, widow and heir at law of William Dunn, late a soldier in the Regular Army of the United States (24th Regular, commanded by Col. Anderson in Capt. William Butler's Company), makes application for bounty land. Recorded June Term 1827. (P. 165)

Robert Ricketts, John Wright, and William Knight indicted for "riot." Recorded 27 June 1827. (P. 170)

Joseph Berry entered a plea of guilty of affraying. Fined $2.50 and Joseph L. Wilson agreed that the fine be issued jointly against him. Recorded 27 June 1827. (P. 174)

Thomas Bradley versus Richard, David, and Catherine Fields, Redden Fields, Charles and Nancy Bradberry,

Julias and Parthena Sanders, Philip and Mary Koonce, John and Rachel Fields, heirs of David Fields. Recorded June Term 1827. (P. 191)

William McHaney appointed guardian to Richard, Robert, and Suckey Craddock, the minor heirs of Richard C. Craddock. Recorded September Term 1827. (P. 198)

John S. Kennedy charged James Campbell and others with trespassing. Recorded September Term 1827. (P. 221)

David Knight charged with being the father of Mary B)'s bastard child. Recorded September 1827. (P. 230)

Stokes Edwards found guilty of being the father of Mary Patterson's bastard child. Recorded 27 September 1827. (P. 233)

James C. Drake failed to appear in court on a charge of an affray. Recorded September Term 1827. (P. 234)

Elihu McMinn found guilty of assault and battery. Recorded September Term 1827. (P. 235)

Thomas S. Green entered a plea of guilty to the charge of an affray. Recorded September Term 1827. (P. 236)

Tabner Spradley ordered to keep the peace toward all the good citizens of this State, and particularly toward Samuel Hill. Recorded September Term 1827. (P. 236)

Samuel Hill ordered to keep the peace toward all the good citizens of this State, and particularly toward Tabner Spradley. Recorded September Term 1827. (P. 236)

Thomas Burks, Charles Bruce, Allen Goodwin, Adam Cowger, and Burchett Douglass indicted by the Grand Jury. Recorded September Term 1827. (Pp. 240,241,243,245)

Be it remembered that at this day John Muirhead, aged 27 years, born in Sterlingshire in Scotland within the Kingdom of Great Britain, came into court and prayed to be admitted to the rights and privileges of the citizens of the United States. So ordered. Recorded September Term 1827. (Pp. 245-246)

John Wright and William Knight indicted by the Grand Jury. Recorded September Term 1827. (Pp. 246,248)

Sally Nailor says that she is guilty as charged, and submits to the mercy of the court. Fined one cent. Recorded September Term 1827. (P. 248)

Jesse Berry indicted by the Grand Jury. Recorded September Term 1827. (P. 251)

Patrick H. Hegerty charged Lawrence Sypert with trespassing. Recorded December Term 1827. (P. 253)

Thomas B. Aust, aged about 17 years, bound to Freder

ick Aust. Recorded December Term 1827. (P. 265)

Thomas Ubanks and George Wier charged with an affray. Recorded December Term 1827. (P. 289)

Spencer W. Talley and William W. Talley charged with tipling. Recorded December Term 1827. (P. 290)

William Wilkerson and John Ragling charged with an affray. Recorded December Term 1827. (P. 291)

James K. Eason charged with tipling. Recorded December Term 1827. (P. 293)

John Merritt charged with assault and battery. Recorded 29 December 1827. (P. 297)

John Sanders charged with assault and battery. Recorded 29 December 1827. (P. 298)

William Thaxton, a resident of Wilson County, aged 67 years, who being first sworn doth on his oath made the following declaration in order to obtain the provisions made by the Congress on 18 March 1818. Said Thaxton enlisted for eighteen months on the ___ day of July in the year 1780 in the State of Virginia in the Company commanded by Col. Green and ___ Hall in the State of Virginia on the Virginia Continental, that he continued to serve in the corpse untill the 31st day of December in the year 1781. That he was discharged from service on the 10th day of January 1822 in Salsbury in the State of North Carolina by Capt. John Anderson and Major Sneed. He is making application for a pension. He states that he is unable to work because of age and bodily infirmity and that he has no family now, all his children having married and left, and that he is indigent. He states that he is worth $65. The Court is satisfied that he served in the Revolutionary Army. Recorded December Term 1827. (Pp. 305,403-405)

Robert M. Burton charged with an affray. Recorded December Term 1827. (P. 315)

Ira E. Eason ordered to pay for the support of Patsy Corder's bastard child. Recorded December Term 1827. (P. 316)

William R. D. Phelps, George A. Huddleston, and Charles W. Cummings charged with gaming. Recorded 2 January 1828. (Pp. 322-323)

Matthew Dew and Thomas Cox charged with tipling. Recorded December Term 1827. (P. 342)

James Porterfield appointed guardian of John, James, Thomas Greenberry, Loving, David, Sally, and Delafayette Wier, the minor heirs of Dudley Wier. Recorded December Term 1827. (P. 344)

William Alsup charged John Mason with trespassing. Recorded 26 March 1828. (P. 387)

QUARTERLY COURT MINUTES 1826-1828

Robert Cole charged with an affray. Recorded March Term 1828. (P. 388)

James Ward and Littleberry Belcher charged with gaming. Recorded March Term 1828. (P. 391)

Joseph Hight fined one dollar for an affray. Recorded 27 March 1827. (P. 392)

Patrick Youree found guilty of usuary. Recorded 27 March 1828. (P. 392)

Martin Talley found guilty of gaming. Recorded 28 March 1828. (P. 397)

John Bond charged with assault and battery. Recorded 28 March 1828. (P. 399)

Jacob Keaton entered a plea of not guilty to larceny. Recorded 29 March 1828. (P. 400)

Brantley Burns charged with tipling. Recorded March Term 1828. (P. 414)

Henry Liggan charged Josiah Guill and Judieth Guill with trespassing. Recorded 3 April 1828. (P. 435)

Ransom H. Byrn charged with gaming. Recorded 4 April 1828. (P. 437)

Absolum Gleaves found guilty of assault and battery. He submitted himself to the mercy of the Court. Recorded June Term 1828. (P. 475)

Elijah Jones and Bennett Guill charged with assault and battery. Recorded June Term 1828. (Pp. 485-486)

Dennis Hegerty charged with assault and battery. Recorded 26 June 1828. (P. 489)

Adam Harpole charged with tipling. Recorded 26 June 1828. (P. 489)

Thomas H. Hunt charged with bastardy. Recorded June Term 1828. (P. 494)

Fountain Robertson, Jacob Hill, and Thomas Burk charged with gaming. Recorded June Term 1828. (Pp. 495-496)

Richard Townsend charged with bastardy. Recorded June Term 1828. (P. 496)

A deed from (Carwell) Johnson to Clem Johnson for his interest in the estate of Jeremiah Johnson. Recorded 12 February 1846.

A deed of gift from Samuel E. Eason to his wife, Elizabeth Jane Eason, during her lifetime, and then to his children. Recorded 1846.

A bill of sale from Joseph Hays to Samuel Hays for his interest in a family of negroes belonging to the estate of Charles Hays. Proved by James L. Hays and by the handwriting of John R. Hays who has moved out of this state. Recorded 6 April 1846.

A conveyance from Joshua Cannon to Pierce Walker and his wife, Elizabeth Jane Walker. Recorded 16 April 1846.

A deed of gift from Thomas Williamson to his daughter, Perlina Ann Williamson. Recorded April 1846.

A contract and obligation between James Godfrey and James N. Patton on the subject of a tract of land and how it should be paid. Recorded 2 May 1846.

A deed of gift from William Corley to his son, Elisha Corley. Recorded 7 September 1846.

A deed from Samuel L. Hickman to Snowden Hickman for his undivided interest in a tract of land in the 21st District. Recorded 5 October 1846.

A deed of partition between Nancy Crunk and Willis Bradshaw and his wife, Lavisa. Recorded 8 October 1846.

A deed from Alfred B., Benjamin W., and George W. Payne to Daniel F. Payne. Recorded 24 October 1846.

A deed from John O. Poyner to Thomas J. Smith for 82 acres in the 22nd District. Recorded 1846.

A bill of sale from A. D. Duke and his wife, Nancy, (and also Wood S. Shearin) to John J. Crittenden for their undivided interest in slaves. Nancy Duke, being one of the daughters of Thomas Bradshaw. Recorded 1846.

A deed from S. J. Kittrell to John Hunt for 37 acres on Spring Creek. Recorded 28 December 1846.

A deed from Joel Swindell to Thomas A. Swindell for 100 acres in the 8th District. Recorded 1 March 1847.

A deed from Samuel Bryant and wife, Harriet Avery Mitchell, to Garret G. Mitchell for their interest in a tract of land belonging to Robert R. Mitchell deceased. Recorded 1 March 1847.

A deed from Warner Lambert to Isham Kittrell for 18 acres. Recorded 3 May 1847.

A deed of gift from Robert Reed and wife, Margaret, to their daughters Mary D. Bett, wife of Jeremiah Bett; Millison Helen Beadles, wife of Abram A. Beadles; and

*Book has no page numbers

and Margaret Ann Williams, wife of Howel J. Williams. Recorded 6 May 1847.

A bill of sale from Jacob Earheart to David Baird. Recorded 23 May 1847.

A deed from Harrison A. Goodall and wife, Frances M. Goodall, to Daniel Seay for their undivided interest in 87 acres in Smith County. Said interest is one fifth. Recorded 3 July 1847.

A deed from Edmund Melvin to Joseph and Andrew Melvin for 16 acres on Stone's Creek. Recorded 2 August 1847.

A deed from Henry F. Johnson to James H. Johnson for a town lot in Lebanon. Recorded 9 August 1847.

A deed from John Telford and wife, Sarah, to William H. Telford for all their interest in the estate of Parks Goodall. Recorded 2 September 1847.

A deed of gift from Hughes Morton to William Moore, the trustee for the estate that is coming to him in Virginia from his grandfather and grandmother for the support of his father, William Morton. Witnesses: Abram Huguely and Drury Lain. Thomas B. Lain and Armstead Lain state that Drury Lain has left the country and his residence is unknown. Recorded 9 October 1847.

A deed from Elijah B. Drake to Edmund B. Drake for two tracts of land willed to the said Elijah B. by his father, Brittain Drake. Recorded 8 November 1847.

A deed from James A. Roach and wife, Elizabeth H., to James W. Barton for their undivided interest in a tract of land in the 24th District, it being the land which Stephen Barton lived and died. Recorded 12 November 1847.

A deed of gift from Martha Jones to Elizabeth B. Crutchfield. Recorded 3 January 1848.

A bill of sale from Warner Lambert to John W. Bettes. Recorded 7 March 1848.

A deed from M. L. Sims to James Haw for 66 acres. Recorded 20 May 1848.

A deed from George A. Evans and wife Thursey Ann to Leroy B. Settle. Said Thursey Ann Evans is an heir of Patrick Hegerty. Said land is located in the 5th District. Recorded 6 July 1848.

A deed from James W. Hearn to Mary F. Hearn, his granddaughter. Recorded 1848.

A deed from John Allen and Gary Steele to A. J. Dillard for their interest in 20 acres of land. 5 December 1848.

Be it remembered that on the fourth Monday in December-

*Book has no page numbers

ber 1848. . . (last page of book)

*Book has no page numbers

JOHN W. JARRELL Widow's Allotment. 10 February 1866. Jane Jarrell given her allotment for one year. (P. 1)

JOHN ANDREWS Sale. Recorded 20 March 1866. (P. 1)

WILLIAM L. LEE Widow's Allotment. Elizabeth Lee given her allotment for one year. (P. 1)

CARROL LEWIS Sale. 13 January 1866. A. S. Young, administrator. Recorded 20 March 1866. (P. 2)

Z. TATE Inventory. A. J. Tate, guardian of Z. Tate, a lunatic. Recorded 21 March 1866. (Pp. 1-2)

JOHN DUKE Will. 13 June 1860. Heirs: daughters Nelly Garrett, Cinthia Briant, and Evaline Russell; heirs of Anna McDearman deceased; sons Alfred Duke and John Duke deceased; grandsons Winfield, son of Sally Ann McDearman, John, son of Sion Duke; heirs of Samuel Duke (I have given to my daughter in law, Darthula Duke, mother of said heirs); granddaughter Sally Ann McDearman; and son in law Thomas Tuggle. James Hamelton, executor. Witnesses: D. D. Hamelton, W. B. Hewgley, and M. D. L. McFarland. Recorded 22 April 1866. (P. 2)

J. M. ARMSTRONG Sale. G. W. Armstrong, administrator. Recorded 20 March 1866. (P. 3)

RICHARD D. GRAVES Will. 18 November 1863. Walker County, Georgia. "I Richard D. Graves of the County of Ellis, State of Texas. Heirs: sister Matilda Taylor; brothers E. Graves, Williamson Stokes Graves, John Graves, and Lester Graves; niece Puss; nephew Alexander Wright; and brother John's sons Bernice and Makajah Graves. Executors: brother John E. Graves and James W. Wright. Witnesses: Lawson Black and B. R. McCutcheon. Recorded 22 April 1866. (Pp. 3-4)

W. MARLER Sale. R. Marler, administrator. Recorded 20 March 1866. (P. 4)

WILLIAM M. JOHNS Sale. 27 October 1865. H. G. Johns, administrator. Recorded 20 March 1866. (P. 4)

SIMON ADAMSON Sale. 20 March 1866. S. C. Hamelton, administrator. Recorded 22 April 1866. (P. 4)

CAROLINE P. BOWERS Will. 4 November 1862. "I set apart the interest from my mother, Mary Nolin, to her son William H. Nolin. Said William H. Nolin now being dead, I leave to my sister in law Elizabeth B. Towson. Witnesses: John Chambers and Robert Joplin. Recorded 22 April 1866. (P. 5)

A. J. THOMPSON Inventory. Recorded 21 March 1866. (P. 5)

JAMES M. ARMSTRONG Widow's Allotment. 17 February 1866. (P. 5)

CARROL LEWIS Widow's Allotment. (P. 5)

DICY McFARLAND Will. 24 December 1859. "I Dicy McFarland, widow of James McFarland." Heirs: son John P. McFarland; six daughters; and grandson P. McFarland. James Hamelton, executor. Witnesses: J. B. White and A. R. Davis. Recorded 23 May 1866. (P. 6)

ROBERT MITCHELL Will. 21 March 1866. Heirs: wife Martha Mitchell; son Paulding Mitchell; and other children. Joseph Mottley, executor. Witnesses: J. B. Cooksey and Giles G. Glenn. Recorded 23 May 1866. (Pp. 6-7)

NATHAN GREEN Will. 26 March 1866. Heirs: wife E. A. Green; sons John A. Green (Austin, Texas),Robert Green, Nathan Green, and Dr. J. H. Green (near Oakalony, Mississippi); daughters Ann A.Bowden, the wife of Rev. James C. Bowden, and Mary Field. Mentions my brother, William Green, who died in the State of Virginia in 1862. Executors: son Nathan Green and wife E. A. Green. Witnesses: Andrew Martin and Horace Rice. Recorded 23 May 1866. (Pp. 7-8)

J. W. L. BETTES Sale. 10 January 1866. Martha E. Bettes, administratrix. Recorded 23 May 1866. (P. 8)

MERRIT CARAWAY Widow's Allotment. Sophia Caraway given her allotment for one year. Recorded 23 May 1866. (P. 8)

W. B. WRIGHT Sale. Recorded 23 May 1866. (P. 9)

JOHN WALKER Sale. Recorded 23 May 1866. (P. 10)

MARY M. JACKSON Inventory. 30 April 1866. Isham Jackson, administrator. Recorded 24 May 1866. (P. 11)

AARON GIBSON Will. Heirs: wife Elizabeth Gibson; sons Thomas J. and Aaron B. Gibson; daughters Ruth J., Margaret L., and Martha A. Gibson. Elizabeth Gibson, executrix. Witnesses: W. L. Putman and A. A. Puckett. Recorded 24 May 1866. (P. 12)

MARGARET DONNELL Sale. 20 March 1866. R. B. Donnell, administrator. Recorded 24 May 1866. (P. 13)

SMITH BLOODWORTH Sale. 5 May 1866. Among buyers: William Bloodworth and Wilson Bloodworth. Recorded 25 May 1866. (P. 14)

ISAAC N. STEVENSON Sale. 5 May 1866. L. N. M. Cook, administrator. Recorded 24 May 1866. (P. 14)

ASAPH BOND Widow's Allotment. 11 October 1862. Mary Bond given her allotment for one year. Recorded 24 May 1866. (P. 15)

JAMES H. JOHNSON Widow's Allotment. 10 March 1866. Recorded 24 May 1866. (P. 15)

B. A. GOOSEN Inventory. Recorded 30 May 1866. (P. 17)

ROBERT MALONE Will. 20 October 1865. Heirs: wife Ann Malone; my seven children Lemuel, Jerry, Nancy,

Tennessee, John, Robert, and Mary Malone. Joseph Young, Jr., executor. Witnesses: G. A. Neal, Jasper Fowler, and George Neal. Recorded 10 June 1866. (P. 18)

WILLIAM A. POWELL Sale. D. J. Powell, executor. Recorded 10 June 1866. (P. 19)

REBECCA PHILIPS Sale. 22 May 1866. The record also refers to her as Rebecca Williams. Recorded 12 June 1866. (Pp. 20-21)

WILLIAM L. MARTIN Inventory. Recorded 20 June 1866. (Pp. 22-23)

JAMES BRYANT Inventory. 8 July 1865. Recorded 20 June 1866. (P. 24)

LAMBERT VANHOOZER Sale. Recorded 20 May 1866. (P. 24)

JOHN A. McCLAIN Will. 18 May 1866. Heirs: wife Manerva McClain; children Jo, Panthia, and William McClain. Mentions other children. Executor: son Rufus P. McClain. Witnesses: J. B. Vivrett and L. L. Robertson. Recorded 20 July 1866. (P. 25)

WILLIAM E. HUGHEY Inventory. Recorded 21 July 1866. (P. 26)

JOHN L. PATTERSON Inventory. Recorded 21 July 1866. (P. 26)

WILLIAM BENNETT Will. Heir: wife Ideson Bennett. The graveyard on my land is reserved. I am a member of Union Baptist Church. Having no children, I leave to Union Church. If said church should cease to exist, then my estate to pay for the support of a school at Sugar Grove which is located near Cainsville. J. W. Edwards, executor. Witnesses: J. A. Major and E. L. Lindsey. Recorded 20 July 1866. (P. 29)

W. A. DAWSON Widow's Allotment. 16 July 1866. Recorded 16 August 1866. (P. 29)

CARNES LOGUE Sale. L. G. Logue, administrator. Recorded 10 August 1866. (Pp. 30-31)

W. C. KNOX Widow's Allotment. Bette Knox given her allotment for one year. Recorded 15 August 1866. (P. 31)

ELIJAH WAMMACK Sale. L. D. Wammack, administrator. Recorded 15 August 1866. (Pp. 32-33)

J. C. McCULLOCK Inventory. G. L. Gleaves, administrator. Recorded 15 August 1866. (P. 34)

JESSE COOK Widow's Allotment. Mary A. Cook given her allotment for one year. Recorded 15 August 1866. (P. 36)

BENJAMIN ALEXANDER Will. 27 July 1859. Heirs: wife; children Ezekiel Alexander, Thomas B. Alexander,

Joseph L. Alexander, George G. Alexander, John N. Alexander, Polly Tate, Margaret M. Roach, Catherine W. James, and Elizabeth Wood. Thomas B. Alexander, executor. Recorded 11 September 1866. (Pp. 37-38)

P. P. BENSON Sale. Recorded 11 September 1866. (Pp. 38-39)

DAVID JENKINS Sale. 19 January 1863. (P. 39)

HENRY HASS Will. 24 May 1866. Heirs: wife Sarah Hass; son James A. Hass; daughters Martha Williamson, Elizabeth Gatton, Eliza Ann Sadler, Hannah C. Dunn, Mary F. Sadler, Sarah D. Adams, Margaret A. Hass, and Susanah H. Hass. Recorded 18 October 1866. (Pp. 40-41)

PARTHENA WATSON CAWTHON Will. 18 July 1866. Heirs: son John R. Cawthon; and daughter Eliza Watson Cawthon. John R. Cawthon, executor. Witnesses: Alex Brett and R. C. Lane. Recorded 18 October 1866. (P. 41)

GEORGE PRICHETT Widow's Allotment. Sophrona Prichett given her allotment for one year. Recorded 18 October 1866. (P. 41)

GEORGE OAKLEY Widow's Allotment. 26 September 1865. (P. 42)

ROBERT C. HATTON Will. 9 August 1866. Heir: wife Margaret Hatton. Witnesses: Nathan Green and Maggie H. Riddle. Recorded 18 October 1866. (P. 42)

BENJAMIN PRITCHETT Sale. Recorded 19 October 1866. (P. 43)

ARCHIBALD CARVER Sale. Recorded 20 October 1866. (Pp. 44-46)

LEWIS CHAMBERS Inventory. 27 June 1864. Recorded 20 October 1866. (P. 47)

DANIEL GLENN Inventory. Recorded 23 October 1866. (Pp. 48-49)

ANDREW THOMPSON Widow's Allotment. 25 October 1866. Milly Thompson given her allotment for one year. Recorded 10 November 1866. (P. 49)

JOSEPH P. WHARTON Will. 13 September 1866. Heirs: wife Caroline C. Wharton; sons Robert H. Wharton and his two brothers; daughters Ann Buchanan, Matilda Emma Price, Betty Wharton, and Mary Wharton. Witnesses: J. S. McClain, Giles H. Glenn, and Thomas Norman. Recorded 10 November 1866. (P. 50)

LEVI FISHER Will. 10 August 1866. Heirs: wife Susan Fisher; children Richard W. Fisher, Cloe Atkinson, and John Fisher; American Bible Society. Executors: Lewis W. Robertson and James S. Cartmell. Witnesses: S. C. Jackson and William H. Jackson. Recorded 22 September 1866. (Pp. 51-52)

ALICE BURKE Will. 26 July 1866. Heirs: son

William H. Burke; daughters Louiza Burke, Martha Lane, and Mary Dandridge. The three children of James Burke will receive their deceased father's share. William H. Burke to receive my interest in my mother's, Elizabeth Hagerty, land. William H. Burke, executor. Witnesses: B. J. Tarver and W. H. L. Baird. Recorded 12 November 1866. (P. 52)

ALEXANDER BRIDGE Widow's Allotment. Recorded 12 November 1866. (P. 54)

WILLIAM H. GRAVES Sale. Recorded 12 November 1866. (P. 54)

S. E. BELCHER Widow's Allotment. Recorded 15 November 1866. (P. 57)

WILLIAM VANTREASE Inventory. J. J. Ford, administrator. Recorded 26 December 1866. (P. 58)

P. C. BAIRD Sale. Recorded 26 December 1866. (P. 59)

ROBERT P. SWEATT Sale. 22 November 1866. Recorded 26 December 1866. (Pp. 59-60)

ISABELLA ALSUP Will. Heirs: Mrs. Isbel Cummings; Susan Alsup, wife of Nelson Alsup; Mrs. Perk Robertson; Lavina Zackery; Caroline Shaw; Jane Brown; Isabella J. A. Zackery; Dicy Alsup; Callie Alsup; Aunt Jane Duke; and Domestic Board of Missions of Methodist Episcopal Church South. A. H. Alsup, executor. Witnesses: R. B. Zackery and Isabella Cummings. Recorded 26 December 1866. (P. 61)

N. CARTMELL Inventory. Widow Sarah Cartmell, the administrator. Recorded 12 January 1867. (Pp. 63-66)

JOHN G. LIGON Inventory. James E. Scobey, administrator. Recorded 13 January 1867. (P. 69)

DAVID JENKINS Widow's Allotment. Elizabeth Jenkins given her allotment for one year. Recorded 16 January 1867. (P. 72)

MRS. E. A. TAYLOR Sale. 17 February 1865. Recorded 16 January 1867. (P. 73)

ELLEN OUTLAW Will. 13 June 1867. Heirs: daughter Mary Elizabeth Donnell and children. Peter Thompson, executor. Witnesses: E. L. Thompson and William Bailey. Recorded 7 August 1867. (P. 74)

JOHN A. CLOPTON Sale. 24 August 1865. Recorded 7 August 1867. (P. 74)

STEPHEN H. HEARN Sale. E. D. Hearn, administrator. Recorded 17 January 1867. (P. 75)

JOHN EDWARDS Inventory. Recorded 17 January 1867. (P. 76)

JOHN G. LIGON Widow's Allotment. 17 December 1866.

Recorded 17 January 1867. (P. 76)

JULIA DODSON Inventory. Recorded 17 January 1867. (P. 76)

JOHN W. CARVER Widow's Allotment. 10 November 1866. Martha C. Carver given her allotment for one year. Recorded 18 January 1867. (P. 77)

PURNEL LANE Inventory. Recorded 18 January 1867. (P. 77)

WILLIAM GILLIAM Will. 15 December 1858. Heirs: Edmund Gilliam; Margaret Brown's children, she being dead; and Sarah M. Alsup. Edmund Gilliam, executor. Witnesses: A. J. Ivey, W. C. Clemmons, and John A. Clopton. Recorded 10 February 1867. (P. 78)

JOHN E. BAKER Inventory. Recorded 10 February 1867. (P. 79)

NANCY KOONCE Sale. James L. Murry, administrator. Recorded 12 February 1867. (P. 80)

B. F. LAIN Inventory. Recorded 12 February 1867. (P. 81)

THOMAS K. WHITLOCK Sale. Robert F. Whitlock, administrator. Recorded 15 March 1867. (P. 81)

MRS. SUSAN WHITE Inventory. James W. White, administrator. Recorded 15 March 1867. (P. 82)

ISAAC SMITH Sale. 31 January 1867. Recorded 18 March 1867. (Pp. 83-86)

JOHN W. WHITE Sale. 2 December 1865. Recorded 18 March 1867. (P. 87)

EZEKIEL BASS Inventory. Recorded 18 March 1867. (Pp. 87-88)

ELIHU McMINN Will. Heirs: son Samuel N. McMinn; daughters Lavina Lasater, Martha Bone, Jane Francina Donnell, and Lavice Hill. Recorded 17 April 1867. (P. 89)

JAMES M. BLALOCK Will. 14 March 1867. Heirs: wife Margaret M. Blalock; daughter Annie Laura Blalock; and son Felix Haynes Blalock. Executors: wife Margaret M. Blalock and Henry J. Lockett of Sumner County. Recorded 21 April 1867. (P. 90)

WILLIAM B. ANDERSON Will. 20 May 1861. Heirs: sister Mary Jane Roach; and brother L. T. Anderson. L. T. Anderson to receive 167 acres of land in Monroe County, Arkansas. Witnesses: J. B. Vivrett and H. L. Bass. Recorded 21 April 1867. (P. 90)

J. H. WILLIAMS Inventory. Recorded 22 April 1867. (Pp. 91-92)

HENRY PARTEN Inventory. 6 March 1867. Tempy Parten, widow. Recorded 22 April 1867. (P. 92)

WILLS & INVENTORIES 1866-1871

MARTHA CLEMMONS Sale. 18 February 1867. Recorded 23 April 1867. (Pp. 93-94)

ARCHIBALD TALLEY Sale. 1 March 1867. D. G. Talley, administrator. Recorded 23 April 1867. (P. 94)

JAMES DRENNAN Sale. Thomas J. Drennan, administrator. Recorded 23 April 1867. (P. 95)

MARY ANN WHITE Sale. 1 April 1867. William Bradley, administrator. Recorded 23 April 1867. (P. 96)

C. W. GAINES Sale. Recorded 23 April 1867. (P. 96)

JOHN W. HAMILTON Widow's Allotment. Susanna Hamilton given her allotment for one year. Recorded 10 May 1867. (P. 96)

JOHN BATES Sale. Recorded 12 May 1867. (Pp. 99-101)

MRS. ELIZABETH SHAW Widow's Allotment. 12 April 1867. Also called Elizabeth Moseley. Recorded 24 May 1867. (P. 102)

RALPH MARTIN Widow's Allotment. 13 December 1866. Elizabeth C. Martin given her allotment for one year. Recorded 12 June 1867. (P. 103)

SOLOMON SWAIN Settlement. J. B. Marks, administrator. Recorded 12 June 1867. (P. 103)

REBECCA N. CASON Will. 20 April 1867. Heirs: brothers Favor, Jeremiah H., Joseph M., and John M. Cason; sister Fannie Baird; Ann M. Cason; Indianna Cason, daughter of Favor Cason. Favor Cason, executor. Recorded 12 June 1867. (P. 104)

LEWIS W. PARHAM Widow's Allotment. 15 May 1867. Martha Parham given her allotment for one year. Recorded 12 June 1867. (P. 105)

HENRY R. COX Inventory. Recorded 12 July 1867. (P. 106)

SARAH JANE ROGERS Will. 24 April 1867. Heirs: children Frank, Jenny, and Milly's part to be held by their father for them. "I have a brother." Recorded 10 August 1867. (P. 108)

HENRY PARTIN Sale. B. C. Partin, administrator. Recorded 10 August 1867. (P. 109)

SAMUEL COLES Widow's Allotment. 16 May 1867. Recorded 10 August 1867. (P. 110)

THOMAS L. HOLMAN Inventory. W. H. McDonald, administrator. Recorded 10 August 1867. (P. 110)

WILLIAM ESKEW Sale. 27 June 1867. B. J. Eskew, administrator. Recorded 10 August 1867. (P. 111)

JAMES SHANNON Will. 27 March 1860. Heirs: children Etheldred J. Shannon, Henry J. Shannon, Mary Jane

Martin, George W. B. Shannon, and Rebecca Brown. W. B. Tatum, executor. Witnesses: J. S. Haralson and W. B. Goldstone. Recorded 18 September 1867. (Pp. 111-112)

WILLIAM B. CAMPBELL Will. 23 November 1865. Heirs: children Mary A., Margaret H., William B., Fannie A., Joseph A., John A., and Lemuel R. Campbell. Executors: Mary A., Margaret H., and William B. Campbell. Witnesses: M. H. Campbell and C. B. Scales. Recorded 18 September 1867. (P. 112)

FRANCES B. HARRISON Will. 9 March 1867. Heirs: brothers and sisters Mary Word, Lavisa Green, Catherine C. Gordon, Samuel B. Moore, Alexander Moore, Armstead Moore, and Robert Moore deceased, that is his children. Said brothers and sisters to receive the land that I lived upon in Shreveport, Louisiana. I desire a sufficient amount of money reserved to fix a railing around the grave of my former husband, Dr. Hardwick, and the grave of my husband, Col. Harrison. My river land in Louisiana is to go to Joyce (Bersford), sister of my former husband, Dr. Hardwick. I leave to Dr. Tompson who married Tabitha Word, my sister's daughter. An amount is to be set apart to improve my father's grave in Smith County. Witnesses: Mary L. Martin and W. H. Campbell. Recorded 19 September 1867. (P. 113)

WILLIAM TOMLINSON Inventory. Recorded 19 September 1867. (P. 114)

G. W. JENNINGS Inventory. Recorded 19 September 1867. (P. 114)

ETHELDRED CLEMMONS Sale. Recorded 19 September 1867. (P. 115)

P. P. HUDSON Widow's Allotment. 19 November 1864. Alafair Hudson given her allotment for one year. Recorded 19 September 1867. (P. 115)

GEORGE McDONALD Sale. Recorded 19 September 1867. (P. 116)

MRS. JANE BARTON Sale. W. J. Barton, administrator. Recorded 19 September 1867. (P. 116)

PATRICK H. ANDERSON Will. 26 September 1867. Heirs: wife Mary Ann Anderson; all my children. Executors: wife Mary Ann Anderson and father P. Anderson. Witnesses: D. C. Kelly and Eudora McGregor. Recorded 10 October 1867. (P. 118)

WILLIAM R. HOLMAN Sale. Recorded 10 October 1867. (P. 119)

WILLIAM R. SHANNON Sale. 14 September 1867. Recorded 12 October 1867. (P. 122)

A. M. HUNT Widow's Allotment. Recorded 12 October 1867. (P. 122)

SAMUEL L. MOORE Widow's Allotment. Recorded 12

October 1867. (P. 123)

GEORGE W. MARTIN Will. Heirs: son James B. Martin; daughter Mary S. Hickerson. I desire to be buried in the family graveyard on the premises on which I now live. Witnesses: S. H. Ewing and J. W. Putman. Recorded 19 November 1867. (P. 124)

WILLIAM B. JENKINS Will. 20 September 1867. Heirs: wife Elizabeth Jenkins; sons John R. and Obadiah Jenkins; daughters Elizabeth and Eliza Jenkins; and grandson William J. Dice. Witnesses: H. A. Goodall and J. T. Goodall. Recorded 19 November 1867. (P. 125)

ROBERT HUFFMAN Will. Heirs: sisters Constantine Grogan, Elizabeth Huffman, and Nancy Huffman. After the death of my sisters, the estate is to be divided among the three heirs of Archibald Huffman, to wit, Robert, William, and Nancy Huffman. Robert Huffman, executor. Witnesses: James G. Swann and J. F. Wilkinson. Recorded 19 November 1867. (Pp. 125-126)

MATILDA LOYD Sale. Recorded 19 November 1867. (P. 126)

THOMAS VIVRETT Sale. 26 August 1867. J. L. Cluck, administrator. Recorded 20 November 1867. (P. 127)

B. F. BRIGGS Sale. 24 October 1867. Recorded 20 November 1867. (P. 127)

JOHN SCOBY Will. 11 July 1862. Heirs: sons Robert C. Scoby and James M. Scoby; daughters Susan Stone and Frances Sims; and the children of my daughter Eliza Hawkins deceased. Executors: Robert C. Scoby and James M. Scoby. Witnesses: Joseph M. Miller and Samuel Smithwick. Recorded 15 January 1868. (P. 128)

JACK BLOODWORTH Sale. Recorded 15 January 1868. (Pp. 128-129)

ROBERT C. NEAL Will. 22 April 1867. Heirs: wife and children. W. W. Luck, administrator. Recorded 15 January 1868. (P. 129)

SUSAN BASS Inventory. 19 October 1867. William Bass, administrator. Recorded 11 May 1868. (Pp. 130-132)

JOHN BASS Inventory. 19 October 1867. William Bass, administrator. Recorded 11 May 1868. (P. 132)

WILLIAM McMILLEN Will. 25 May 1867. Heirs: wife Jensy McMillen; my youngest children Mary, Peggy, Jane, Sarah, Thomas, Tennessee, Lily, Frances, Andrew, and Joseph McMillen; all my children. Z. McMillen, executor. Witnesses: C. W. Neal and J. T. Talley. Recorded 11 May 1868. (P. 133)

COLEMAN PUCKETT Sale. Recorded 11 May 1868. (P. 134)

LUCRETIA HOLT Will. 31 August 1867. Heirs: Martha Holt and B. Holt. Recorded 12 May 1868. (P. 136)

GUY T. GLEAVES Will. 21 October 1867. Heirs: wife Julia A. Gleaves; my four youngest children by her; sons John, Benjamin, Jesse, and Tavel Gleaves; daughter Michey A. Gleaves. Executor: son J. W. Gleaves. Witnesses: John Crudup and John T. Gleaves. Recorded 13 May 1868. (Pp. 137-138)

W. L. ESTES Will. 8 November 1867. Heir: wife Nancy M. Estes to have all coming from my deceased brother, Robert E. Estes. C. R. Dillon, administrator. Witnesses: C. C. H. Burton and C. R. Dillon. Recorded 13 May 1868. (P. 138)

T. W. WHITLOCK Widow's Allotment. Martha J. Whitlock given her allotment for one year. Recorded 13 May 1868. (P. 138)

J. F. DISMUKES Widow's Allotment. Recorded 13 May 1868. (P. 139)

J. G. PUCKETT Sale. Recorded 13 May 1868. (P. 139)

ISHAM JOLLY Sale. Recorded 14 May 1868. (P. 140)

JAMES AYRES Widow's Allotment. Recorded 14 May 1868. (P. 140)

MICAJAH VIVRETT Sale. 20 November 1867. P. H. Vivrett, administrator. Recorded 14 May 1868. (P. 141)

BENJAMIN GRAVES Sale. Recorded 14 May 1868. (P. 142)

JAMES T. JEWELL Inventory. A. M. Jewell, administrator. Recorded 14 May 1868. (P. 143)

W. J. ESTES Inventory. Recorded 15 May 1868. (P. 144)

HENRY MOSER, SR. Sale. 7 June 1861. Recorded 15 May 1868. (Pp. 145-146)

J. L. KNIGHT Widow's Allotment. Recorded 16 May 1868. (P. 146)

HICKSEY SHAW Inventory. Recorded 16 May 1868. (P. 147)

S. H. PORTERFIELD Inventory. 21 November 1867. P. Thompson, administrator. Recorded 16 May 1868. (P. 148)

ROBERT HUGHES Sale. 12 April 1868. Robert Hughes, administrator. Recorded 15 May 1868. (P. 153)

WILLARD LAIN Will. 15 June 1865. Heir: nephew Milton Lain. Witnesses: J. P. Cawthon and Jeptha Clemmons. Recorded 18 May 1868. (P. 154)

THOMAS B. LAIN Sale. 28 January 1869. Administrators: James S. Lain and G. B. Lain. Recorded 18 May 1868. (P. 155)

PETER MIERS Will. 25 September 1856. Heirs: wife Dinnah Miers; sons Washington, Morgan, and William Miers; all my children. Executors: Washington Miers and Morgan Miers. Witnesses: Thomas C. Martin and Absolom Earheart. Recorded 19 May 1868. (P. 157)

S. M. DONNELL Will. 10 June 1867. Heirs: wife Catherine Donnell; nieces and nephews John A. Major, A. M. Major, W. B. Major, Lucy Lindsey, Elizabeth Major, Martha Turner, Jane Dement, Martha Hearn, Francis L. Philips, and Wilson B. Major. Witnesses: David Young and Samuel Corley Donnell. Recorded 19 May 1868. (Pp. 159-160)

WILLIAM YOUNG Widow's Allotment. Recorded 22 May 1868. (P. 161)

MARGARET AYRES Sale. 13 March 1868. Nathan Oakley, administrator. Recorded 22 May 1868. (P. 162)

ANDREW GWYNN Widow's Allotment. 17 January 1868. Esther Gwynn given her allotment for one year. Recorded 22 May 1868. (Pp. 164-165)

B. S. PEYTON Sale. Recorded 23 May 1868. (Pp. 166-167)

DANIEL JAMES Widow's Allotment. Malinda James given her allotment for one year. Recorded 22 May 1868. (P. 167)

CATHERINE CAMPBELL Will. 4 March 1859. Heirs: son David H. K. Campbell; and daughters Mary H. Scales and Margaret Hamilton Campbell. Son William B. Campbell and daughter V. L. Shelton not provided for because of the ample provisions for them by their uncle Governor Campbell of Virginia. Executors: Margaret H. Campbell and David H. Campbell. Witnesses: Orville Green. Recorded 24 May 1868. (Pp. 169-170)

CATHERINE CAMPBELL CODICIL. "When this will was written, I thought that my son John was dead, as he is living it is my wish that he be included." January 1867. Recorded 24 May 1868. (P. 170)

MARY J. KING Sale. Recorded 8 June 1868. (P. 170)

HARDY BRETT Will. Heirs: brother A. Brett; other brothers and sisters. A. Brett, executor. Witnesses: W. F. Todd and J. J. Banks. Recorded 8 June 1868. (P. 174)

WILLIAM C. DEW Will. 6 April 1866. Heirs: wife; three daughters of William C. Sypert, to wit, Roxalany Straughn, Jane Bowers, and Mary Ann Risen; John C. Sypert; and Mrs. Betsy Cook. Executors: wife and John C. Sypert. Witnesses: B. J. Tarver and Alexander W. Vick. Recorded 8 June 1868. (Pp. 175-176)

ELIZABETH PUCKETT Sale. 13 March 1868. John Wright, administrator. Recorded 9 July 1868. (P. 178)

ISAAC H. HUNTER Inventory. Recorded 9 July 1868. (P. 179)

LEWIS W. EASON Will. 30 May 1868. Heirs: wife Ann Eason; my two children James F. and Lavicy F. Eason. Ann Eason, executrix. Witnesses: David Clark and B. G. L. Warren. Recorded 15 August 1868. (P. 180)

JOHN H. JOHNSON Will. 29 June 1868. Heirs: wife Martha Johnson to receive my land in Logan County, Kentucky. John L. Simpson, executor. Witnesses: E. L. Smith, H. C. Matthews, and M. Martin. Recorded 15 August 1868. (P. 180)

MARTHA MARRS Inventory. R. A. Marrs, administrator. Recorded 10 October 1868. (P. 181)

TYRE LAIN Widow's Allotment. 11 September 1868. Nancy Lain given her allotment for one year. Recorded 10 October 1868. (P. 181)

HENRY CARVER Settlement. Heirs: children James, Mary, and Trephrena Carver. Recorded 10 October 1868. (P. 182)

GIDEON G. GAINES Sale. Recorded 10 October 1868. (P. 183)

W. S. ALEXANDER Widow's Allotment. Recorded 10 October 1868. (Pp. 183-185)

MARTHA H. DOUGLASS Sale. John C. Kirkpatrick, administrator. Recorded 17 October 1868. (Pp. 186-187)

JULIA CARTER Sale. Recorded 17 October 1868. (Pp. 188-190)

JAMES W. ROBINSON Widow's Allotment. 16 September 1868. Stephen Robinson, administrator. Recorded 12 October 1868. (P. 196)

J. G. SIMS Widow's Allotment. Recorded 17 October 1868. (P. 190)

NANCY NEAL Inventory. Recorded 12 October 1868. (P. 191)

ANDERSON JENNINGS Will. 23 May 1868. Heirs: wife Malinda Jennings; all my children. Samuel Jennings, administrator. Witnesses: J. P. Cawthon and J. H. Jennings. Recorded 10 November 1868. (P. 193)

MILES McCORKLE Will. Heirs: wife Kitty Ann McCorkle; son William McCorkle; daughter in law Emma J. McCorkle; and grandson Henry H. McCorkle. Executors: J. Y. Blythe and son William McCorkle. Witnesses: Nathan Green and T. H. Bostick. Recorded 10 November 1868. (P. 194)

WILLIAM R. BOYD Widow's Allotment. 23 April 1868.

Synthia Boyd given her allotment for one year. Recorded 11 November 1868. (Pp. 194-195)

FLEMMING P. WOOD Sale. Recorded 16 November 1868. (Pp. 195-196)

REBECCA HAMILTON Sale. Recorded 17 November 1868. (P. 197)

LEVI D. HOLLOWAY Will. 22 October 1868. Heirs: wife; child; brother A. J. Holloway. William Hancock, executor. Witnesses: A. C. Kidder, Levi Holloway, and R. B. Castleman. Recorded 12 November 1868. (P. 198)

PERMELIA W. HUNT Noncupative Will. 17 October 1868. Heirs: mother Penelope E. Hunt; brothers James M. Hunt and John Thomas Hunt. Witnesses: A. H. Moser and Nancy L. Moser. Recorded 15 December 1868. (P. 203)

BENJAMIN WARREN Sale. 7 November 1868. W. G. Warren, executor. Recorded 15 December 1868. (P. 203)

WILLIAM CLEMMONS Inventory. 30 November 1868. A. C. Bettes, administrator. Recorded 16 December 1868. (P. 204)

F. P. WOOD Widow's Allotment. 8 October 1868. Mary Wood given her allotment for one year. Recorded 16 December 1869. (P. 204)

ELIZABETH JENKINS Inventory. Recorded 16 December 1868. (P. 204)

JOHN G. THOMAS Sale. Recorded 16 December 1868. (P. 205)

DR. ED DONOHO Inventory. John W. Price, administrator. Recorded 26 December 1868. (Pp. 206-208)

AMON EAGAN Will. 16 September 1868. Heirs: wife Judey Eagan; sons Martin Hancock and Jack Wray; Edney Wray; William Hall; Milberry Eagan; and granddaughter Louiza Stewart. John H. McLarin, executor. Witnesses: John H. McLarin and John J. Smith. Recorded 15 January 1869. (P. 209)

S. O. TARPLEY Inventory. Recorded 15 January 1869. (P. 209)

J. C. SMITH Sale. Recorded 16 January 1869. (P. 211)

J. H. MOSELEY Widow's Allotment. Manerva Moseley given her allotment for one year. Recorded 16 January 1869. (P. 211)

ROBERT KNIGHT Widow's Allotment. 17 December 1868. Sophronia Knight given her allotment for one year. Recorded 16 January 1869. (P. 212)

MOSES ELLIS Sale. 28 December 1868. An account of sale of Moses Ellis and of Elizabeth Ellis, his widow. Recorded 16 January 1869. (Pp. 212-213)

HANNAH HANCOCK Inventory. Recorded 16 January 1869. (P. 213)

WILLIAM McMILLEN Inventory. Recorded 16 January 1869. (P. 214)

JAMES L. TOMPKINS Will. 28 June 1867. Heirs: wife; son Samuel W. Tompkins; daughter Elizabeth A. J. Turner; children of Edmund H. Tompkins; wife's sister Catherine Dunn; widows and orphans. Executors: Alfred M. Turner and L. N. M. Cook. Witnesses: H. S. Kennedy and M. R. Eagan. Recorded 19 February 1869. (P. 216)

JOSIAH PHILIPS Will. 24 October 1868. Heirs: wife L. Philips; seven sons John, William, Harden, David, Benjamin, and Wilson Philips. "I have made no reference to the lands which my wife inherited from her father." John Philips, executor. Witnesses: H. Ragland, J. W. Philips, and W. S. Philips. (This will was contested in Circuit Court under John S. Philips, Ex. vs. John Oakley and others.) Recorded 19 February 1869. (Pp. 217,221)

JAMES H. MOSELEY Sale. 12 December 1868. W. J. Moseley, administrator. Recorded 18 January 1869. (Pp. 219-220)

IRVIN TOMLINSON Sale. Recorded 19 January 1869. (P. 220)

NORA J. HUNT Will. 2 December 1868. Heirs: mother P. E. Hunt; sisters Maria W., Sarah H., and Leddy C. Hunt; brothers James M., Thomas, P. E., and William D. Hunt. "I am an heir of James Madison Hunt." Executrix: mother P. E. Hunt. Witnesses: A. H. Moser and J. M. Moser. Recorded 20 February 1869. (P. 224)

E. H. TOMPKINS Sale. Recorded 21 February 1869. (Pp. 226-228)

MARY BURCHETT Inventory. Recorded 21 February 1869. (P. 229)

JOSIAH PHILIPS Widow's Allotment. Malinda Philips given her allotment for one year. Recorded 21 February 1869. (P. 231)

W. C. BOND Widow's Allotment. Martha Bond given her allotment for one year. Recorded 21 February 1869. (P. 231)

BURRELL TARVER Will. 26 January 1869. Heirs: wife Matilda Tarver; children Jane, Malissa, Robert, John, Adaline, and Almeda Tarver; grandchild William Cartwright. Executors: J. B. Tarver and B. J. Tarver. Witnesses: J. B. Burdine, William Eddins, and J. B. Tarver. Recorded 10 March 1869. (P. 232)

ELIZABETH HEARN Sale. O. D. Hearn, administrator. Recorded 16 April 1869. (Pp. 239-241)

SAMUEL HAYS Widow's Allotment. Rebecca Hays given her allotment for one year. Recorded 6 July 1869. (P.

244)

SYLVANIA SULLIVAN Widow's Allotment. Malvina F. Sullivan given her allotment for one year. Recorded 6 July 1869. (Pp. 244,248-249)

MARTHA POSEY Sale. Recorded 6 July 1869. (P. 245)

STANHOPE WHITLOCK Inventory. 16 February 1869. A. B. Whitlock, administrator. Recorded 6 July 1869. (P. 245)

W. G. ROBERTSON Inventory. John H. Robertson, administrator. Recorded 7 July 1869. (P. 247)

DR. LAWRENCE LINDSEY Inventory. H. S. Lindsey, administrator. Recorded 7 July 1869. (P. 247)

MARY GRANDSTAFF Sale. Recorded 8 July 1869. (Pp. 249-250)

MARY BASS Sale. Recorded 8 July 1869. (Pp. 250-251)

SARAH WATERS Sale. Recorded 8 July 1869. (Pp. 252-253)

ANNA THOMPSON Inventory. Recorded 8 July 1869. (P. 255)

DAVID BUCHER Will. 25 February 1867. Heirs: children; grandchildren Sophrona and David Bucher, the minor heirs of Henry Bucher; son in law Lea Wharton. Lea Wharton, executor. Recorded 8 July 1869. (P. 255)

MASON TILLER Will. 16 November 1867. Heirs: wife Virginia Tiller; children Virginia Tiller, Mason Tiller, Mary Tiller, and Amanda Williams. Daughter Amanda Williams is now a resident of Georgia and a child by my first marriage. Executors: wife Virginia Tiller and friend Samuel L. Moseley. Recorded 8 July 1869. (Pp. 256-257)

G. G. HUDDLESTON Will. 15 April 1869. Heirs: wife; and children. Executor: brother William A. Huddleston. Recorded 9 July 1869. (Pp. 257-258)

JOHN McCAFFREY Widow's Allotment. Rebecca McCaffrey given her allotment for one year. Recorded 12 July 1869. (Pp. 264-265)

JANE NELSON Sale. Recorded 12 July 1869. (P. 267)

MARK DODD Will. 30 October 1867. Heirs: daughter Narcissa Wier. Other children excluded, to wit, John Dodd, Jane Hodge, David Dodd, William Dodd, Mary Wright's children she being dead, and the children of Elizabeth Hodge deceased. Recorded 8 August 1869. (P. 269)

JAMES S. WOOD Will. 12 January 1869. Heirs: wife J. F. Wood; children; business partner James Compton. Moses Wood, executor. Recorded 17 September 1869. (P. 270)

JONATHAN EATHERLY Will. 14 August 1868. Heirs:

51

children Thompson Eatherly, Frances A. Eatherly, Mary E.
Davis, and Samantha C. Thompson; children of my son
Rufus Eatherly, to wit, Alexander F., Ewing M., and
William J. Eatherly; and children of my daughter Martha
Visey, to wit, Valnius L., Virginia A., William H.,
Sargant P., Richard R., and John Visey. Recorded 17
September 1869. (P. 271)

MRS. CALVARY JOHNSON Inventory. Recorded 12 September 1869. (Pp. 272-274)

THOMAS W. LYONS Widow's Allotment. Recorded 12
September 1869. (P. 275)

J. N. PATTON Sale. Recorded 12 September 1869.
(P. 275)

W. D. SMITH Inventory. Recorded 12 September 1869.
(Pp. 275-277)

TABITHA WOOD Sale. Recorded 12 September 1869.
(Pp. 280-281)

L. W. SHERRILL Widow's Allotment. 24 July 1869.
Eliza Sherrill given her allotment for one year. Recorded 12 September 1869. (Pp. 284-285)

SUSAN JENNINGS Inventory. Recorded 12 September
1869. (Pp. 285-287)

SAMUEL DAVIS Will. 30 August 1869. Heirs: daughter Sarah M. Lowe; two children of my deceased daughter
Mary E. Lowe, to wit, Margaret E. and Rosabella Lowe;
and children of my son James E. Davis, to wit, James W.,
Emma M., and Samuel Davis, Jr. Witnesses: John L.
Gleves, Harris Adams, and B. T. Alexander. (P. 290)

SAMUEL DAVIS Codicil. 2 September 1869. My executor, William B. Jennings, is to set aside one fourth of
an acre as a family burying ground and have the same
walled, and that he have placed at my grave and that of
my son, Harvy, a headstone and foot stone. Recorded 8
October 1869. (P. 291)

OSBORN THOMPSON Sale. Recorded 12 October 1869.
(Pp. 295-299)

NANCY E. VANHOOZER Estate. November 1869. Heirs:
children Miss L. J. Vanhoozer and F. Vanhoozer. Recorded 18 November 1869. (P. 299)

H. J. FERRELL Inventory. Recorded 18 November
1869. (P. 300)

GEORGE BROWN Sale. Recorded 18 November 1869. (P. 300)

C. C. SMITH Widow's Allotment. Recorded 19 November 1869. (P. 301)

EZEKIEL BASS Will. 28 January 1868. Heirs: wife
Sarah Bass; youngest daughters Harty P. and Rachel F.
Bass; children Dolphan, Archemack's heirs, John, Nancy,

Henry, and Warren Bass. Nancy Jane Bass, the daughter of Washington Bass, to receive twenty dollars. W. L. Waters, executor. Recorded 19 December 1869. (Pp. 305-307)

WILLIAM McGREGOR Widow's Allotment. 11 February 1869. Frances McGregor given her allotment for one year. Recorded 19 December 1869. (P. 310)

B. L. POSEY Sale. Recorded 24 January 1870. (P. 311)

JOHN H. BAIRD Will. 27 July 1869. Heir: wife Fannie Baird. Fannie Baird, executrix. Recorded 24 February 1870. (P. 313)

GEORGE W. JENNINGS Widow's Allotment. Recorded 24 February 1870. (P. 314)

ELIZABETH GREEN Sale. Recorded 24 February 1870. (Pp. 316-317)

JOHN B. SNOW Will. 18 February 1870. Heirs: wife Martha A. Snow; daughters Lilla D. and Josey M. Snow. T. B. Chapman, executor. Witnesses: R. H. Morris and J. L. Golden. Recorded 24 March 1870. (P. 318)

AMOS MARTIN Will. 18 July 1867. Heirs: wife Sarah Martin; my six children Elijah, Caleb, Sarah, Samuel, Catherine, and Thomas Martin. I have given James M., Elizabeth M., and Jane Martin land in the Western District. Witnesses: J. L. Castleman and James H. Lain. Recorded 24 March 1870. (Pp. 318-319)

E. A. DAVIS Widow's Allotment. Recorded 14 April 1870. (P. 321)

HARRIEL COPPAGE Sale. Recorded 14 April 1870. (Pp. 321-322)

ISABELLA WILLIAMS Sale. Recorded 14 April 1870. (Pp. 322-323)

MARTHA JANE CARVER Will. 14 February 1870. Heirs: sisters Sarah E., Nicey E., and Trephena A. Carver; brothers David H. and James H. Carver. Executor: my beloved uncle William H. Carver. Witnesses: J. H. Guill and P. M. Carver. Recorded 14 April 1870. (Pp. 323-324)

ELIJAH WILLIAMS Will. 4 March 1870. Heirs: wife Sarah Williams; my lawful heirs Laurel Morris, Elizabeth Tucker, Hyram Williams, Cynthia Emaline McDearman, Benjamin Williams, Aquilla Williams, John Williams, William J. Williams, Martha J. Coram, Elisha Williams, and Mary Frances Williams. Executor: son John W. Williams. Recorded 14 April 1870. (Pp. 324-325)

MRS. MARY BROWN Sale. 26 February 1870. F. A. Chandler, administrator. Recorded 24 May 1870. (P. 326)

THOMAS VIVRETT Inventory. 2 April 1870. J. D.

Vivrett, administrator. Mentions the widow. Recorded 24 May 1870. (P. 327)

WILLIAM E. BUCY Widow's Allotment. 16 April 1870. Martha Bucy given her allotment for one year. Recorded 24 May 1870. (P. 327)

NANCY BRIDGES Inventory. Recorded 24 May 1870. (P. 328)

WILLIAM YOUNG Widow's Allotment. 13 April 1868. Hannah Young given her allotment for one year. Recorded 24 May 1870. (P. 328)

JAMES H. CASON Sale. Recorded 24 May 1870. (Pp. 328-329)

MRS. E. A. BEDFORD Sale. Recorded 24 June 1870. (P. 333)

R. R. BARTON Inventory. 20 May 1870. William D. Hamblen, administrator. Recorded 24 June 1870. (P. 333)

NANCY G. CLEMMONS Sale. 14 January 1870. J. D. Bettes, administrator. Recorded 24 June 1870. (Pp. 335-336)

SALLY A. E. JACKSON Will. 22 April 1870. Heirs: husband John B. Jackson; daughter Nancy L. F. Jackson; children of my sister Esther Sanders, to wit, Sally, Andrew, and Joseph Sanders; children of Susan Robbin to receive my interest in the dower where my mother now lives, Elnora and Cora; Nancy Foster, the wife of Robert Foster, to receive the bed and bed clothing that she gave to James Foster, my former husband. John B. Jackson, executor. Witnesses: J. M. Hedgpeth and James H. Rice. Recorded 24 June 1870. (Pp. 336-337)

J. H. SHANNON Will. 28 February 1870. Heirs: wife Isabella Shannon; sons E. K., A., and C. F. Shannon; daughters Emarilda E. Green and Nancy C. Forbis. Executors: sons E. K. and A. Shannon. Recorded 25 July 1870. (P. 338)

SIMON ADAMSON Will. 6 May 1865. Heirs: son William Adamson; each family of my grandchildren; and one sixth interest to the children of Simon P. Adamson deceased who are my great grandchildren. William Adamson, executor. Recorded 25 July 1870. (P. 339)

JOHN JOHNSON Will. 21 May 1870. Heirs: wife Elizabeth Johnson; children Casandria Cason, Clementy Shannon, Delianna Walker, and Paulding Johnson. Recorded 26 July 1870. (P. 339)

MATTHEW HAMMONS Will. 9 May 1870. Heirs: sons Andrew Jackson, James Landerford, and John Hammons; daughters Mary Ann Bryant, Manervy Elizabeth Jane George, Araminta Ann Anderson, and Sarah Frances Stewart; George Washington Lafayette Hammons. James K. P. Bryant, executor. Recorded 26 July 1870. (Pp. 340-341)

JEFFERSON SPRINGS Sale. 14 June 1870. Administrator: father William Springs. Recorded 26 July 1870. (P. 341)

NANCY HILL Inventory. Recorded 26 July 1870. (Pp. 342-343)

MARTHA E. POWELL Will. 6 July 1870. Heirs: mother Sarah J. Powell; brothers and sisters John M., George F., Silas T., Robert D., Price P., Ruth A., Edward S., Sally H., and German G. Powell. William T. Powell, executor. Witnesses: John J. Pittman, E. P. Horn, and James Hamilton. Recorded 14 September 1870. (P. 347)

ELIZABETH BOND Will. 5 August 1870. Heirs: daughters Mahala Jane Knight, Martha Ann Bond, and Pheoba Moser. Recorded 14 September 1870. (P. 348)

JAMES H. McFARLAND Will. 13 June 1870. Heirs: wife Charlotte McFarland; my five children John W., James H., Ada B., Mattie E. McFarland, and older daughter Sally D. Rucks. Executors: John W. McFarland and Matt W. Comin. Recorded 14 September 1870. (P. 349)

BENJAMIN DAVIS Sale. Recorded 14 September 1870. (P. 350)

E. DAVIDSON JOHNSON Inventory. Recorded 14 September 1870. (Pp. 350-353)

REBECCA WRIGHT Sale. Recorded 14 September 1870. (Pp. 353-354)

WILLIAM F. LAIN Widow's Allotment. Recorded 14 September 1870. (P. 356)

MARY MASSEY Inventory. Recorded 14 September 1870. (Pp. 356-360)

PHILIP FISHER Sale. 15 January 1858. Phebe Fisher, administratrix. Recorded 14 September 1870. (Pp. 361-362)

J. E. DAVIS Widow's Allotment. 19 September 1870. Anna Davis given her allotment for one year. Recorded 20 October 1870. (P. 363)

WILLIAM K. PHILLIPS Widow's Allotment. Recorded 20 October 1870. (Pp. 363-364)

N. G. ALEXANDER Widow's Allotment. Recorded 20 October 1870. (P. 364)

RICHARD HORN Widow's Allotment. Clarissa Horn given her allotment for one year. Recorded 20 October 1870. (P. 365)

J. P. WRIGHT Sale. Recorded 20 October 1870. (Pp. 367-368)

JOHN C. SYPERT Inventory. Recorded 20 October 1870. (P. 368)

JOHN OWEN Sale. Recorded 20 October 1870. (Pp. 368-369)

HARRISON THOMAS Inventory. Recorded 20 October 1870. (P. 370)

THOMAS E. WILLIAMSON Widow's Allotment. Recorded 10 December 1870. (P. 371)

L. A. GREEN Widow's Allotment. Recorded 10 December 1870. (P. 371)

G. W. BOND Sale. Recorded 10 December 1870. (Pp. 372-373)

WILLIAM H. HAWKINS Inventory. 27 November 1869. Elizabeth H. Hawkins, administratrix. Recorded 10 December 1870. (P. 373)

ANDERSON JENNINGS Widow's Allotment. Recorded 24 January 1871. (P. 377)

CLARISA HORN Sale. Recorded 24 January 1871. (P. 383)

LEVY McCAFFREY Will. 22 October 1869. Heirs: wife Elizabeth McCaffrey; children Sary Ann, John, and James McCaffrey. There was one fourth of the tract willed to my sister, Sary McCaffrey, by my father, Robert McCaffrey. Elizabeth McCaffrey, executrix. Recorded 24 January 1871. (P. 383)

REBECCA RIGHT Will. 31 May 1870. Heirs: My beloved granddaughter, Fanny Right, daughter of Benjamin Right to have twenty-five dollars over and above all my other heirs. R. B. Zachary, executor. Recorded 24 January 1871. (P. 384)

A. E. DONNELL Inventory. 28 January 1871. F. M. Donnell, administrator. Recorded 20 February 1871. (P. 385)

DAVID L. WILEY Inventory. Recorded 20 February 1871. (P. 386)

MARY REECE Inventory. Recorded 20 February 1871. (Pp. 386-387)

JERRY BOND Will. 2 September 1870. Heirs: wife Elizabeth Bond; my children. J. M. Martin, executor. Recorded 14 March 1871. (Pp. 388-389)

JAMES McCULLOCH Inventory. Recorded 14 March 1871. (P. 389)

ELIZA MEREDITH Inventory. 6 March 1871. Administrator: husband William B. Meredith. Recorded 14 March 1871. (Pp. 389-390)

JACOB FITE Will. 9 February 1860. Heirs: wife Matilda Fite; sons Leonard B., Samuel M., Albert, Jacob C., John, James, and Edwin M. Fite; daughter Dorcas R. Scott, the wife of Leander Scott; and granddaughter

Amanda Scott. Executors: Leonard B. Fite and Samuel M. Fite.

JACOB FITE Codicil. Daughter Roena Scott is not to be subject to the debts or control of Leander Scott or any future husband. Witnesses: Edwin C. Fite and J. W. Fite. Recorded 14 March 1871. (P. 391)

ADAM KEMPER Will. 11 June 1870. Heirs: son James Madison Kemper; daughter Jemimah Kemper. Executors: S. T. Mottley and Joseph Mottley. Recorded 14 March 1871. (P. 391)

JAMES WALLACE Will. 2 August 1860. Heirs: wife; son James F. Wallace; daughters Mary Ann Vanhoozer, Louiza Wallace, and Elizabeth Thompson. Executors: James F. Wallace and Lambeth Vanhoozer. Recorded 14 March 1871. (P. 392)

ASA JACKSON Sale. Recorded 14 March 1871. (Pp. 393-396)

RICHARD MOUNT Will. Heirs: wife Lively Mount; children Sarah Hight, Susan Knight, Jane Bond, Polly Ann Patterson, Richard A. Mount, and Mathias Mount; children of my daughter Elizabeth Copeland; children of my son Amos Mount; children of my son William Mount; and children of my grandson, John R. Harris. Executors: Mathias Mount and A. J. Patterson. Witnesses: Lewis Patterson and E. S. Smith. Recorded 14 March 1871. (Pp. 397-398)

MARTHA A. CORDER Will. 6 August 1861. Heirs: brothers William G. and Robert A. Corder. William G. Corder, executor. Recorded 14 March 1871. (P. 398)

ALFRED ESKEW Sale. Recorded 14 March 1871. (P. 399)

KINNEY PRICE Will. 13 August 1870. Heir: wife Milly Price. The will is intended to include all property which may come to me from the estate of my brother Isham Slaughter who died in Cincinatti, Ohio. Recorded 10 May 1871. (P. 400)

WILLIAM L. CLEMMONS Inventory. Recorded 10 May 1871. (Pp. 401-402)

STACY YOUNG Sale. Recorded 14 May 1871. (Pp. 402-404)

E. B. VIVRETT Widow's Allotment. 11 February 1871. Indiana Vivrett given her allotment for one year. Recorded 24 May 1871. (P. 407)

ALLEN ROSS Will. 17 November 1866. Heirs: wife Margaret Ross; children Fountain P. Ross, Manerva McClain, Mitchell Ross (who is now dead, but had two children, to wit, Sarah and John William), Henry P. Ross, Sarah Freeman, Lavonia A. Pitman, William A. Ross, E. T. Ross, James G. Ross, and Elizabeth Patton. I have had three wives and three sets of children. My first wife was a Motheral. My second wife was a Proctor (six children by her). Executor: grandson Rufus McClain. Recorded 24 May 1871. (Pp. 408-409)

TRUMAN HARRINGTON Will. 29 May 1871. Heir: wife Elizabeth Harrington. Elizabeth Harrington, executrix. Recorded 24 May 1871. (P. 410)

SARAH F. MILLER Will. 4 September 1868. Heirs: adopted daughter Lavina Miller; niece, Ann Young, the daughter of my sister, Betsey Young; and sister Ann McKinney and her husband, Wesley McKinney. Recorded 24 May 1871. (Pp. 410-411)

LETTISHA SANDERS Will. 7 April 1870. Heirs: sons R. C. and D. L. Sanders. R. C. Sanders, executor. Recorded 24 June 1871. (P. 412)

D. B. MOORE Sale. Recorded 24 June 1871. (Pp. 412-414)

GEORGE WILLIAMS Sale. Recorded 24 June 1871. (Pp. 414-415)

C. W. NEAL Inventory. Recorded 24 June 1871. (Pp. 417-422)

O. G. FINLEY Widow's Allotment. 28 April 1871. Bettie Finley given her allotment for one year. Recorded 24 June 1871. (P. 422)

ANN DEW Sale. Recorded 10 July 1871. (Pp. 423-424)

JOHN GREEN Inventory. Recorded 15 July 1871. (Pp. 425-429)

DANIEL FITE Will. 23 February 1871. Heirs: wife Margaret Jane Fite; our eight children John H., Mary V., William, Martha E., Henry A., Thomas M., Edmond L., and Helen A. Fite. Executor: brother Moses H. Fite. Witnesses: Isaiah B. David, James Allen, and Joseph Clarke. Recorded 15 July 1871. (Pp. 429-430)

SUSAN CURD Will. 8 May 1871. Heirs: son John N. Curd; daughters Elizabeth Dotson and Nancy Freeman; granddaughter Ida Freeman. William Dotson, executor. Witnesses: John Crudup and J. P. Cawthon. Recorded 15 July 1871. (P. 430)

FOSTER LOYD Widow's Allotment. Recorded 15 July 1871. (P. 436)

LAWRENCE SYPERT Will. 17 March 1870. Heirs: wife Betsy Sypert; son William Carroll Sypert; daughter Mary D. Anderson; granddaughter Sally Coleman, the daughter of my daughter Eliza H. Hays; children of Thomas Gibson, born to him by Martha Jane Gibson. Dr. J. M. Anderson, executor. Recorded 14 August 1871. (Pp. 439-440)

LUCINDA TARVER Will. 9 January 1867. Smith County,

Tennessee. Heirs: two step sons Benjamin J. and John B.
Tarver; Mrs. Lucy Tarver, the wife of step son John B.
Tarver; nephews Thomas J. S. and John B. Burdine;
nieces Flora, Mary Elizabeth, Laura Lee, Mary D., and
Martha Jane Burdine; brothers Nathan B. and John B.
Burdine; sister in law Euphenia E. Burdine; sister
Mary A. Owen; niece Fountainella Ward; the legitimate
heirs of John B. Burdine. Step sons to receive of the
estate of my husband Silas Tarver. Nathan B. Burdine,
executor. Recorded 14 August 1871. (Pp. 440-442)

WILLIAM M. BARROW Will. 19 June 1871. Heirs:
wife Mary Ann Barrow; sons James J. and Cullen P. Barrow; and daughter Henrietta Barrow. Recorded 14 August
1871. (Pp. 442-443)

E. A. TURNER Widow's Allotment. 14 July 1871.
Anice Turner given her allotment for one year. Recorded
14 August 1871. (Pp. 443-446)

JAMES NEAL Inventory. Recorded 14 August 1871.
(Pp. 446-447)

CATHERINE VANTREASE Will. 29 November 1855. Heirs:
daughter Polly Neal; sons John, William, Nicholas, and
Jackson Vantrease; sons of deceased son Jacob Vantrease,
to wit, William and Ezekiel Vantrease. Recorded 14 September 1871. (P. 448)

BERDOTTA HEWGLEY Will. 10 August 1867. Heirs:
mother Nancy Bridges; brothers and sisters. Executor:
brother John Hewgley. Witnesses: T. B. Stroud and
C. P. Eskew. Recorded 14 September 1871. (P. 449)

ELIZABETH HAGARTY Will. 20 September 1871. Heir:
sister. Executors: R. M. Whitescarver and O. L. Martin.
Recorded 14 October 1871. (P. 449)

MARY WRIGHT Will. 16 April 1862. Heirs: niece
Sarah Jane Wright to receive the land I bought of
Samuel M. Wright; niece Nancy Ann Wright to receive the
land I bought of Lemuel Wright. Executor: brother
Josiah Wright. Recorded 14 October 1871. (Pp. 452-453)

JAMES M. BENTLEY Will. 6 August 1871. Heirs: wife
and children. Executor: brother J. F. Bentley. Recorded 14 October 1871. (P. 453)

R. H. ANDERSON Widow's Allotment. 3 October 1871.
Mary Ann Anderson given her allotment for one year. Recorded 14 October 1871. (Pp. 453-454)

W. D. THOMPSON Widow's Allotment. Recorded 14
October 1871. (P. 454)

ASAPH ALSUP Inventory. Recorded 14 October 1871.
(P. 455)

MARTHA E. LIGON Inventory. 12 September 1871.
W. B. Ligon, administrator. Recorded 14 October 1871.
(P. 456)

WILLIAM L. SYPERT Will. 17 July 1869. Heirs: daughter Elizabeth Cook; Rockerlany Straughn; John Bowers and wife Jane; Mary Ann Rison, widow of James Rison; Thomas Sypert, Jr., son of Thomas Sypert; and Josephine Callaway. Mathew W. and John C. Sypert to receive my lands in Texas, a portion of which is in the hands of H. Sypert, administrator of Thomas Sypert deceased. John C. Sypert, executor. Recorded 26 January 1872. (P. 459)

THOMAS TURNER Noncupative Will. 11 October 1871.
Heirs: wife: children J. W., E. A., L. L., Joel P.
Hamilton, T. M., Marion H., and Rufus W. Turner. Execu-
tor: son Marion H. Turner. Recorded 10 November 1871.
(Pp. 1-2)

HOWELL W. WILLIAMS Will. 16 October 1871. Heirs:
wife Sarah Williams; son W. W. Williams; daughters
M. H. Williams and Ann R. Jones; granddaughter M. J.
Thompson. Executors: sons R. N. and A. L. Williams.
Recorded 10 November 1871. (Pp. 2-3)

WILLIAM JAMES ROGERS Will. 6 January 1871. Heirs:
wife Eliza Jane Rogers; children Martha C. Eskew,
James M. Rogers, Henry A. Rogers, Mary C. Chandler,
Houston L. Rogers, Louiza Rogers, Viola Rogers, Maggie L.
Rogers, and John C. Rogers. Mentions my father. Henry
A. Rogers, executor. Recorded 10 November 1871. (Pp.
3-4)

W. W. PRICE Widow's Allotment. Recorded 10 November
1871. (P. 5)

N. W. MOORE Inventory. Recorded 10 November 1871.
(P. 5)

ELIZABETH BAIRD Will. Heirs: mother; sister Jane
C. Sherrill; niece Emma Thompson, the daughter of my
sister Mary F. Thompson. I am one of the children of
J. D. Martin. Executor: husband A. W. Baird. Recorded
10 November 1871. (P. 7)

L. H. BASS Widow's Allotment. Recorded 10 December
1871. (P. 9)

GEORGE WILLIAMSON Will. 19 August 1867. Heirs:
wife Sarah A. Williamson; sons P. K. and T. E. Williamson; and grandson John M. Williamson. William Williamson, executor. Recorded 24 January 1872. (P. 10)

DAVID PROCTOR Inventory. Recorded 24 January 1872.
(P. 12)

VICTORIA PHELPS Inventory. Recorded 24 January
1872. (Pp. 12-14)

SIDNEY WILLIAMS Sale. Recorded 24 January 1872.
(Pp. 14-16)

SAMUEL SPERRY Inventory. Recorded 24 January 1872.
(Pp. 16-17)

D. COOK, JR. Will. 27 January 1872. Heirs: father;
mother; sisters; brothers George and Clark Cook;
children of brother George Cook. Executors: friends
John H. Owen and Andrew B. Martin. Witnesses: R. L.
Caruthers, Richard Beard, and J. M. Anderson. Recorded
14 February 1872. (Pp. 18-19)

JOHN PEMBERTON Sale. Recorded 14 February 1872.
(Pp. 19-21)

ANNY MURRY Sale. Recorded 14 February 1872. (Pp. 23-24)

REBECCA PARTLOW Will. 12 January 1872. Heirs: mother; sister Sary Jane Partlow. Jasper Martin, executor. Witnesses: J. F. Hooker and J. N. Partlow. Recorded 14 March 1872. (P. 25)

R. H. QUESENBURY Sale. Recorded 14 March 1872. (Pp. 27-28)

CHARLES G. CARTER Widow's Allotment. Recorded 14 March 1872. (P. 31)

N. L. LINDSLEY Inventory. Recorded 14 March 1872. (P. 32)

J. W. CRAWFORD Sale. Recorded 14 March 1872. (P. 32)

R. L. LIGON Inventory. R. R. Ligon, administrator. Recorded 10 April 1872. (Pp. 34-35)

J. H. DICKASON Sale. Recorded 10 April 1872. (Pp. 37-38)

WILLIAM RICE Inventory. Recorded 10 May 1872. (P. 39)

JOHN TRIBBLE Inventory. 14 March 1872. A lunatic. Recorded 10 May 1872. (P. 39)

WILLIAM P. BARRY Noncupative Will. 13 May 1872. Heirs: children. Mentions Jordan and Tennie. Recorded 10 June 1872. (P. 47)

D. A. WHITSETT Will. 29 April 1872. Heirs: sons William H. and John B. Whitsett; and daughter M. B. Whitsett. James Hamilton, executor. Witnesses: James P. McFarland and N. M. Major. Recorded 10 June 1872. (P. 47)

LUCY PRUETT Sale. Recorded 10 June 1872. (P. 48)

W. C. KNOX Sale. Recorded 10 June 1872. (P. 50)

WILLIAM JENNINGS Widow's Allotment. 27 April 1872. Polly Jennings given her allotment for one year. Recorded 10 June 1872. (P. 50)

JONATHAN BAILEY Will. 26 December 1871. Heirs: wife Cassandra Bailey; sister Syllava Walker; nieces Susan James, Cinderella Turner, Syllava Donnell, Lucy Mitchell, Elizabeth Smith, Cleopatra Moore, Sally Hart, Harriet Harris, and Mandy Hubbard; nephew B. S. Bailey; Jany Donnell's son James A. Donnell; and Jane Barbee. Executors: David Young and W. W. Seay. Recorded 10 July 1872. (Pp. 51-52)

FELIX H. TAYLOR Inventory. Recorded 11 July 1872. (P. 61)

SARAH BACHUS Sale. Recorded 10 July 1872. (P. 61)

WILLS & INVENTORIES 1871-1878

JOHN ODUM Widow's Allotment. Frances Odum given her allotment for one year. Recorded 10 July 1872. (Pp. 64-65)

D. W. QUARLES Inventory. Recorded 10 July 1872. (P. 66)

JAMES EATHERLY Will. July 1865. Heirs: wife Rebecca Eatherly; sons Ervin, William, and James Eatherly; daughters Roxy Telford, Harriet, Jane, Mary, and Rebecca A. Eatherly; granddaughter Mary E. Smith; grandson Maxwell Smith; deceased son Yewell Eatherly's children, to wit, Lucinda Ellen and John Bowie Eatherly; son in law William B. Smith. Mentions James Telford deceased. Executors: wife Rebecca Eatherly and son James Eatherly. Recorded 10 August 1872. (Pp. 68-69)

REBECCA ADKINSON Will. 13 November 1871. Heirs: daughters Matilda Adkinson, Elizabeth Martha McConnell, Mary Indiana Shryer, and Eliza Frances Horn; grandchildren John Julian and Amanda Ann Adkinson. Executors: James Hamilton and B. W. G. Winford. Recorded 10 August 1872. (Pp. 69-70)

BENJAMIN SULLIVAN Will. 27 November 1871. Wagon maker and tanner. Heirs: wife Mary Sullivan; daughters Amanda M. Gates, Mary R. Sullivan, and Nancy Caraway; my other children; grandchildren of Christopher C. S. Rogers and his sister, Elizabeth F. Baird, wife of Rufus Baird, now a citizen of Collins County, Texas. Recorded 10 June 1872. (Pp. 70-71)

MATTHEW ESTES Widow's Allotment. Recorded 10 August 1872. (P. 75)

BENJAMIN BARCLAY Sale. Recorded 10 August 1872. (P. 75)

R. F. HARLAN Sale. 21 January 1872. Green Hobbs, administrator. Recorded 10 August 1872. (P. 78)

ADAM KEMPER Sale. Recorded 10 August 1872. (Pp. 78-79)

WILLIAM HANCOCK Will. 13 July 1872. Heirs: wife Frances A. Hancock; sons David T., John E. Hancock; daughters Mary E. A., Nancy C., Louisa E., Sally J. C., and Sophia B. Hancock. Executors: brother James H. Hancock and son John E. Hancock. Witnesses: J. B. Baird, Martin Hancock, and J. B. Hancock. Recorded 10 September 1872. (Pp. 80-83)

ALLAPHAIR HUDSON Will. 28 March 1872. Heirs: nieces Mary P. Collier and Allaphair H. Chapman. T. B. Chapman, executor. Recorded 10 September 1872. (Pp. 83-84)

GEORGE W. MOTHERAL Will. 10 April 1872. Heirs: mother Elizabeth A. Motheral; brother L. J. Motheral; sisters Vandalia and Martha R. Motheral. Recorded 10 September 1872. (P. 84)

RICHARD BASS Widow's Allotment. 16 November 1870. Emily Bass given her allotment for one year. Recorded 10 September 1872. (Pp. 85-86)

THOMAS H. ESTES Will. 11 May 1859. Heirs: wife Lucy Estes; children. Executors: wife Lucy Estes and Robert Estes. Recorded 10 October 1872. (P. 86)

G. W. O'NEAL Will. 8 August 1872. Heirs: my three children. Executor: father Asa O'Neal. Witnesses: J. W. Dill and James Lester. Recorded 10 October 1872. (P. 87)

JOHN HARLAN Widow's Allotment. Recorded 10 October 1872. (P. 88)

ISAAC SMITH Inventory. Recorded 10 October 1872. (Pp. 91-92)

NEIL KEATON Sale. 4 September 1868. James Keaton, administrator. Recorded 4 December 1872. (P. 97)

ROBERT COLEMAN Widow's Allotment. Mary J. Coleman and her three children given their allotment for one year. Recorded 4 December 1872. (P. 101)

SALLY SIMS Will. 15 February 1872. Heirs: four daughters Nancy, Sally Ann, Susan Eugenia L., and Diretha Agnes Sims. Mentions other children. Witnesses: B. F. Knox and Matthew Eatherly. Recorded 10 December 1872. (P. 102)

JOHN C. HUNT Will. 19 February 1869. Heirs: wife Jane Hunt; sons Elijah C., Josiah, William C., Hartwell Hunt; daughters Susan Campbell and Emily Hale; children of deceased son George Hunt; and children of deceased daughter Jane Willis. Recorded 10 December 1872. (P. 103)

LEONARD FITE Will. 4 September 1868. Heirs: sons Thomas D. and Lemuel Fite; deceased son L. D. Fite's widow Caroline Fite; daughter Margaret Martin and children; granddaughters Lavina Hays and Mary J. Martin; heirs of Lawrence Reed; Nancy Davis; and Mary Williams. Executors: sons Thomas D. and Lemuel Fite. Recorded 10 December 1872. (Pp. 103-104)

ISAAC DAVIS Will. 4 May 1872. Heirs: sons L. H., G. W., and Isaac T. Davis; daughters Lara J., Mary R., Rachel, and Elmira Davis. Eli R. Green, executor. Recorded 14 January 1873. (P. 105)

SUE A. HEARN Will. Heirs: mother Ellen Kerby; M. L. Walsh; R. D. Hearn; sister Brunette R. Walsh. O. D. Hearn, executor. Recorded 14 January 1873. (Pp. 105-106)

MILBERRY P. HEARN Noncupative Will. 17 December 1871. Heirs: Hardy F. Hearn to receive the old James W. Hearn tract, and the land given to his mother by his grandfather, Robertson Johnson. Mentions Purnel Hearn and wife, Bettie. Recorded 14 January 1873. (P. 107)

JOHN DRENNAN Sale. Executors: J. D. Drennan and
D. C. Drennan. Recorded 14 January 1873. (Pp. 112-113)

M. L. VAUGHAN Will. 20 December 1870. Heirs: wife
Sarah A. Vaughan; son Talleyrand L. Vaughan; Mary W.
Vaughan, wife of William W. Vaughan and their children
James T., Edward D., and John D. Vaughan; Anna Hundley
Vaughan, infant daughter of my son H. L. Vaughan deceased.
Executors: Talleyrand L. Vaughan and Edward D. Vaughan.
Witnesses: John C. Kirkpatrick, William G. Thompson,
and C. H. Oldham. Recorded 14 March 1873. (P. 118)

ELIZABETH A. VANTREASE Sale. 22 February 1873.
J. J. Vantrease, administrator. Recorded 14 March 1873.
(Pp. 120-121)

THOMAS NORMAN Will. 6 March 1873. Heirs: daughters
Matilda C., Annie F., and Sallie H. Norman. Daughter
Kate M. Martin is the wife of J. M. Martin. Annie F. is
now Annie F. Swain. Executors: J. L. Fite and H. T.
Norman. Recorded 28 April 1873. (Pp. 122-123)

JESSE JENNINGS Will. 1 August 1872. Heirs: wife
Temperance Jennings; sons Clem and George Jennings;
daughter Louisa May Jennings. James H. Jennings, executor. Recorded 28 April 1873. (Pp. 123-124)

VALENTINE VANHOOZER Will. 27 April 1861. Heirs:
present wife Delila Vanhoozer; all my children by said
wife, to wit, Lavinia, Arena, Ardena, Gentry L., Amanda,
Rutherford G., and William R. Vanhoozer. Andrew J.
Winters, executor. Recorded 28 April 1873. (P. 124)

W. A. SIMMONS Inventory. Recorded 28 April 1873.
(P. 125)

MARY C. CARUTH Inventory. Recorded 28 April 1873.
(Pp. 125-127)

R. L. LIGON Sale. 30 January 1873. Second sale.
Recorded 28 April 1873. (P. 128)

MARY TUCKER Sale. Recorded 28 April 1873. (Pp.
129-131)

MARY WOODS Sale. Recorded 28 April 1873. (P. 133)

JAMES CARUTH Sale. Recorded 28 April 1873. (Pp.
134-135)

G. L. ARMSTRONG Widow's Allotment. Recorded 28
April 1873. (P. 135)

SARAH ALSUP Will. 10 June 1867. Heirs: three sons
W. G., A. B., and H. C. Alsup; children of deceased son
C. B. Alsup, to wit, Indiana and William Alsup; Mary G.
Moore, the wife of C. B. Alsup. Executors: A. B. and
H. C. Alsup. Recorded 14 May 1873. (P. 136)

MRS. EDA SKEEN Sale. Recorded 14 May 1873. (Pp.
137-139)

THOMAS P. HOLMAN Inventory. Recorded 10 June 1873. (Pp. 141-142)

FRANCINA WILLIAMS Inventory. Recorded 10 June 1873. (P. 142)

MRS. ANNIE HOLMAN Inventory. Recorded 10 June 1873. (P. 142)

JOSEPH D. YOUNG, SR. Inventory. Recorded 2 October 1873. (Pp. 146-147)

NICHOLAS VANTREASE Sale. 22 February 1873. James P. Doss, administrator. Recorded 8 October 1873. (Pp. 149-150)

H. C. SHORTER Widow's Allotment. 30 August 1873. Delia Shorter given her allotment for one year. Recorded 8 October 1873. (P. 151)

ELIZABETH BAIRD Inventory. 1 September 1873. Administrator: husband B. Baird. Recorded 8 October 1873. (P. 151)

S. B. PATTERSON Widow's Allotment. 30 June 1873. Polly Patterson given her allotment for one year. Recorded 14 October 1873. (P. 155)

GEORGE ALLEN Widow's Allotment. 23 August 1873. Sarah Allen given her allotment for one year. Recorded 15 October 1873. (P. 155)

WILLIAM HARRIS, SR. Will. 28 June 1873. Heirs: wife Hannah R. Harris; and daughter Martha Harris. Said William was a joint owner with W. F. Harris of a town lot in Cainsville. Executors: Hannah R. Harris and P. W. Harris. Recorded 15 October 1873. (P. 156)

ELMIRA J. SMITH Will. 22 September 1873. Heirs: husband Thomas J. Smith; my brothers and sisters; my husband's brothers and sisters. Dr. James M. Smith to look after my husband's part. Recorded 16 October 1873. (P. 157)

MARTHA H. ANDERSON Will. Heirs: daughter Elizabeth C. Martin; and niece Rachel Donaldson. Mentions two sons. Elizabeth C. Martin, executrix. Recorded 18 October 1873. (P. 158)

BIRD DEBOW Will. 26 September 1873. Heirs: wife Ann Debow; sons Hugh C. and John Debow; daughters Mary Ann Debow and Rachel J. Justice. Executors: Ann Debow and John Palmer. Recorded 18 October 1873. (P. 159)

SUSAN F. MOORE Sale. Recorded 28 October 1873. (P. 160)

JOHN W. SMITH Sale. Recorded 20 November 1873. (Pp. 163-165)

MARION WHITEHEAD Widow's Allotment. Annie J. Whitehead given her allotment for one year. Recorded 25 November 1873. (P. 167)

JACOB GRIMMETT Sale. Recorded 6 December 1873. (Pp. 172-176)

NANCY DONNELL Widow's Allotment. Recorded 9 December 1873. (P. 176)

JOSIAH DONNELL Sale. Recorded 8 December 1873. (P. 177)

SARAH BOND Will. 21 April 1866. Heirs: children Leland F. Clemmons, Presley L. Clemmons, and Nancy P. Phillips; minor heirs of Harvey H. Bond, to wit, Mary Francis, Louiza Jane, and Elizabeth Susan Bond. Leland F. Clemmons, executor. Recorded 10 December 1873. (P. 178)

EUNICE CARVER Will. 1 March 1871. Heirs: niece Emily A. Clemmons; brother Archibald Carver's children, to wit, Pleasant J., Martha E., Pemelia C., Samuel L., and Lucy A. Carver; brother Samuel Carver's children, to wit, Pleasant P., Rhoda A., and Mary J. Carver; sister Elizabeth L. Clemmons children, to wit, Mary F. and Emily A. Clemmons. Recorded 10 December 1873. (P. 179)

JORDAN CHANDLER Sale. Recorded 18 December 1873. (P. 185)

JAMES JOHNSON Widow's Allotment. Recorded 2 January 1874. (P. 190)

TAVEL GLEAVES Inventory. Recorded 13 January 1874. (P. 191)

EDWARD JONES Sale. Recorded 22 January 1874. (Pp. 192-198)

SAM GOLLADAY Inventory. 4 December 1873. S. G. Stratton, administrator. Recorded 27 January 1874. (Pp. 200-201)

R. T. HAYS Sale. Recorded 27 January 1874. (P. 202)

W. A. SIMMONS Widow's Allotment. Recorded 31 January 1874. (P. 202)

COL. S. JARMAN Widow's Allotment. Recorded 31 January 1874. (Pp. 203-204)

NANCY E. HILL Will. 7 January 1874. Heirs: husband F. T. A. Hill; brother W. F. Todd; Sallie P. Todd, daughter of William F. and Juliette H. Todd; A. E. Ligon, daughter of W. B. and Mary C. Ligon; and the Silver Springs Congregation. Mentions money coming to me from the estate of J. B. Scobey. The money coming to me from the estate of my dear deceased sister, M. E. Ligon, to go toward erecting tombstones at the graves of my dear little Earl and my dear little boys. Executor: husband F. T. A. Hill. Recorded 5 March 1874. (Pp. 207-208)

JAMES D. WHITE Will. Heirs: children Lorenzo, Sue S., Frank L., Jennie B., and Nellie R. White. Men-

tions my children by my first wife, Lucy Shelton White,
to receive from the estate of James Shelton. I owe my
three youngest children as the executor of Sarah J.
Rogers. Executors: David C. Scales and H. Y. Riddle.
Recorded 5 March 1874. (Pp. 208-209)

H. R. GWYNN Widow's Allotment. Recorded 5 March
1874. (P. 209)

JAMES TOMLINSON Widow's Allotment. Recorded 7
March 1874. (P. 211)

SAMUEL B. SMITH Will. 8 May 1873. Heirs: wife
Elizabeth Smith; son Samuel Houston Smith. Executor:
friend James H. Jennings. Witnesses: James J. Blair
and J. M. Maxwell. Recorded 7 March 1874. (P. 212)

THOMAS PHILIPS Sale. 19 February 1874. John Philips,
administrator. Recorded 21 March 1874. (Pp. 216-217)

MISS SARAH J. ROGERS Inventory. Recorded 4 April
1874. (P. 218)

D. J. BASS Widow's Allotment. Recorded 4 April
1874. (P. 219)

D. C. HIBBITTS Will. 13 February 1869. Heirs:
children James Hibbitts, Mary P. Webb, Penelopy W. Beaumont, and David C. Hibbitts; children of Ann E. Fakes;
and the children of Josiah R. Hibbitts. Executor: brother John J. Hibbitts.

D. C. HIBBITTS Codicil. 17 August 1871. Son James
Hibbitts' share to go to his son, Walter Hibbitts, and
daughter, Elizabeth Hibbitts. Daughter Ann E. Fakes
share to go to her daughters, Mary and Sally Fakes to
the exclusion of her male children. Recorded 25 April
1874. (P. 225)

J. J. SMITH Widow's Allotment. 24 February 1874.
The widow and her eight children given their allotment
for one year. Recorded 25 April 1874. (P. 225)

JOHN W. PRICE Will. 11 September 1871. Heirs:
wife; sons William and John Price; daughter Sallie
Price. Mentions younger children. Recorded 16 May
1874. (Pp. 226-227)

DOKE YOUNG Widow's Allotment. Sallie given her
allotment for one year. Recorded 23 May 1874. (P. 227)

DARREL FREEMAN Widow's Allotment. Recorded 23 May
1874. (P. 229)

B. B. BRETT Widow's Allotment. Recorded 23 May
1874. (P. 229)

HENRY D. LESTER Will. 16 April 1873. Heirs: son
John A. Lester; daughter Betsy Foust; children of daugh-
ter Mickey Gillespie who is dead. Executors: sons John
A. and Joshua Lester. Recorded 4 June 1874. (P. 233)

JAMES YOUNG Widow's Allotment. Recorded 8 June 1874.

WILLS & INVENTORIES 1871-1878

(P. 234)

WILLIAM LANIUS Will. 27 November 1873. Heirs: sons Richard P. and J. C. Lanius; heirs of Catherine E. Wallace; and granddaughter Nannie E. Jackson. Executors: P. C. and J. C. Lanius. Recorded 8 June 1874. (Pp. 235-236)

MAHALA H. HUDDLESTON Will. Heirs: children. Executors: Mother Huddleston and brother in law William A. Huddleston. Recorded 8 June 1874. (Pp. 237-238)

ELIZABETH SMITH Widow's Allotment. Recorded 16 July 1874. (P. 239)

ELIZA M. HIBBITT Will. September 1869. Heir: granddaughter Mary E. Helm. Mentions an article of separation between D. C. Hibbitt and myself on the 27th June 1869. Thomas J. Stratton, executor. Recorded 11 July 1874. (P. 241)

TOM TUGGLE Sale. Recorded 11 July 1874. (P. 242)

PATRICK JOHNSON Widow's Allotment. Recorded 24 October 1874. (P. 244)

DANIEL KELLY Sale. Recorded 24 October 1874. (Pp. 245-247)

BERRY MOSER Inventory. Recorded 24 October 1874. (Pp. 249-251)

JOSIAH SMITH Widow's Allotment. Sarah A. Smith given her allotment for one year. Recorded 29 October 1874. (P. 252)

WILLIAM JOHNS Inventory. 24 August 1874. Mentions Mrs. Johns and Bluford Johns. F. M. Russell, administrator. Recorded 20 October 1874. (P. 252)

TEMPA L. MORRIS Widow's Allotment. Recorded 31 October 1874. (P. 257)

JAMES M. GRAVES Widow's Allotment. Elizabeth A. Graves given her allotment for one year. Recorded 31 October 1874. (P. 257)

WILLIAM S. CLEMMONS Widow's Allotment. Recorded 31 October 1874. (P. 258)

SARAH JOPLIN Sale. Recorded 31 October 1874. (P. 259)

*TOP KELLY Sale. Recorded 7 November 1874. (Pp. 264-265)

JANE ROBB Will. 15 July 1874. Heirs: daughters Margaret E. and Jane Robb. They are to receive because they stayed with me. Margaret E. Robb, executrix. Recorded 7 November 1874. (Pp. 266-267)

WILLIAM ROBB Sale. Recorded 9 November 1874. (Pp. 267-268)

*Black

WILLS & INVENTORIES 1871-1878

HENRY MOORING Will. 24 September 1873. Heirs: brother William Mooring; sisters Jane Hardaway and Nancy Rains. L. N. M. Cook, executor. Witnesses: J. L. Lane and William D. Hamblin. Recorded 16 December 1874. (Pp. 268-269)

JOHN W. MABRY Will. 1 December 1874. Heirs: wife Miranda Mabry; children; grandchildren John and Catherine Dill. Miranda Mabry, executrix. Recorded 16 December 1874. (Pp. 269-270)

SMITH HEARN Widow's Allotment. Recorded 16 December 1874. (Pp. 270-271)

JAMES F. WRIGHT Widow's Allotment. Recorded 16 December 1874. (P. 271)

EMMA BELL Inventory. Recorded 16 December 1874. (P. 271)

NANCY RUTLEDGE Inventory. Recorded 16 December 1874. (Pp. 272-275)

J. W. SMITH Children's Allotment. The children are alloted one year's provisions after the deaths of their father and mother. Recorded 19 December 1874. (P. 277)

SUSAN E. GRIGG Sale. Recorded 19 December 1874. (Pp. 277-278)

YOUNG GRISSOM Inventory. Recorded 9 March 1875. (P. 283)

WHITFIELD MOORE Sale. Recorded 4 February 1875. (P. 284)

JOHN W. CLAY Sale. Recorded 4 February 1875. (P. 285)

JOSEPH MOTTLEY Inventory. Recorded 9 March 1875. (P. 285)

JOHN C. BROWN Will. 21 December 1874. Second Civil District. Heirs: wife Susan Brown; sons Albert, J. E., G. W., William, and James Brown; daughters Leander and Nancy Brown, Elizabeth Young, Harriet Baker, and Mary Drennan. William D. Hamblin, executor. Witnesses: James F. Wallace and Ed Curd. Recorded 12 April 1875. (P. 287)

ISAIAH COE Will. 28 November 1867. Heirs: wife; older children; younger daughter Julia Word. Executor: friend H. A. Goodall. Witnesses: H. A. and John T. Goodall, Jr. Recorded 12 April 1875. (P. 288)

MARY DONNELL Will. 21 January 1875. Heir: daughter Betty Ann Sellars. Witnesses: S. S. Preston and Asa O'Neal. Recorded 12 April 1875. (P. 289)

FRANCIS ANN HANCOCK Will. 12 October 1872. Heirs: husband's children D. T., J. E., M. A. E., N. C., L. E., S. J., and S. B. Hancock; sister Sarah J. Castleman, the wife of John L. Castleman; sister Harriet A. Hancock, the wife of James H. Hancock; and brother Andrew J. Holloway. I want Brother James Sewell to preach my funeral. I want houses to be built over my grave, and those of my mother and father. I want to be buried next to my husband. James H. Hancock, executor. Recorded 12 April 1875. (Pp. 289-290)

MARTIN F. HUGHES Sale. Recorded 12 April 1875. (P. 292)

ELI GOLDSTON Inventory. Recorded 12 April 1875. (Pp. 292-298)

W. B. JOHNSON Sale. 22 December 1874. J. C. Johnson, administrator. Recorded 12 April 1875. (P. 293)

BENJAMIN H. DAVIS Noncupative Will. 1 April 1875. Heir: wife. Recorded 1875. (P. 294)

J. M. McMURRY Will. 3 April 1875. Heirs: wife Elizabeth McMurry; daughter Ann Eliza McMurry; nieces and nephews. Three hundred dollars to be applied to the portraits of my brother in law, Dr. T. C. Anderson, and my own. They are to hang in the picture gallery of Cumberland University. Mentions my land in Montague County, Texas. Also, my land in Warren County, Tennessee where I formerly resided for many years. Executrixes: wife Elizabeth McMurry and daughter Ann Eliza McMurry. Witnesses: Robert L. Caruthers and J. Y. Blythe. Recorded 6 May 1875. (Pp. 294-295)

EDWIN R. PENNEBAKER Will. 18 February 1875. Heirs: mother Sarah Wiseman; wife; and children. Mentions son Edwin R. Pennebaker, Jr. Alex W. Vick, executor. Recorded 11 June 1875. (Pp. 296-297)

BENJAMIN L. BELL Will. 21 July 1874. Heirs: wife Lotty Bell; daughter Eliza Jane Terry; son Isaac Bell; other children William L., Harding, Thomas J., Martha H. and Mary F. Bell; daughters Sarah Ann Eason and Susan E. Smith. Executor is to be appointed by the County Court. Witnesses: John C. Jackson, Samuel Dies, and Beverly D. Hagar. Recorded 11 June 1875. (P. 298)

HENRY ROGERS Will. 22 December 187_. Heirs: wife Jane Rogers; Lorinda F. Spradlin; son John A. Rogers; daughter Mary Lain; children of William J. Rogers; children of Nancy Lain; Mary B. and William L. Fonville; children of Alfred B. Rogers; children of son Henry J. Rogers, to wit, Christopher C., Frances E. Rogers, and Catherine F. Taylor; grandchildren Catherine F. Rogers, Martha Ann Wade, William Henry Wade, and Polly Taylor. Executors: friends George W. Layne and John C. Eskew. Recorded 24 April 1875. (Pp. 299-300)

W. J. HALE Will. 18 April 1875. Heirs: wife Parilee Hale; children John H., Lina, Edgar, and Stella Hale. Executors: brothers C. W. S. and J. R. Hale. Recorded 12 June 1875. (Pp. 300-302)

R. D. REED Widow's Allotment. Recorded 12 June 1875. (P. 305)

ETHELDRED BASS Widow's Allotment. Recorded 14 June 1875. (Pp. 306-313)

BETTIE DONOHO Will. 11 May 1875. Heir: sister Mary Donoho. Executor: my brother. Witnesses: James L. Thompson and Mary W. Thompson. Recorded 7 July 1875. (P. 314)

JEREMIAH MARTIN HEDGEPATH Will. 3 May 1875. Heirs: wife Margaret Hedgepath; sons Robert F., James M., and John Hedgepath; children of daughter Susan Robins. J. F. Hooker, executor. Witnesses: J. C. Taylor and P. C. Hooker. Recorded 3 August 1875. (Pp. 316-317)

J. B. LINDSEY Will. 3 August 1868. Heirs: wife Malinda Lindsey; sons Lucelius, Eli, Melan, James, and Josiah Lindsey. Eli Lindsey, executor. Recorded 3 August 1875. (Pp. 317-318)

A. S. SULLIVAN Will. 10 July 1875. Heirs: wife; and son Ambros Sullivan. J. N. Partlow, executor. Witnesses: Frank Summerhill and J. N. Partlow. Recorded 3 August 1875. (Pp. 318-319)

JAMES L. HEARN Widow's Allotment. Recorded 6 August 1875. (P. 321)

JOEL BEADLE Widow's Allotment. Said Joel Beadle died 7 June 1875. Susan Beadle given her allotment for one year. Recorded 6 August 1875. (P. 322)

SARAH BAIRD Noncupative Will. 26 April 1875. Heirs: children of daughter Mary Fakes, to wit, Mary and Ella Fakes; grandchildren of daughter Emeline Baird; grandchildren Samuel, Mollie, Edward, Annie, James H., Terza, and Kate Baird. Recorded 24 November 1875. (Pp. 323-324)

SALLIE A. PAYNE Will. 12 August 1875. Heirs: children Ellen, Douglas, Permelia, Emily, Mary, Alice, Jesse, Lea, Mar), Corah, and Solurah B. Payne; sisters Pamelia and Eliza Hamblin. Executors: W. F. Hamblin and J. N. Sullivan. Recorded 12 August 1875. (P. 325)

JORDAN CHANDLER Will. 22 May 1873. Heirs: my six children. Recorded 25 November 1875. (P. 326)

JAMES P. RUCKER Will. 5 April 1875. Heirs: mother Elizabeth Rucker; and brothers S. B. and J. H. Rucker. S. S. Preston, executor. Recorded 26 November 1875. (P. 327)

ELIZABETH MARKS Will. 25 March 1869. Heirs: sons George and Bailey Marks; daughter Louiza J. Clark, wife of John Clark; granddaughter Elizabeth Johnson. Nathaniel Murry, executor. Recorded 26 November 1875. (P. 328)

A. S. SULLIVAN Widow's Allotment. 20 August 1875. Mary Sullivan given her allotment for one year. Recorded

26 November 1875. (P. 332)

WILLIAM KING Widow's Allotment. Susan King given her allotment for one year. Recorded 27 November 1875. (P. 337)

T. C. McSPADDEN Sale. Recorded 27 November 1875. (Pp. 337-338)

JOHN C. BURNS Inventory. Recorded 27 November 1875. (Pp. 338-339)

JOHN SHORTER Widow's Allotment. Recorded 27 November 1875. (P. 341)

JAMES WATERS Sale. Recorded 28 December 1875. (Pp. 347-351)

THOMAS H. TAYLOR Sale. Recorded 28 December 1875. (P. 351)

S. R. McKEE Sale. Recorded 29 December 1875. (P. 356)

R. W. CRADDOCK Widow's Allotment. Recorded 29 December 1875. (P. 358)

MARY DONOHO Will. 14 November 1875. Heirs: sister Bettie Donoho; brother Henry M. Donoho; and beloved friend Mary Thompson. Thomas J. Stratton, executor. Recorded 15 January 1876. (Pp. 359-361)

ANDERSON T. DAVIS Will. 4 November 1866. Heirs: wife Mary T. Davis; children of sister Nancy D. Reeves. Mary T. Davis, executrix. Recorded 15 January 1876. (P. 361)

H. W. PICKETT Inventory. Recorded 18 January 1876. (P. 368)

SUSANNAH LYONS Sale. Recorded 18 January 1876. (P. 369)

THOMAS WATKINS Widow's Allotment. Nancy Watkins given her allotment for one year. Recorded 20 January 1876. (P. 376)

S. W. MACON Widow's Allotment. Recorded 20 January 1876. (Pp. 376-377)

JOHN CUNNINGHAM Sale. Recorded 18 January 1876. (Pp. 385-388)

MARGARET B. YOUNG Sale. Recorded 14 February 1876. (Pp. 388-390)

W. C. BAIRD Widow's Allotment. 16 October 1875. Martha Baird given her allotment for one year. Recorded 14 February 1876. (Pp. 391-392)

MARGARET CARTMELL Sale. Recorded 10 March 1876. (Pp. 393-394)

ANN MALONE Children's Allotment. Recorded 10 March 1876. (P. 394)

PLEASANT GEER Widow's Allotment. Recorded 10 March 1876. (P. 394)

CHARLES BRUCE Sale. Recorded 10 March 1876. (P. 396)

Z. TOLLIVER Sale. 14 January 1876. Recorded 11 April 1876. (Pp. 398-402)

THOMAS COLEMAN Sale. Recorded 12 April 1876. (P. 403)

A. H. HARRIS Widow's Allotment. Recorded 12 April 1876. (P. 404)

RICE GRAVES Will. 26 February 1873. Heirs: Edna A. and Reuben Graves. Executors: Edna A. and Reuben Graves. Recorded 24 April 1876. (Pp. 405-406)

JOSIAH S. McCLAIN Will. 17 November 1873. Heirs: wife Martha McClain; daughters Bettie Green and Martha Bostick; Martha Bostick's two children, to wit, Mary Sitton and Kate Bostick. Executor: son in law Nathan Green. Recorded 8 May 1876. (Pp. 408-409)

WILLIAM LACKS Sale. Recorded 8 May 1876. (Pp. 410-411)

LEMUEL LOYD Will. 7 February 1873. Heir: wife Harriet Loyd. Executors: R. H. Laine and J. H. Johnson. Recorded 9 June 1876. (Pp. 414-415)

E. C. CHANDLER Will. 19 August 1875. Heirs: sisters Jane B. Hays, Sarah A. Jackson, and Rachel Thompson; William D., John G., and Sarah E. Sharp. J. W. Shreeve, executor. Recorded 9 June 1876. (Pp. 415-416)

ISAAC E. GIBSON Will. 23 December 1876. Heirs: wife; children Thomas W. Gibson, Ira B. Gibson, Polly A. Haralson, Elizabeth E. Barnett, Ardena F. Chandler, and Sarah J. Russell. Ira B. Gibson, executor. Recorded 9 June 1876. (Pp. 416-417)

MARTHA HANCOCK Widow's Allotment. Recorded 5 July 1876. (P. 419)

GREEN B. COOK Will. 16 March 1868. Heir: daughter in law Elvira Cook. Executor: friend William B. Penning. Recorded 6 July 1876. (P. 419)

W. M. CARTMELL Will. 10 January 1875. Heirs: brother James S. Cartmell and wife Mary Elizabeth; niece Mary Ella Cartmell; nephew Henry H. Cartmell; John M. Powell, a son of a deceased sister (if I treated him as he deserved, I would not give him anything. He has treated me so badly.); brother James S. Cartmell's children, to wit, William H., Sophia, and Isabella Cartmell; Ann Eliza Ramsey, formerly Ann Eliza Cook, and Green Cook who are children of a deceased sister. Executors: brother James S. Cartmell and friend Benjamin J. Tarver. Witnesses: James A. Wynne, J. K. Wynne, P. Lipscomb, and H. M. Cartmell. A scholarship is to be for students to attend Vanderbilt University. Said students must have been members of Baptist, Methodist Episcopal Church, or Presbyterian Church at least one year before receiving said scholarship. (Pp. 420-424)

W. M. CARTMELL Codicil. 6 September 1875. Friends Mrs. Martha Blair and daughter Betty Blair to be included. I have just now heard of the death of Ann Eliza Cook, a daughter of my sister Eliza Jane, who married Ramsey, and lately married a man by the name of McPeak, I believe. Recorded 6 July 1876. (Pp. 424-426)

NANCY PROCTOR Will. 26 March 1874. Heir: son J. A. Proctor. I being 84 years last May. Witnesses: L. D. Smith and Samuel C. Bell. Recorded 19 July 1876. (P. 429)

MARTHA H. DOUGLASS Will. 26 November 1865. Heirs: Martha D. Davis; nephew George William Boddie to receive the land I inherited from my father in Sumner County. Executors: James Vaughan and John F. Harkreader. (P. 430)

LITTLEBERRY WRIGHT Will. 24 April 1871. Heirs: wife Elizabeth Wright; daughter Rebecca Ann Wright who is afflicted; other children. Recorded 11 August 1876. (P. 431)

MOSES M. CURREY Will. 12 June 1876. Heirs: wife Peggy Currey; James H. Currey; my lawful heirs. Executor: William S. Woodrum. Witnesses: J. N. Partlow and J. H. Dikes. Recorded 11 August 1876. (P. 432)

ROBERT MOTHERAL Will. 25 October 1872. Heirs: wife Jane Motheral; son John R. K. Motheral; and daughter Luiza Ann Taylor. Jane Motheral, executrix. Recorded 13 September 1876. (P. 433)

G. W. COLES Sale. Recorded 14 September 1876. (P. 441)

ELIZABETH CLAY Inventory. Recorded 30 October 1876. (P. 442)

SARAH J. DAY Noncupative Will. 5 September 1876. Heirs: children Samuel J., Thomas A., and Ella Day; sisters Mildred S. Smithwick and Melissa; brothers Sam and Tommy. Said Sarah J. Day was 36 years old at the time of her death. Mentions her father. Recorded 31 October 1876. (Pp. 446-447)

MATILDA FITE Will. 15 December 1875. Heirs: sons Edwin C. and J. L. Fite; and daughter Margaret E. Witt. Recorded 11 October 1876. (P. 448)

W. B. BOON Widow's Allotment. Recorded 11 November 1876. (P. 450)

JAMES F. WRIGHT Widow's Allotment. 7 October 1876. Josephine Wright given her allotment for one year. Recorded 11 November 1876. (P. 451)

JOHN H. BRYANT Inventory. Recorded 11 November 1876. (P. 451)

H. A. BAXTER Sale. Recorded 11 November 1876. (P. 453)

HENDERSON ESTES Sale. Recorded 11 November 1876. (Pp. 454-458)

MAHALA HUDDLESTON Sale. 17 October 1876. Mentions seven children. Recorded 1876. (P. 458)

HENRY TRUETT Will. 16 November 1874. Heirs: grand-daughters Martisha Barr and Frusannah Hamilton. T. B. Chapman, executor. Witnesses: E. D. and J. H. Clemmons. Recorded 1876. (P. 461)

LUCINDA F. DAVIS Will. Second Civil District. Heir: Octavia Ann Davis. James C. Freeman, executor. Recorded 7 February 1877. (P. 467)

SALLIE HIGHT Sale. Recorded 9 February 1877. (Pp. 468-469)

JOHN M. BERRY Widow's Allotment. Recorded 9 February 1877. (P. 472)

JOHN DEBOW Will. 12 June 1874. Heir: adopted daughter Eula Lee Debow. H. C. Debow to be her guardian until she comes of age. Witnesses: J. D. Corum and F. Whitesides. Recorded 31 January 1878. (P. 481)

WILLIAM PAUL Will. 5 November 1870. Heirs; daughter Rebecca Berry; sons of deceased son B. H. Paul, to wit, John W. and William B. Paul. Peter Thompson, executor. Recorded 9 March 1878. (P. 482)

JOHN T. SIMPSON Sale. Recorded 9 March 1877. (P. 483)

*WILLIAM JARMON Will. Heir: deaf and dumb daughter Issabella Jarmon and her two children, Frances and Easter. H. C. Matthews, executor. Recorded 10 April 1877. (P. 485)

W. A. GREEN Widow's Allotment. Polly Green given her allotment for one year. Recorded 9 March 1877. (P. 486)

LEWIS PATTERSON Widow's Allotment. Recorded 9 March 1877. (P. 489)

JAMES S. HARRISON Sale. Recorded 18 April 1877. (P. 491)

N. D. HANCOCK Sale. 17 March 1877. W. D. Hancock, administrator. Recorded 1877. (P. 493)

MITCHELL CLAY Will. 2 January 1869. Heir: Carlos G. Clay. Carlos G. Clay, executor. Recorded 11 May 1877. (P. 493)

J. A. ROLAND Will. 16 March 1877. Heir: My wife Jenny Roland to have my house of North College Street in

*Black

Lebanon. Edgar Waters, executor. Recorded 12 May 1877. (P. 494)

NANCY L. MOXLEY Sale. Recorded 16 May 1877. (Pp. 495-496)

SIMPSON HUGHES Widow's Allotment. Recorded 12 June 1877. (Pp. 497-498)

ESTHER GWYNN Sale. Recorded 12 June 1877. (Pp. 498-499)

L. B. GREEN Widow's Allotment. Recorded 13 June 1877. (Pp. 500-506)

THOMAS B. AUST Will. 6 June 1877. Heirs: wife Sarah Aust; sons James and William H. Aust; daughters Tennessee Aust, and Martha Susan Lane who is the wife of Thornton Lane. James Aust, executor. Recorded 4 July 1877. (Pp. 506-507)

THOMAS HOWELL Will. 6 August 1872. Heirs: wife Quincey Howell; daughters Rebecca Ann and Joanna Howell; all my other children. Recorded 5 July 1877. (Pp. 508-509)

WRIGHT HICKMAN Sale. 25 June 1877. Mathias Johnson, administrator. Recorded 10 July 1877. (P. 510)

MARY DAVIS Inventory. Recorded 10 July 1877. (P. 511)

ELIZABETH CLAY Sale. Recorded 1877. (P. 511)

MARY P. SULLIVAN Will. 31 May 1877. Heirs: sisters Martha J. and Almeda B. Sullivan. Martha J. Sullivan, executrix. Recorded 8 August 1877. (P. 512)

NANCY HALLUM Will. 23 July 1877. Heirs: son Robert E. Murphy and his wife Mary Murphy. Robert E. Murphy, executor. Recorded 9 August 1877. (P. 513)

RUFUS W. TURNER Noncupative Will. Heir: niece Bettie Turner. Recorded 9 August 1877. (Pp. 513-514)

LEWIS LINDSEY Will. 1 July 1876. Heirs: wife Elizabeth Lindsey; son George Lindsey; daughter Ellen Lindsey; other children. Recorded 8 September 1877. (P. 522)

E. W. COLE Will. 1 July 1876. Heirs: son William H. Cole; daughters Ann Vaughan, Jo Seay, and Luvina Birgett. J. W. Shreeve, executor. Recorded 8 September 1877. (P. 523)

MRS. WINEFRED BETTES Sale. J. M. Johnson, administrator. Recorded 14 September 1877. (P. 524)

SAMUEL C. ANDERSON Inventory. Recorded 14 September 1877. (Pp. 525-526)

P. LIPSCOMB Will. 7 June 1877. Heirs: my three children. Executors: James Hamilton and B. W. G. Winford. Recorded 16 October 1877. (P. 527)

SALLIE WISEMAN Inventory. Recorded 30 October 1877. (P. 531)

DRURY HALL Widow's Allotment. Recorded 30 October 1877. (Pp. 531-533)

DR. B. H. DAVIS Sale. Recorded 30 October 1877. (Pp. 533-534)

MILEY HAGERTY Will. 18 August 1857. Heir: sister Jane Hagerty. Recorded 22 November 1877. (P. 535)

WILLIAM R. SANDERS Will. 6 October 1877. Heirs: wife Susan B. Sanders; sons F. J. and Charles H. Sanders; daughter Amanda Elizabeth Cawthon who is the wife of D. C. Cawthon. F. J. Sanders, executor. Recorded 22 November 1877. (Pp. 536-537)

ELIJAH CREEL Sale. Recorded 11 December 1877. (P. 538)

N. D. HANCOCK Widow's Allotment. Recorded 11 December 1877. (P. 538)

SUSAN E. GRIGG Child's Support. 17 October 1874. Lue P. Grigg, the daughter of Susan E. Grigg, given her allotment for one year. Recorded 11 December 1877. (P. 539)

ISAAC CARVER Sale. Recorded 11 December 1877. (P. 539)

VESTER GEORGE Sale. Recorded 22 January 1878. (P. 542)

SARAH SMITH Sale. Recorded 22 January 1878. (P. 543)

MRS. C. H. BAILEY Sale. Recorded 22 December 1878. (Pp. 544-545)

BAIRD'S MILL BAPTIST CHURCH
R#2 466
     Fannie Swingley one acre of land in the 21st Dis-
trict for a colored Baptist Church and school. Dated 18
November 1882.

CEDAR GROVE BAPTIST CHURCH
X#2 99
     B. P. Collier and M. D. Collier to Joseph Holman,
Dug Walker, Jasper Harris, Wilson Chambers, and Joseph
Wharton one acre of land in the 5th District on Cumber-
land and Stone's River Turnpike "in trust for members of
the Cedar Grove Colored Missionary Baptist Church."
Dated 14 November 1889.

GLADE MISSIONARY BAPTIST CHURCH
V#2 360
     John Pittman and wife, Caroline Pittman, to Solomon
Price and George Mace, trustees of the Missionary Baptist
Church Colored, known as the Glade Church, one half acre
"for moral development of our race and the up-building of
Christianity in our community." Bounded by Wash Wilson,
John Pittman, and east by the road leading from B. M.
Mace's house to the pike. Dated 15 October 1887.

GLADEVILLE CHAPEL AFRICAN M-EPISCOPAL CHURCH
W#2 413
     A. L. Chandler and wife, J. K. Chandler, two acres
of land to the trustees of the Gladeville Chapel Church
African M-Episcopal Church. Dated 4 March 1889.

LAGUARDO METHODIST EPISCOPAL CHURCH
F#2 485
     Jesse T. Davis to Andrew Booker, Lue Davis, and I.
Davis, trustees of Colored Methodist Episcopal Church,
land at fork of Laguardo and Bull's Branch Turnpike "for
school and church purposes." Dated 27 August 1867.

LINWOOD MISSIONARY BAPTIST CHURCH
W#2 438
     Martin New and wife, Bettie New, to Missionary Bap-
tist Church at Linwood in the 11th District. Dated 19
April 1889.
W#2 468
     W. E. Wilson and wife, Victoria Wilson, deed of gift
to the Missionary Baptist Church at Linwood in the 11th
District. Bounded by Mary Carter to a rock in the Leba-
non and Commerce Road. Dated 5 September 1887.

AFRICAN METHODIST CHURCH
55 243
     Maria Moore to African Methodist Church. No loca-
tion given. Dated 28 May 1898.

PICKETT'S CHAPEL CHURCH
H#2 83
     Daniel Fite and Allen Hancock "for colored members
of said church in Lebanon. Dated 21 February 1870.

CHURCH DEEDS

F#2 161

Allen A. Gee to B. J. Turner, Thomas J. Stratton,
A. W. Vick, G. Y. Blythe, A. G. Muirhead, and John Owen
for Pickett's Chapel Church. Dated 18 July 1866.

— — W. F. M. Betty to J. Braden, C. Pickett, J. Pickett,
H. W. Key, J. P. Gregg, H. Phillips, Jesse P. Price, and
Berry Anderson, trustees of Tennessee Conference of Methodist Episcopal Church. Dated 9 October 1886.
52 221

Lillard Thompson to the President and Secretary of
the Board of Trustees of the Tennessee Conference of the
Methodist Episcopal Church. President Calvin Pickett;
Secretary Jessie R. Price. Dated 7 February 1894.

SEAY'S CHAPEL CROSSROADS

— — A. J. Sherrill to Page Seay, Jack Harris, and Charley Seay, trustees of the Seay's Chapel Methodist Episcopal Church of Tucker's Cross Roads on Big Springs
Road. Dated 6 October 1889.

TWELVE CORNER'S BAPTIST CHURCH
W#2 486

J. S. Womack to Jo Bass, Doak Young, Abe Young,
George Phillips, Demps Harris, T. J. Bryan, and Louis
Young one acre in the 16th District "to be used for
church purposes or the building of a school to be at op-
tion of the officers or deacons. Dated 13 May 1889.

WILLIAMSON CHAPEL

— — Richard Williamson and Chaney Williamson to Joe
Johnson, Hiram Williamson, Jessie Parker, Col. Gordon,
and John Houston, trustees of Williamson Chapel. Dated
6 July 1886.

WINTER'S CHAPEL A. M. E. CHURCH
S#2 408

J. T. Lane to Reuben Drake, Caesar Winston, Harvey
Gannon, Sandy Haralson, and Henry Denton, trustees of
Winter's Chapel A. M. E. Church in Lebanon. Dated 11
March 1884.

BARTON'S CREEK BAPTIST CHURCH
Q 191

William Davis to R. B. Sypert, John M. Davis, and
Marcus Walker a parcel of land lying and being on the
waters of Barton's Creek for one dollar. Dated 29 August
1835.
Y#2 166

John Fields and Nancy Fields to Baptist Church on
Barton's Creek. Dated 39 May 1891.

BIG SPRING BAPTIST CHURCH
55 188

J. M. Bradshaw and W. A. Rushing to William Haley,
James Oldham, and John Shannon, deacons of Big Spring

CHURCH DEEDS

Baptist Church, located on the Rome Pike. Dated 8 February 1898.

CARMEL FREE WILL BAPTIST CHURCH
Q 596
Robert M. Baskins to Joshua Woolen, Leven Woolen, and James Knight, Jr. land for a Free Will Baptist Church. Dated 5 December 1836.

CEDAR CREEK BAPTIST CHURCH
I 471
Jonas Bradley one acre of land on the waters of Cedar Creek for a Baptist Church. Dated 1822.
Y#2 168
Cedar Creek Baptist Church one acre of land on the Averitt's Ferry Road to J. D. Bass, T. F. King, J. C. McDonald, and J. W. Walker, trustees for a Primitive Baptist Church. Dated 1 June 1891.

LEBANON UNITED BAPTIST CHURCH
X 15
James Turner to Deacon Simon Adamson one acre of land. Dated 27 September 1848.

GLADEVILLE BAPTIST CHURCH
O#2 572
E. H. Thornton et ux one acre of land on Stewart's Ferry Road for a Baptist Church. Dated 6 March 1880.

HARRIS CHAPEL BAPTIST CHURCH
N#2 475
William H. Carter et ux to Lee Caplenor, Willie Rucks, and Larkin Page for a Baptist Church in the 7th District. Dated 16 December 1878.

HURRICANE BAPTIST CHURCH
Z#2 491
J. T. Huddleston and wife, Elizabeth Huddleston, to W. A. Hobbs, W. A. Patterson, and B. S. Cluck, deacons of Baptist Church in 20th District. Dated 1 April 1893.

FALL CREEK BAPTIST CHURCH
F#2 496
Samuel Copeland to Baptist Church.
Q#2 501
H. L. Henderson et ux to the deacons of Fall Creek Baptist Church, located in the 18th District. Dated 7 April 1881.

LEBANON FIRST BAPTIST CHURCH
K 284
David Marshall to trustee Thomas Edwards. The three acres is bounded by the schoolhouse, Edward Tucker, and Peyton Randolph. Dated 27 November 1824.
Z 466
Paulding Anderson, power of attorney for Baptist Church in Lebanon, to J. W. Franklin a town lot for five hundred dollars. Corner of lot in which Abbe Institute is situated. Later sold to the Cumberland Presbyterians.

CHURCH DEEDS

Dated 9 November 1853.

LIBERTY BAPTIST CHURCH
X 467
    Rebecca George to Liberty Baptist Church one acre in which "all denominations can preach, provided they do not interfere with their meetings. Dated 29 July 1848.

LINWOOD BAPTIST CHURCH
W#2 468
    E. Wilson and wife, Victoria Wilson, land to Linwood Baptist Church. Dated 5 September 1887.
W#2 438
    Martin V. New and wife, Betty New, to Baptist Church in the 11th District. Dated 19 April 1889.

LITTLE CEDAR LICK BAPTIST CHURCH
V 43
    John G. Ligon to William Bilbro and James McFarland, deacons of Little Cedar Lick Baptist Church, located in the 1st District.

MOUNT OLIVET BAPTIST CHURCH
H 427
    John McNairy of Davidson County a parcel of land for a Baptist Church at Leeville. This is the same deed as that of the Cedar Lick Baptist Church. Dated 29 December 1809.

PLEASANT GROVE UNITED BAPTIST CHURCH
R 474
    John Buchanan to Joshua Kelley, David Campbell, and John W. Peyton land "for society for public and divine worship." Land located near where road from Gallatin to Murfreesboro crosses road leading from Lebanon to Nashville.
V 107
    Isaac Green to Pleasant Grove Church "for friendship for people." Dated 10 November 1842.

RIDGE CHURCH UNITED BAPTIST
R 454
    Phillip Smart and William Wray to William Hill, William Terrill, and Thomas Willis one acre "for the Ridge Church of United Baptist being disconnected from the Baptist State Convention for love and affection." Dated 10 February 1838.

ROCKY BRANCH MISSIONARY BAPTIST CHURCH
P#2 188
    Samuel A. Ricketts to the Missionary Baptist Church on Rocky Branch in the 16th District. Dated 3 August 1882.

ROCKY VALLEY BAPTIST CHURCH
Z 336
    James Clemmons and S. F. Steed, for love and affection, two acres to the Baptist Church. Dated 9 April 1853.

CHURCH DEEDS

T#2

James L. Clemmons and Lucretia Hearn et al to W. D. Martin, John Davis, E. A. Clemmons, J. H. Lane, and R. B. Castleman, deacons of Rocky Valley Church, a parcel of land. Dated 27 August 1883.

ROUND LICK BAPTIST CHURCH
L#2 460

Chancery Court to deacons of Round Lick Church.
V#2 246

Alexander Young to Round Lick Baptist Church a parcel of land. Dated 6 June 1887.

RUTLAND BAPTIST CHURCH
I 216

Blake Rutland, Benjamin F. Stevenson, and Elizabeth Stevenson to John H. Ligon in trust for the Baptist Church a tract of land for a church. Dated 4 September 1820.

SHOP SPRINGS BAPTIST CHURCH
Q#2 527

Nelson J. Bryan to David Young, William M. Bryan, William Bass, and John W. Bryan, deacons of Shop Springs Baptist Church, two acres of land on the Sparta Turnpike. Dated 15 March 1882.

SMITH'S FORK BAPTIST CHURCH
F 212

Jesse Hodges to Smith's Fork Baptist Church.

SPENCER'S CREEK BAPTIST CHURCH
R 369

Thomas Bradshaw, Jr. four and three-fourths acres to Alford Dukes, William Modglin, and James S. Tompkins, trustees of Spencer's Creek Church. Dated 5 October 1837.

BELLWOOD CHURCH OF CHRIST
Q#2 139

B. W. Harris gave land in the 8th District for "the religion of Christ and Church of God rejecting all creeds or disciplines made by man. Dated 4 June 1881.

BETHLEHEM CHURCH OF CHRIST
Y#2 310

J. P. Collier and wife, Florie Collier, to I. A. Coe, William Watson, Robert Lane, John H. Smith, and Leonard Beard one acre in the 9th District. Dated 11 September 1891.

COMMERCE CHURCH OF CHRIST
55 727

F. B. Hastings and wife, Nancy Hastings, to the Church of Christ at Commerce in the 12th District. Dated 11 February 1898.

JENNINGS' FORK CHURCH OF CHRIST
V 308

Robert Sweatt gave two acres of land in the 8th District for a Church of Christ. Dated 11 July 1844.

CHURCH DEEDS

LAGUARDO CHURCH OF CHRIST
X#2 397

W. L. Bradshaw and wife, S. J. Bradshaw to George Oldham, William Oldham, and Samuel Bradshaw, trustees of the Christian Church at Laguardo where a church is already erected. Dated 10 September 1883.

MOUNT JULIET CHURCH OF CHRIST
57 8

Jessie H. Gleaves and wife, Annie Gleaves, a tract of land to Mount Juliet Church of Christ. Dated 25 November 1899.

SARDIS CHURCH OF CHRIST
52 30

J. A. Barrett and wife, Betty Barrett, one acre of land in the 20th District to trustees "combined church and school for the Christian people." Dated 11 November 1892.

TAYLORSVILLE CHURCH OF CHRIST
68 498

John White and Sallie White to the Church of God at Taylorsville who take the Word of God alone for their faith and practice to the exclusion of all creeds gotten up by man. Located beside the Taylorsville Academy. Dated 20 July 1893.

CHRISTIAN CHURCH, NINTH DISTRICT
Y#2 310

J. P. Collier and wife, Florie Collier, one acre of land for a Christian Church in the 9th District. Dated 11 September 1891.

ALEXANDRIA METHODIST EPISCOPAL CHURCH SOUTH
P#2 211

Thomas M. Edwards a parcel of land to William B. Gundall, Thomas Seay, Martin New, O. D. Hearn, J. W. McDaniel, M. C. Hankins, W. P. Hearn, Thomas M. Edwards, and William Hamer, trustees of Methodist Episcopal Church. Dated 1 May 1880.

BEECH LOG METHODIST EPISCOPAL CHURCH
M#2 442

John Grandstaff land for a Methodist Episcopal Church to N. Murry, G. L. Hearn, and J. B. Haley, trustees. Dated 7 January 1881.

CAINSVILLE METHODIST CHURCH
V 455

William Williams to Burrell Patterson, Isaac Winston, Charles Abernathy, Anthony W. Huddleston, Matt Matthews, Ezekiel Martin, and Shad Jarman, trustees of Methodist Church. Dated 3 October 1835.

COMMERCE METHODIST CHURCH
T 495

Joshua Taylor, Sr. lot #11 in the town of Commerce to John Rains, Benjamin F. Bartlett, Joshua V. Taylor,

CHURCH DEEDS

Matthew Cartwright, Thomas Barbee, Edward Cartwright, and Richard Midgett, trustees of Methodist Church. Dated 31 March 1832.

DRAKE'S LICK METHODIST CHURCH CAMPGROUND
R 464

Caleb Taylor to Allen Ross, John Rieff, Ross Webb, Alford Moore, and Samuel Morriss, trustees of Methodist Church. Dated 1 October 1834.

EBENEZER METHODIST EPISCOPAL CHURCH SOUTH
C 224

Daniel Pross one acre of land to John Jarrett, John Hobson, John Brown, John Dill, William Dill, Reuben Jackson, and Matthew Hawk, trustees for Methodist Church. Dated 24 September 1808.

GLADEVILLE METHODIST EPISCOPAL CHURCH
Q 485

Benjamin Hooker, Sr. six acres with always wood and water for a school to Thomas Chambers, Jonathan Hooker, Thomas Partlow, and Joshua Hooker. Later, a Methodist Church was erected here. Dated 28 November 1833.
W 202

Thomas Chambers and Jonathan Hooker to Thomas Chambers, Thomas Partlow, Jonathan Hooker, and Joshua Hooker, trustees. The six acres is to be used for both school and church. Dated 1 May 1847.

GILLIAD METHODIST CHURCH
P 530

Benjamin Nicholas one acre on Pond Lick for a Methodist Church. Dated 13 March 1830.

HEBRON METHODIST CHURCH
Q#2 582

William W. Adams a parcel of land in the 15th District to Thomas Patton, James Haas, George Huchison, and James Williamson for the Methodist Church. Dated 4 August 1880.

HOPEWELL METHODIST EPISCOPAL CHURCH
P#2 1

Samuel Hamlett and Mary Hamlett three-fourths of an acre in the 7th District to Manuel Taylor, Wesley Page, and Thornton Beasley, trustees of Hopewell Methodist Church. Dated 24 January 1880.

JACOB'S HILL METHODIST EPISCOPAL CHURCH
U 264

Dawson Hancock five acres to William L. Warren, E. R. Russell, Stephen Hearn, and Wesley Hancock for a Methodist Church on Pond Lick. Dated 20 November 1842.

LEBANON METHODIST CHURCH
M 471

Joseph Johnson town lot #15 to E. P. Horn, James Frazier, Edward Myers, John Jarrett, William Moore, and George F. McQuisten for a Methodist Episcopal Church.

Dated June 1829.
V 2

Robert Caruthers to Morgan Gardner, Crutcher, John Kelly, Alford Moore, Green B. Cook, Darrell Freeman, J. B. Wynne, Allen Ross, and Lemuel N. M. Cook, trustees of the Methodist Episcopal Church. Dated 8 January 1844.
C#2 61

Joseph Mottley to Methodist Episcopal Church South a town lot on the north side of Main East Street for one thousand dollars. Dated 1857.
O#2 412

Johnson Harding and wife, Carrie C. Johnson, to Methodist Episcopal Church a tract of land on Market and Cedar Streets in Lebanon.

LIBERTY HILL METHODIST PROTESTANT CHURCH
R#2 264

Mark Whitaker two acres to the members of the Associated Methodist Church at Liberty Hill. Dated 10 November 1860.

MOUNT PISGAH METHODIST EPISCOPAL CHURCH
V 121

Purnell Hearn to Methodist Church a tract of land where Purnell Hearn now lives. Located on road from Lebanon to Cainsville. Dated 25 October 1844.

PIRTLE'S CREEK METHODIST CHURCH
P 318

Aaron Ruyle to Joseph Fite, Leonard Fite, John M. Bennett, Edward Robinson, and William Anderson, trustees. Dated 12 June 1834.

POND LICK METHODIST CHURCH
E 626

Benjamin Hichols to George Avery, William Anderson, and John Hancock, trustees of Methodist Church on Pond Lick. Dated 18 November 1815.

ROUND LICK METHODIST CHURCH
O 30

John Garner three acres of land to Elijah Vant, Benjamin Puckett, Thomas Hearn, Thomas Jackson, and William Campbell, trustees. Dated 28 September 1827.
N 270

Abner Springs a parcel of land in 1st District to George L. Swan, William Gill, William Seay, Daniel Seay, Samuel Spring, William Spears, and John Seay, Sr. for a Methodist Church. Dated 24 July 1829.
Y 71

A. A. Massey and J. Alexander a parcel of land on Round Lick Creek to Jacob S. Hearn, Edward Jacobs, Edward G. Jacobs, Hugh Campbell, John Booker, Nelson G. Alexander, and Thomas Tracy, trustees of the Methodist Church. Dated 15 December 1841.

SHILOH METHODIST EPISCOPAL CHURCH
J#2 560

CHURCH DEEDS

William B. Pursley a parcel of land in center of Lebanon and on the Big Spring Turnpike to Shiloh Methodist Church. Dated 21 December 1870.

SPRING CREEK METHODIST EPISCOPAL CHURCH SOUTH
V 322

P. P. Hudson a parcel of land on Spring Creek to the Methodist Episcopal Church South. Dated 4 October 1845.

UNION METHODIST CHURCH
T#2 106

R. C. Scobey and wife, A. E. Scobey, for love and affection a parcel of land in the 21st District to Freeland Comer, L. J. Reed, Green Reed, R. C. Scobey, and W. A. Johnson, trustees of Union Methodist Church. Dated 8 September 1884.

ZION METHODIST EPISCOPAL CHURCH
I 524

John Hearn one acre on the waters of Jennings' Fork to John Maholland, William New, and Ebenezer Hearn, trustees of the Methodist Church. Dated 22 December 1824.

WATERTOWN UNITED METHODIST CHURCH
P#2 434

Joseph Berry one fourth acre of land (the Abram Massey tract) to N. Murry, George Hearn, and J. B. Haley, trustees of Methodist Episcopal Church South. Located in the 16th District. Dated 7 January 1881.

METHODIST EPISCOPAL CHURCH SOUTH, FIRST DISTRICT
K#2 40

John D. Taylor one acre of land in the 1st District to Edward Smith, Benjamin B. Britt, Fountain G. Taylor, George W. Nokes, and Samuel D. Taylor, trustees of Methodist Episcopal Church South. Dated 10 April 1873.

METHODIST EPISCOPAL CHURCH SOUTH, THIRD DISTRICT
V 579

John Powell to Methodist Episcopal Church South, Third District one acre of land. If not used for five years, land reverts back to the original tract. William Powell and Alfred M. Hunt, witnesses. Dated 21 September 1846.

METHODIST EPISCOPAL CHURCH, SIXTH DISTRICT
H#2 133

John J. Carter three acres of land in the 6th District to Methodist Episcopal Church. All cedar rails reserved. Dated 2 March 1870.

METHODIST EPISCOPAL CHURCH, TENTH DISTRICT
S#2 245

John Seay a tract of land in Lebanon to the Methodist Episcopal Church. Joins the Baird block on Public Square, the Webb Hotel, North Cumberland Street, Market Street on to the creek. Price: one dollar. Dated 21 December 1883.

CHURCH DEEDS

METHODIST EPISCOPAL CHURCH, TWENTY-SECOND DISTRICT
O 433

    J. W. Peyton one and a half acres of land in the 22nd District to the Methodist Church. Dated 8 January 1846.

METHODIST EPISCOPAL CHURCH, TWENTY-FIFTH DISTRICT
J#2 62

    Hollis Wright one acre of land in the 25th District to Shadrack Jarman, Joseph Barclay, William Jarman, Dobson, James Steel, Sterling Hardy, S. W. Hewgley, T. H. Gleaves, George R. Padgett, and Gassaway Peach, trustees of the Methodist Episcopal Church. Dated 4 May 1870.

METHODIST CHURCH
M 471

    Joseph Johnson a tract of land for a Methodist Church to E. P. Horn, James Frazier, Edward Moore, John Jarrett, William Moore, and George F. Wheeler, trustees. Dated 29 June 1829.

M 162

    Joseph Johnson two acres for a Methodist Church to Simon Hancock, James Guthrie, John Skein, Abediah Freeman, Hope Hancock, Alford H. Harris, and Thomas S. Green, trustees. Dated 9 February 1828.

METHODIST CHURCH
H 134

    George White one acre of land and a house of worship for use of Methodist Episcopal to Charles Ledbetter, Hezekiah Woodward, and Wallis Cofield and their successors in office. Price: eight dollars. Corner of George White's land. Dated 12 November 1819.

BARTON'S CREEK CUMBERLAND PRESBYTERIAN CHURCH
O 359

    Thomas Conyers to George H. Bullard, Isaac Golladay, Edward A. White, and John S. Tapp, trustees, three acres on a small branch which runs into Barton's Creek for a Cumberland Presbyterian Church. Dated 4 April 1832.

BEESLEY'S BEND CUMBERLAND PRESBYTERIAN CHURCH
Q 292

    John Bonner, Sr., Henry Jackson, and Mary Jackson for a Cumberland Presbyterian Church. Dated 3 November 1835.

BETHESDA CUMBERLAND PRESBYTERIAN CHURCH
O 250

    William Donnell, Sr. four acres on west fork of the spring to Alexander Foster, John Bone, and Jesse Jackson, trustees. Also, included a graveyard and campground. Dated 7 August 1832.

BETHEL CUMBERLAND PRESBYTERIAN CHURCH
P#2 240

    John B. Jackson, agent and attorney for trustees of Methodist Episcopal Church South of Gallatin District, to E. A. Marshall, John Johnson, Rufus Clark, Ephraim Beasley, and William Webster, trustees of Bethel Church in Beasley's Bend of Cumberland River. Dated 11 October 1880.

BIG SPRING CUMBERLAND PRESBYTERIAN CHURCH
E 572
James Winchester of Sumner County to Thomas Calhoun, Andrew Foster, David McMurry, William Steele, and Alexander Aston, trustees in trust of Cumberland Presbyterian Church, part of the land Winchester purchased from Nicholas Coonrod who held it by premption on the east bank of Cedar Creek one half mile below the Big Spring. Land consisted of three acres. Dated 8 August 1815.

CEDAR GROVE CUMBERLAND PRESBYTERIAN CHURCH
U#2 568
E. R. Womack and wife, M. L. Womack, to the elders of Mount Union and Bethesda Churches to be called Cedar Grove in the 19th District on corner of G. W. Thompson and E. Berry's corner of the road. Dated 23 September 1886.

CLOYD'S CUMBERLAND PRESBYTERIAN CHURCH
P 40
Ezekiel Cloyd two acres of land for twenty-five cents to the elders of the Cumberland Presbyterian Church on Stoner's Creek. Dated 1 January 1832.

COMMERCE CUMBERLAND PRESBYTERIAN CHURCH
J#2 353
Albert Wood, Thomas F. Smith and wife, Elizabeth Smith three acres of land at Commerce to John Boone, O. T. Barbee, Sr., J. S. Chastain, D. B. Hastings, J. S. Barbee, and Britton Marks for a Cumberland Presbyterian Church. Dated 28 June 1872.

GOSHEN CUMBERLAND PRESBYTERIAN CHURCH
54 354
William H. Carter and Mary Carter two acres in the 7th District to J. A. Shipp, H. W. Grissim, and R. L. C. Young, trustees of Goshen Cumberland Presbyterian Church. Dated 27 July 1895.

LAGUARDO CUMBERLAND PRESBYTERIAN CHURCH
G#2 110
Samuel W. Davis to Laguardo Masonic Lodge #237 and to John R. Davis, Saul Smith, E. M. H. Wright, Hundley L. Vaughan, and P. G. Williamson as a Session of Laguardo Congregation of the Cumberland Presbyterian Church where said Lodge and Congregation have erected a building with church below and Masonic Lodge above. Should there cease to be a Session of the Cumberland Presbyterian Church at this place, then the interest of said Congregation shall go to the Lebanon Presbytery of the Cumberland Presbyterian Church or to whichever presbytery of said church said property may be situated at the time. Located in the 4th District. Dated 7 May 1861.

LEBANON CUMBERLAND PRESBYTERIAN CHURCH
O 39

CHURCH DEEDS

Joseph Johnson to Isaac Golladay, Edward A. White, and John S. Tapp, trustees of the Cumberland Presbyterian Church in Lebanon, one lot of ground on which a church is now erected for twenty dollars. Dated 3 January 1832. Z 466

Paulding Anderson, power of attorney for the Baptist Church in Lebanon, to Lebanon Cumberland Presbyterian Church in Lebanon, a corner town lot in which the Abbe Institute is situated. The alley is located near Dr. Anderson's. Dated 9 November 1853.

Joseph W. Allen, Andrew Allison, and Robert L. Caruthers to Lebanon Cumberland Presbyterian Church town lot #5 in Lebanon. Dated 6 August 1857. G#2 371

Andrew B. Martin and J. J. D. Hinds to Mrs. Lillard Thompson the town lot adjoining Judge Robert L. Caruthers' lot. Deed is from the Cumberland Presbyterian Church.

LOCUST GROVE CUMBERLAND PRESBYTERIAN CHURCH
W 447

Robert S. Tate one and a half acres on the waters of Stoner's Creek for a Cumberland Presbyterian Church. Dated 7 October 1836.

MARIAH CUMBERLAND PRESBYTERIAN CHURCH
X 184

William H. Smith, George F. Smith, Robert Marshall, William Hooker, Robert W. Lansden, and John C. Marshall six and one fourth acres to John J. Winston, Comm. of Mariah Church. Dated 24 April 1844.

MOUNT MARIAH CUMBERLAND PRESBYTERIAN CHURCH
Z 418

J. R. Jennings for love and affection for the Cumberland Presbyterian Church now established at Mount Mariah to George K. Smith, William Sherrill, John Arnold, and Mack Bone, commissioners. Dated 7 November 1850. Z 419

Jacob Grimmett one acre to Mount Mariah Cumberland Presbyterian Church. Dated 7 November 1850.

MOUNT VERNON PRESBYTERIAN CHURCH
W#2 319

Thomas P. Jones and wife, Elizabeth Jones three acres of land to James T. Patton, Joseph T. Patton, Joseph H. Patton, S. D. Patton, and John Patton, elders of Mount Vernon Church. Dated 10 November 1887.

MOUNT ZION CUMBERLAND PRESBYTERIAN CHURCH
F#2 366

James Shannon to Edmund Crawford, Jesse L. Moore, and Archibald Sherrill, trustees, land where Samuel Moore now lives, also use of the spring. Located in the 22nd District. Dated 4 October 1845.

NEW HOPE CUMBERLAND PRESBYTERIAN CHURCH
O 239

CHURCH DEEDS

Samuel Motheral eight acres to New Hope Cumberland Presbyterian Church. Dated 25 June 1832.
Q 122

David Kirkpatrick two and three-fourth's acres with access to water to New Hope Cumberland Presbyterian Church. Original corner of old New Hope Campground on waters of Cumberland River where Kirkpatrick now lives. Dated 30 May 1834.
M#2 94

John C. Kirkpatrick et al two acres to New Hope Cumberland Presbyterian Church. Dated 26 September 1860.
Q#2 553

H. R. Johnson and wife, Martha Johnson a parcel of land in the 4th District south of Coles Ferry Pike to W. O. Fakes, J. R. Johnson, W. H. Barron, and L. W. Smith, trustees of New Hope Cumberland Presbyterian Church. Dated 15 May 1882.
U#2 311

Elders of New Hope Cumberland Presbyterian Church to Robert Coles and his heirs a tract of land for fifteen dollars. Dated 1 October 1885.

SPRING CREEK CUMBERLAND PRESBYTERIAN CHURCH
G#2 310

J. H. Allen two acres in 5th District to J. M. Fakes, Jr. for a Cumberland Presbyterian Church. Dated 1869.
K#2 122

Richard H. Palmer gave land along Spring Creek which originally belonged to his father, John Palmer. Known as the Harpole Tract. Joins Carroll Academy. Lot not to be used for school purposes, but for Christian denomination. Dated 20 September 1873.
E#2 402

Moses Ellis two acres of land to John H. Allen for a Cumberland Presbyterian Church. Dated 1863.
O#2 291

Quit claim deed. John M. Fakes et al gave land for school purposes and for erecting a Presbyterian Church. Dated 20 February 1879.

SPRING CREEK PRESBYTERIAN CHURCH
J#2 427

G. W. Thompson to Josiah Donnell, J. B. Lindsey, P. Thompson, and F. R. S. Donnell, elders of Spring Creek Presbyterian Church.
N#2 115

Elders of Spring Creek Presbyterian Church sold church land to Robert Cox. Bounded by Chicken Road and Robert Cox's kitchen chimney. Dated 8 February 1872.

SUGG'S CREEK CUMBERLAND PRESBYTERIAN CHURCH
S 24

Elizabeth H. Sugg, Jesse Herring, Mary Herring, Dempsey Dillard, Frances R. Dillard, and Cullin E. Sugg to Hugh Telford, James Drennan, Reuben Wood, and Thomas Telford one and a half acres lying on the waters of Stone's River and Sugg's Creek. Dated 17 June 1829.

CHURCH DEEDS

Wills & Inventories 1832-1834, pp. 182-184
Hugh Telford Will. "I have given the Sugg's Creek Society five acres of land whereon the Meetinghouse stands for the use thereof and campground." Dated 3 December 1832.

N#2 250
John Logue to W. L. Woodrum, John L. Brown, R. F. Wood, Harvey Smith, and A. B. Stone, elders of Sugg's Creek Cumberland Presbyterian Church, a tract of land which joins the land where the church now stands. Dated 25 May 1877.

CUMBERLAND PRESBYTERIAN CHURCH, THIRD DISTRICT
X 514
Thomas Norman and J. Hall gave land which joins Union Schoolhouse (called George Donnell Meetinghouse). Dated 9 December 1848.

CUMBERLAND PRESBYTERIAN CHURCH, EIGHTEENTH DISTRICT
H#2 290
E. S. Thompson, Jr. to Milas Thompson, Andrew Thompson, and James W. Sherrill two acres and four poles. Dated 14 January 1859.

WATERTOWN DISCIPLES OF CHRIST
Y#2 443
John A. Clark to R. H. Baker, William Wood, and Lewis Pendleton, trustees, for the erection of a church for the Disciples of Christ. Dated 21 September 1881.

HOPEWELL CHURCH
P#2 1
Samuel Hamlet and Mary Hamlet three fourth's of an acre in the 7th District to Memiel Taylor, Wesley Page, and Thornton Beasley, trustees. Dated 20 January 1880.

GLADEVILLE CHURCH
53 225
J. F. Harris et al to J. H. Rice, school trustee; and J. H. Rice, Thomas Rice, J. M. Hooker, E. Noble, and W. T. Partlow, church trustees, land in the 23rd District. Dated 11 September 1895.

LITTLE CEDAR LICK FREE CHURCH
I 82
Joshua Tipton "for all Presbyterians, Baptists, and Methodist Societies of county and state one acre of land near Little Cedar Lick." Dated 10 March 1812.

MACEDONIA CHURCH
N#2 116
P. W. Harris and T. R. Harris to R. H. Thompson, Joseph Thompson, John N. Thompson, and Joe K. Thompson, officers of the church, three acres in the 18th District. Dated 20 February 1878.

(A short account of the organization of the first Presbyterian Church at Sugg's Creek Meeting-house with a brief
notice of the origin of the Cumberland Presbyterian Church
at this place. Transcribed from the original records.
13 September 1831. By Elijah Currey, Clerk of Session.)

FIRST PRESBYTERIAN CHURCH
At Sugg's Creek Meeting-house
        In the year eighteen hundred the Reverend Samuel
Donnell of the Presbyterian Body first organized a church
at Sugg's Creek Meeting-house. Elders: William Hannah,
John Hannah, Hugh Telford, and Robert Smith.

        Reverend Samuel Donnell continued his ministerial
labours two years, about this time a great revival of
religion commenced in the neighbourhood, from this time
the Reverend Samuel Donnell declined the pastorate of the
Church at this place, from that time untill the year 1808
the Congregation was supplied with circuit preaching by
Alexander Anderson, Samuel King, and others.

        In the year 1808 David Foster (a Licentiate) took
charge of the Congregation. In 1810 the Cumberland Presbyterians constituted and became a separate body from the
Presbyterians, about this time the Reverend David Foster
reorganized a church at Sugg's Creek Meeting-house called
Cumberland Presbyterians and continued his ministerial
labours untill 1827 at which time he declined the pastoral charge of the Congregation.

        On the 20 day of April 1820 the Church of Sugg's
Creek elected James Law and James Drennan to the office
of Ruling Elder and on Friday the 19 of May following
they were ordained to that office. Upon the 13 day of
May 1826 the Church at Sugg's Creek elected Reuben Wood
and Thomas Telford to the office of Ruling Elders and
shortly after they were ordained.

        The Sugg's Creek Congregation having made choice of
the Reverend John Beard as their stated Pastor. Where-
upon application was made to Nashville Presbytery (accord-
ing to Discipline) that he should preach to them one Sabbath in each month, their petition being granted he proceeded to take charge of the Congregation April 10, 1828.

        By consent of this Session Reverend John Beard ap-
plied to the Nashville Presbytery for a discharge from
his congregation at Sugg's Creek accordingly it was
granted on the 10th day of March 1837. After which the
Congregation was still supplied with the labours of Rev.
John Beard, Rev. Gideon H. Law, and others.

        On Saturday the 15 day of May 1841 the Church of
Sugg's Creek elected Reuben M. Wood and William Woodrum
to the office of Ruling Elders and Moses M. Currey Deacon,
all were ordained the following day by the Reverend John
N. Roach.

        The Sugg's Creek Congregation convened on the 14 day

of October 1841 and elected Reverend John Beard to the pastoral office of the Church and petitioned the Nashville Presbytery for his labours two Sabaths in each month which petition was granted on the 20 day of October 1841.

The Sugg's Creek Church applyed to the Nashville Presbytery for the services of Reverend J. B. Jackson as pastor which was granted 1852. By order of the Session. H. Telford, Clerk.

19 January 1854. The Session convened with J. B. Jackson as moderator. Elders: Thomas Telford, Robert Brown, M. M. Currey, and J. N. Cawthon. H. Telford officiated as Clerk. The Reverend J. B. Jackson offered his resignation to the Session as pastor. After some discussion the matter was postponed untill Spring. The Session resolved that each member ought to feel it their duty to submit to the regulations of our church government and observe the rules of christian propriety. The Session appointed Thomas Telford, Reverend J. B. Jackson, and H. Telford a committee on the c-- book. The Session adjourned to meet on Saturday before the third sabbath in next month in the afternoon. Adjourned by prayer. H. Telford, clerk.

18 February 1854. Two of Session convened and a quorum not being present adjourned untill third Saturday in March. H. Telford, clerk.

27 March 1854. The Session convened. On motion they petitioned the Nashville Presbytery to be released from the obligation between them and Reverend J. B. Jackson as pastor which was granted. Present: Thomas Telford, J. N. Cawthon, M. M. Currey, R. Foster, and absent R. Brown. Closed by prayer. H. Telford, clerk.

22 April 1854. Present: Thomas Telford and Rev. H. Telford only. Absent: R. Foster, R. Brown, M. M. Currey, elders. Recessed untill third Saturday in May. Concluded by prayer. H. Telford, clerk.

20 January 1860. Granted or gave seven letters (to wit) E. A. Miers, G. M. Miers, C. A. Miers, Mary W. Telford, Julia Ann Winters, T. F. M. Telford, and L. E. Telford. H. Telford, clerk.

18 February 1854. Reverend J. B. Jackson, M. M. Currey, and H. Telford met and as a quorum was not present recessed untill March 27th 54. Closed by prayer.

An account of the various scenes through which the Churches passes is a very desirable object, and should be a matter of record for the rising generations and the world. H. Telford.

Since my boyhood I know nothing of a lack of faithful preaching up to 1827 by the Reverend David Foster. Some of the greatest revivals of religion have been here, and some of the sorest of dark and destructive coldness. One of the great revivals was in 1820. Reverend John

94

Provine traveled the circuit a great time for the Church.
One night Esther Rice, Jun'r. professed and next year--
21 or 22-- at Fall Creek two other sisters and Betsy Rice
also a great many others I cannot now name at Stoner's
Creek. In September 23 I embraced Christ as my Savior
and in October 1836 there I was received by the Nashville
Presbytery as a candidate for the holy ministry and in
1842 at Ewing C., Rutherford County, was set apart to the
whole work of the ministry. By the laying on of the hands
of the Presbytery. My ministerial course has been one of
trial and difficulty through poverty and want of education
and in all that time I have been sacrifiseing my time and
health for the good of my fellow men.

Whereas certain scandalous reports injurious to the
cause of religion having been circulated upon Henry J.
Binkley (viz. fornification with his sister in law) therefore the Session of Sugg's Creek thought proper to send
two Elders to converse with him upon the subject. They
obeyed the order and he confessed guilt which they re-
ported to the Session. The Session then notified him to
appear before them upon the 14th day of July 1833. He
came forward and acknowledged his guilt. They then admonished, rebuked, and suspended him untill he give satis-
factory evidence of true repentance. Members present:
Reverend John Beard, Reuben Wood, Elijah Currey, Thomas
Telford, and John Roach. Thomas Telford, clerk pro tem.
14 July 1833.

11 June 1836. Whereas William Yandel, a member of
Sugg's Creek Congregation, being charged by comon fame of
using immoral language and fighting upon the 28th day of
April 1836 (previous to citation he was conversed with
upon the subject by two members). Then being regularly
cited to appear before the Session of said Congregation
upon the 11 day of June to answer to said charges. Seven
witnesses being somoned (viz. John H. Cauthon, Eli M.
Bradford, Moses M. Currey, Eli Sinclair, Solomon Carter,
Wilee McDearmon, and James Yandel, Sr. The Session met
on the above date at Sugg's Creek Meeting-house. Members
present: Reverend John Beard, Thomas Telford, A. Gwynn,
and E. Currey. Constituted by prayer. The accused being
ready for trial the Session proceeded.

J. H. Cauthon deposeth and saith that William Yandel
and J. J. Roach commenced quarreling about lifting together. Yandel dared him to collar him. Roach collared
him. Yandel struck him and used the word dadburn you
and gave the lie and they fought.

Eli M. Bradford deposeth and saith William Yandel
accused Roach of taking advantage of a stick in lifting
together. Roach said it was an accident. Yandel charged
him a second time. Roach called him an infernal rascal
and collared him and they fought.

Moses M. Currey deposeth and saith that while Yandel
and Roach was lifting together the stick slipped. Yandel

charged Roach with it. Roach said it was an accident.
Yandel give him the lie. Roach called him a dadburned
rascal and collared him. Yandel said, "Don't collar me."
Roach said, "You have been telling lies on me." Yandel
said, "Let him come. I am as good a man as him." And
they fought.

Eli Sinclair deposeth and saith Yandel and Roach was
lifting at a log together. Yandel charged Roach of taking
the advantage. He charged him a second time and give him
the lie. Roach went towards him. Yandel dared him to
touch him and they fought.

Solomon Carter deposeth and saith Yandel and Roach
lifted together. Yandel said Roach took the advantage of
him. Roach said he did not. Yandel give him the lie.
They made at each other and the struck. We parted them.
Yandel said, "Let him come. I am not afraid of him."
And they fought.

Wilie McDermon deposeth and saith Yandel and Roach
lifted together. Yandel charged him with taking the advantage of him. Roach denied. Yandel give him the lie
and dared him to collar him again and they fought.

James Yandel, Sr. deposeth and saith from some things
that passed he thought a quarrel was coming on. Yandel
and Roach lifted together. Yandel charged him with being
unfair. Roach denied. They contradicted a second time.
Yandel give Roach the lie. Roach collared him. Yandel
steped off some distance and told him to come on and they
fought.

The accused was requested to withdraw. After a few
minutes private conversation amongst the Session the
accused was called in and told by the Moderator that the
Session had found him guilty of both charges against him
and wished to know whether he felt sorry for his conduct.
He said, "I feel sorry it hapned on account of the Church."
When asked if he did feel sorry for giving the lie and
banter he said he did note and would fight when imposed
on (or words to that amount). He was requested to withdraw again when the Session decided as follows. That
William Yandel be excluded from church privileges untill
he give signs of repentance and sorrow for his conduct.
He was called in and told the decission of the Session.
He appeared obstinate and made use of such expressions
as these. "What tame a lion. You can't tame me. It
was born in me." And still persisted in expressing his
justification. The Moderator was requested to publish
the decission the next Sabbath. He has since been conversed with by a majority of the Session and they still
think he is impenitent. Signed by order of Session. 11
June 1836. Elijah Currey, clerk.

Whereas William Yandel thought he had injustice done
him by the Sugg's Creek Session, appealed to the Nashville
Presbytery in Session at Stoner's Creek the 7th day of

November 1836. There decission was as follows. William Yandel, being suspended by the Session of Sugg's Creek for immoral conduct, appealed to this Presbytery. After mature deliberation by a unanimous vote the decission of said Session was ratified in his case. William Yandel apeared before me and said he wanted a letter. He is now under censure. Confirmed by the Nashville Presbytery. H. Telford, clerk.

Whereas it being public that B. C. Brown, a member of Sugg's Creek Congregation, did upon the 5 day of March 1842 engage in fight with Needham Jones. The Session of said Congregation shortly after met and resolved to send a member to converse with him upon the subject. Accordingly, he went. Said Brown agreed to appear before the Session and acknowledge sorrow for his offense. He came forward upon the 22 day of May and expressed sorrow and penitence. The Session admonished him and restored him to church privileges again. Elijah Currey, clerk.

It being made publick that B. C. Brown, a member of the Cumberland Presbyterian Church at Sugg's Creek, engaged in fight with Mr. Hitton. The Session of said church summoned said Brown to appear before them upon the 7 day of September 1842. Also, three witnesses (viz.) Thomas A. Puckett, G. Peach, and Thomas Osborn.

Session being convened, constituted by prayer. Thomas A. Puckett being called upon and sworn testafieth that Mr. Brown was siting at the shop of Drs. Osborn and Logue and that Mr. Hitton came up within a few feet of him and said, "How are you, Mr. Eight Dollars and a Half," and abused him concerning an old matter between him and Mrs. Jones and her son, Needham. Mr. Brown said that he had better mind his own business. Mr. H. said that Mr. Brown was not too good to steal, that any man that would do as he had done would steal. Mr. B. stated that he had tho't. that he would have nothing to do with him. Mr. H. used very abusive language giving him the d--n-d lie frequently. Mr. B. arose and told him that he could not suffer such language to be heaped upon him, and struck him with his fist.

Question by Mr. B. "Did you see in me during the time of his abuse a disposition to wave the matter?" Witness: "I did all the time."

Mr. Peach being sworn testifyed that Mr. Brown was siting before the shop door of Drs. Osborn and Logue and that Mr. Hitton spoke to him and said, "How are you, Mr. Eight Dollars and a Half, dam you," giving him the d--n-d lie frequently and said that any body that would treat a widow woman as he had done would steal. About this time Mr. B. told him that he had thought that he would have nothing to do with him. But after Mr. H. had repetedly give him the lie Mr. B. arose and said he could not stand it any longer and struck him.

Question by the accused. "Did you see in me a disposition to wave the matter?" Witness: "I did."

Question by the Session. "Did Mr. B. give him any
cause at that time for the abuse?" Witness: "He did not."

T. C. Osborn being duley sworn testifieth that Mr.
Brown was siting before his office door in company with
several gentlemen who were entirely peaceable. "I was in
my office at the time Mr. Hitton came up and therefore did
not see the approach but heard Mr. Hitton in a loud voice
accost Mr. Brown with, "how are you, Mr. Eight Dollars and
a Half?" To which Mr. B. made no answer. "Mr. Hitton
made several such attacks as this before. Mr. Brown seemed
disposed to resist. I then came to the door and heard
Mr. B. remark to Mr. H. that he had thought he would not
have any thing more to do with him to which Mr. H. re-
torted in an angry and abusive manner. At which Mr. B.
seemed to get offended and said he would not stand that
and puled off his coat and prepared for combat. Mr.
Hitton's abuse rested upon an old grudge. Mr. H. said
that any person that would do as he had done would steal.
I have never heard Mr. B. say any thing in reference to
the old grudge previous to the affray that was calculated
to arouse an indignant feeling."

The Session are of opinion that Mr. Brown done rong
in striking the first blow. They therefore admonished
and rebuked him and restored him to church privileges.
Elijah Currey, clerk.

SUGG'S CREEK MINISTERS

Samuel Donnell	(1800-1802)
Alexander Anderson	(1802-1808)
Samuel King	
David Foster	(1808-1828)
John Beard	(1828-1848)
B. D. Moore	(1848-1852)
John B. Jackson	(1852-1856)
Joe L. Alexander	(1856-1866)
John B. Jackson	(1867-1869)
Joe L. Alexander	(1869-1872)
William Wilson	(1874)
A. W. Smith	(1875-1877)
Joe L. Alexander	(1877-1884)
R. T. Phillips	(1884-1887)
R. W. Hooker	(1884-1887)
Thomas B. Rice	(1884-1887)
James Marshall	(1887)
W. R. M. Crump	(1888-1889)
C. C. Russell	(1889-1890)
George M. Oakley	(1890-1892)
F. T. King	(1892)
C. E. Hayes	(1892-1893)
H. L. Walker	(1893-1894)
E. L. McWilliams	(1894-1898)
H. L. Livingstone	(1898)

BARTON'S CREEK BAPTIST CHURCH

(Located three miles southwest of Lebanon on the Barton's Creek Road)

Barton's Creek
21 April 1849

The Presbytery called by the brethren at Clemmons' Schoolhouse, Wilson County, Tennessee met the brethren and congregation there assembled for the purpose of organizing a Christian Church and ordaining Brother Wommack Wilburn to the Gospel Ministry.

On motion, Brother Maddox was chosen Moderator, and C. L. Johns appointed Clerk.

On motion, the Constitution of Cedar Grove Church was read by Brother Maddox and amended and adopted. On motion, the sixteenth article was strickened out, and the following inverted in its stead.

On motion, the Presbytery and brethren desiring the Constitution kneeled in prayer before God for the organization of the Church. Prayer by Brother Maddox. Right hand of fellowship by the Presbytery.

On motion, the meeting adjourned to meet at nine o'clock Sunday morning. E. Maddox, Moderator. C. L. Johns, Clerk. But they met Saturday night, April 21st, and five more joined at that meeting.

Sunday morning, April 22, 1849, the Church met and proceeded to ordain Brother Wilburn who was her first pastor. Presbytery: John Bond, Brother Muse, E. Maddox. E. Maddox, Moderator. C. L. Johns, Clerk.

What other Baptist Church in Wilson County can go farther back in her organization than Cedar Grove and Barton's Creek? Would like to have the date of each church.

A. E. Johnson
23 April 1899

BARTON'S CREEK MINISTERS

Elijah Maddox	(1849)
W. P. Wilburn	(1849-1857)
N. M. Green	(1857-1859)
John Phillips	(1859-1867)
J. C. Brien	(1867-1870)
J. S. Rice	(1870-1872)
William Barton	(1872-1873)
J. C. Brien	(1873-1874)
Lewis Lindsley	(1874-1876)
A. E. Johnson	(1876-1879)
G. A. Ogle	(1879-1882)
A. E. Johnson	(1882-1885)
John S. Rice	(1885-1891)
W. J. Couch	(1891-1892)
W. P. D. Clark	(1892-1900)

MINUTES OF BIG SPRING CHURCH

Soon after the Great Revival of 1800 began, there was a camp meeting held at the Big Spring. Little is now known of this and the succeeding meetings on the first site, except that they were greatly blessed. In the year 1809, the campground was moved to the present site (near Bellwood on the old Rome Pike). In 1811, the house now occupied was built.

The first preacher in charge of this Church was the Reverend Samuel King. From the year 1809 until 1855 or 1856, camp meetings were held annually on this spot. They were kept up out of regard to the feelings of Reverend Thomas Calhoun long after they had ceased to be held elsewhere in the Church (Cumberland Presbyterian). It was not till Calhoun had passed away to his reward that they were finally suspended.

This long series of camp meetings have sent their holy influence over all the field occupied by Cumberland Presbyterians. The ministers converted at these meetings are Calhoun, Baker, McSpeddin, Astor, Provine, Wilson, Dillard, and a whole army besides whose names are not now at hand.

From the converts of these meetings half the churches in the South now owe their most valuable members. But evil days came. Calhoun died. Camp meetings ceased everywhere. Finally, old Big Spring ceased to be a living church.

This summer, a meeting was held on the old spot. Gloom rested over the beginning of the meeting. In the midst of it, a glorious revival resulted in the reorganization of the Congregation. This book begins the second chapter in the history of the Big Spring Church. May its triumphs be equal to those of the first glorious period. 7 October 1869. Written by request of Session. B. W. McDonnold.

NAME	ADMISSION	DEATH
Thomas C. McSpaden	Jul 1869	6 Jul 1875
Mary A. Ferrill	Jul 1869	
Joseph G. Bell	Jul 1869	Mar 1879
Mary P. Bell	Jul 1869	29 Apr 1871
Robert Gann	Jul 1869	1887
Richard Oldham, Sr.	Jul 1869	
Nancy D. Oldham	Jul 1869	
William G. McDonald	Jul 1869	
Manerva H. McDonald	Jul 1869	Apr 1875
Walter W. Melven	Jul 1869	(left disorderly)
Justina S. Melven	Jul 1869	(left disorderly)
Elizabeth W. Gann	Jul 1869	
Anneth R. Ellis	Jul 1869	
Lidia A. Harris	Jul 1869	
Jane A. Fuqua	Jul 1869	
Nancy A. McSpaden	Jul 1869	12 Jul 1875
Martha Reeves	Aug 1869	

100

NAME	ADMISSION	DEATH
Julia A. Caplenor	Jul 1869	
Ann E. Massey	Aug 1869	
Thomas Young	Aug 1869	
Mary A. Young	Sep 1869	
Samuel W. Bell	Sep 1869	
Cynthia H. McSpaden	Sep 1869	
Samuel T. McSpaden	Sep 1869	
Rebecca Johnson	Sep 1869	
Alice B. Melven	Sep 1869 (expelled)	
Edwin C. Melven	Sep 1869 (expelled)	
Thomas H. Phillips	Sep 1869 (withdrew)	
Frances T. McDonald	Sep 1869 (suspended)	
John S. Oldham	Sep 1869	
Emily Carter	Sep 1869	
Julia Ship	Sep 1869	
Mary S. Gaimwell	Sep 1869	1875
Sarah F. McMurry	Sep 1869	
Samuel F. Organ	Sep 1869	
Frances M. Johnson	Sep 1869	
John A. Ship	Sep 1869	
William A. Bell	Sep 1869	
Vilena E. Tomlinson	Sep 1869 (excommunicated)	
Lusana F. Gann	Sep 1869	
Susanna R. Cunningham	Sep 1869	
Mary E. Crowell	Sep 1869	
John F. Shepherd	Sep 1869 (expelled)	
Mary S. Watkins	Sep 1869	
Jane H. Watkins	Sep 1869	
John B. Ellis	Sep 1869	
Moses Watkins	Sep 1869	
Ag Hatcher	Sep 1869	
Robert W. Hendrick	Sep 1869	
Norris J. Osburn	Sep 1869 (left with Baptists)	
Robert S. Watkins	Sep 1869	
Martha Brown	Oct 1869	1880
Martha Dawson	May 1870	
Mary Cooper	May 1870	
Sarah Hankins	Sep 1870	
Ann Ellis	Sep 1870 (to Texas)	
Freelan Dawson	Sep 1870 (left without letter)	
N. Melven	Sep 1870 (left without letter)	
Samuel Oldham	Sep 1870	
Richard Oldham, Jr.	Sep 1870	
Thomas C. Moore	Sep 1870	
Molly A. Brown	Sep 1870	
Elizabeth Hawkins	Nov 1870	9 Jul 1871
Alexander Foster	Sep 1872	23 Mar 1884
Alice Fuqua	Sep 1872	
H. Warren	Nov 1872	1881
Mavias Johnson	Oct 1873	
A tinson Johnson	Oct 1873	
(al Dickens	Oct 1873	
Olyada Cobb	Oct 1873 (removed)	
Lula Suddeth	Oct 1873	

NAME	ADMISSION	DEATH
Mary T. Foster	Oct 1873	
Emma T. Bell	Oct 1873	
Franklin Davis	Aug 1874 (removed)	
Nancy Williams	Aug 1874	
P. G. Calhoun	Sep 1874	
John C. Mitchel	Sep 1874	
Nancy E. Mitchel	Sep 1874	
Sarah Cunningham	1875	
Nancy Cunningham	1875	
Susan Oldham	Sep 1875	
Harry Johnson	Sep 1875	
W. G. Hankins	Sep 1875 (removed)	
Fanny Hankins	Sep 1875 (removed)	
Presley Smith	Jun 1875 (removed)	
James Johnson	Sep 1876	
Mary Carter	Sep 1876	
Frank Calhoun	Sep 1876	20 Apr 1887
Elizabeth Fuqua	Sep 1876 (by letter)	
Betty Cunningham	Sep 1876 (by letter)	
Charly Young	Sep 1876	16 Feb
Nancy Johnson	Sep 1877	
Monroe Rodgers	Oct 1878 (removed)	
Mrs. Sallie Rodgers	Oct 1878	
Robert Gann	Jul 1869	Jul 1887
Nancy Oldham	Jul 1869	13 Oct 1887
Elizabeth W. Gann	Jul 1869	
Lydia T. Farris	Jul 1869	
James H. Fuqua	Jul 1869	
Julea Calhoun	Aug 1869	
Martha H. Johnson	Aug 1869	
Hattie Suddarth	Sep 1879	
Jane Brown	Sep 1879	
Fannie Armistead	Sep 1879	
Alice Suddarth	Sep 1879	14 Aug 1888
Mrs. Hankins	Sep 1879	
Virginia Hudson	Sep 1879	
A. McGee	Oct 1881	
M. Ship	Oct 1881	
Lavinia A. Ship	Oct 1881	
P. B. Calhoun	Oct 1881	
Carrie Calhoun	Oct 1881	
Mattie Calhoun		
William Ferrel	Aug 1883	
Martha E. Dickens	Nov 1883	
James Oldham	Sep 1883	
Fanny Foley	Oct 1883	
Venie Shipp	Oct 1883	
Eliza Shipp	Oct 1883	
John Bell	Oct 1883	
Etta Carter	Oct 1883	
Ellen Dickens	Oct 1883	
William H. Carter	Sep 1885	
Charles T. Carter	Sep 1885	
Alonzo Carter	Sep 1885	

NAME	ADMISSION	DEATH
P. R. Carter	Sep 1885	1886
L. T. Carter	Sep 1885	
Martha Carter	Sep 1885	
Ruth Carter	Sep 1885	
Anderson K. Suddarth	Sep 1885	
Eliza Suddarth	Sep 1885	
Lizzie Johnson	Sep 1885	
Mary Johnson	Sep 1885	
Amanda McGee	Sep 1885	
John Shipp	Sep 1885	
Cora Young	Sep 1885	
T. L. C. Young	Sep 1885	
Bell Dickens	Sep 1885	
Gertina Dickens	Sep 1885	
F. P. Davidson	Sep 1885	
S. T. Davidson	Sep 1885	
Robert D. Grissim	Aug 1887	
Mary E. Grissim	Aug 1887	
Jodie W. Dickens	Aug 1887	
Dr. W. H. Andrews	Oct 1887	
Emma J. Warren	Oct 1887	
Mrs. Dies	Oct 1887	
Mary D. Andrews	Oct 1887	
Eddy Dickens	Oct 1887	
July Bell Carter	Oct 1887	
Leula G. Grissim	Oct 1887	
Robert Donnell Suddarth	Oct 1887	
Clarra Josie Suddarth	Oct 1887	
Henry Stephen Stone	Oct 1887	
Mary E. Bell	Oct 1887	
Mrs. Susan Harris	Oct 1887	
Lilla May Calhoun	Oct 1887	
Virgy V. Corley	Oct 1887	
Ewing G. Calhoun	Oct 1887	
Edward P. Smith	Oct 1887	
William T. Marshall	Oct 1887	
Leora Carter	Oct 1887	
Maggie Corley	Oct 1887	
May Corley	Oct 1887	
L. Dow Conatsy	Oct 1887	
T. J. Bell	Oct 1887	
T. J. Reed	Oct 1887	
M. Proyer	Oct 1887	
Edny Brown	Oct 1887	
Sireany Elzina Dickens	Oct 1887	
David Young	Nov 1887	(from Bethel Church)
W. Hamlet Grissim	Oct 1889	
J. Huby Grissim	Oct 1889	
Samuel Ship	Oct 1889	
Julia Ship	Sep 1890	
C. Grissim	Sep 1890	
Carrie M. Calhoun	Sep 1890	
Paul Dickens	Sep 1890	
L. Bruce	Sep 1890	

MINUTES OF BIG SPRING CHURCH

NAME	ADMISSION	DEATH
Lavina Allen	Sep 1890	
Jennie Grissim	Sep 1889	
Robert Marshal	Sep 1889	
J. William Norris	Sep 1889	
Mrs. Bertha Grissim	Feb 1892 (from M. E. Church)	
John W. Armstead	Sep 1879	
Lewis Dias	Oct 1887	

MARRIAGES

John B. Ellis
Ann Page

Reverend B. Ferrell
24 February 1870

William G. Warren
Rebeca Johnson

Reverend A. W. Hawkins
2 March 1871

William Colquet
Ludie Gann

Reverend A. W. Hawkins
23 March 1871

Sam Cunningham
Martha Reeves

Reverend A. W. Hawkins
25 December 1870

S. E. Baird
Martha A. Johnson

W. W. Suddeth
28 December 1871

John Heflin
Dolly A. Brown

E. F. Tucker
16 September 1873

Edward Marshal
Martha Dawson

W. H. Suddeth
23 October 1873

H. G. McDonald
Nancy McSpedden

W. H. Suddeth
21 January 1874

James G. Grissim
Mattie S. Calhoun

W. W. Suddeth
27 April 1887

Jodie Dickens
Fanny Foley

W. W. Suddeth
1889

Hamlet Grissim
Etta Carter

W. W. Suddeth
1889

B. Parnell
Ela Young

1888

James S. Johnson
Mattie Sudarth

Dr. Kirkpatrick

J. W. Lamb
May Calhoun

Reverend Burns

John Hughs
Luvenia Ship

Green Clay
Emma J. Warren

1889

T. B. Warren
Nannie Johnson

W. W. Suddeth

Henry S. Stone
Eliza North

1889

LEBANON DEMOCRAT EXCERPTS

September 26, 1889
(Below will be found a list of the old men from the 21st District of Wilson County over seventy years of age, where they were born, etc.)

J. B. Baird, born in Wilson County, Tennessee in August, 1813. He has lived in the county all his life, age, 76 years.

S. R. Comer, born at Halifax County, Virginia, September 1808; came to Wilson County, Tennessee when quite young, age, 81 years.

R. B. Castleman, born in Wilson County, Tennessee and has lived in Wilson County all his life, age, 75 years.

John Fields, born in Wilson County, Tennessee, July 1808; has ever been a resident of Wilson County, age, 81 years.

L. Holloway, born, reared, and lived all his life at the homestead where he now lives, born January, 1811, age, 78 years.

W. D. Hancock, born July, 1818, born, reared, and lived in a stone's throw of his present home, age, 71 years.

R. H. Lain, born in Smith County, Tennessee 1817; came to Wilson County, Tennessee while a boy, age, 72 years.

G. H. Merritt, born in Wilson County, Tennessee September, 1814; has lived at his present home from birth, age, 75 years.

J. H. Martin, born near Kingston, Roane County, East Tennessee November, 1816; came to Wilson County a good many years ago, age, 73 years.

C. Osment, born 1811, two miles from Greensboro, Gilford County, North Carolina; came to Tennessee (Wilson County) in 1830 and has lived here ever since, age, 78 years.

Eli Reed, born November 24, 1813, born and lived all his life on the farm where he now lives (Wilson County, Tennessee), age, 75 years.

James Rice, born March 4, 1810; has lived at his present home some 40 or 45 years, age, 79 years.

Frank Saddler, born at Quotoway, Virginia 1816; came to Wilson County when quite young. Mr. Saddler is blind, age, 76 years.

Anders Saddler, born at Quotoway, Virginia 1816; came to Tennessee when young, age, 73 years.

November 7, 1889
(Below will be found a list of those who were once Lebanon boys)

Robert Kirkpatrick is engaged in life insurance at Chattanooga, Tennessee.

Albert Cowan is connected with the Missouri, Kansas, and

Texas Railway Company at Waco, Texas.

Walter Brantley is practicing law in Oregon where he has built up an extensive practice and good reputation.

Brown Peyton is in the lumber business in Texas.

C. H. Pickett is one of Albuquerque's prominent lawyers in New Mexico.

Fred Cabbott is engaged in the dry goods business at Natchez, Mississippi.

J. L. Thompson is one of Nashville's best druggists.

Bailey Cantrell is engaged in the manufacture of woolen goods at McMinnville, Tennessee.

Will and Walter Price are doing business at Jefferson City, Missouri.

Jordan and Walter Stokes stand in the foremost ranks at the Nashville Bar.

Will Lamoine is a prominent real estate agent of Oregon.

Jack Trinum is still engaged in the printing business at Nashville.

W. T. Watson is Principal of Leddin's Business College at Memphis, Tennessee.

Alexander Black lives at McMinnville, Tennessee and is a prosperous farmer.

Bob Burton's home is in St. Louis, Missouri. He is book-keeper for the Jo. M. Hayes Woolen Company.

John Burton is in the lumber business at Murfreesboro, Tennessee.

James Bates is an extensive lumber dealer, and resides at Nashville.

Cling Gribble is doing a good dry goods and clothing business at Woodbury, Tennessee.

Andrew Thompson lives in Sheffield, Alabama and is now superintending the grading of the park drives.

Harry Hill is in the general merchandise business at Honey Grove, Texas and is meeting with success.

Finis Moseley is engaged in the mercantile business at Honey Grove.

Jno. L. Moseley of the Fifth District is chief machinist in a large shop at Gainesville, Texas.

Marshall Young is now living in Cincinatti, Ohio. He is doing well.

Will Cartwright is doing business at Fort Worth, Texas.

Tom Norman is keeping books in Nashville, Tennessee.

Al G. Duffy is in the office of the Grand Keeper of Seal

and Records of Knights Pythias at Nashville.

Bob Russell ranks among the best of Texas farmers.

Harry Haynes is connected with the express office at Dallas, Texas. He is doing well.

November 28, 1889
(Below will be found a list of those who were once Lebanon boys)

Will Whitson is engaged in the clothing house at H. Metz at Nashville, Tennessee.

George Lewis is engaged in the manufacture of carriages at McMinnville, Tennessee.

F. M. Neal is one of the prominent wholesale druggists at Nashville, Tennessee.

Sam Neal is traveling salesman for the wholesale drug firm of Spurlock, Neal, and Company of Nashville.

Ike Finley is proprietor of a large Florida orange grove.

Obe Finley is general manager of the telephone exchange at Clarksville, Tennessee.

Dr. W. M. Finley, Jr. is following his profession in Alabama.

Arch A. Greer is traveling salesman for a St. Louis undertaking establishment.

Willard Haley is engaged in the real estate business in Cincinatti, Ohio.

Dick Allen is engaged in the grocery business in Dennison, Texas.

Ed Stratton is selling dry goods in Mississippi.

Sam Neal is practicing law in Helena, Montana.

William Forrester is collector for the Wrought Iron Range Company in the State of Texas.

Bob Neal has a government position in Arkansas.

Will Neal is engaged in the mercantile business.

A. C. Stewart is attorney for the Wabash Railway with headquarters at St. Louis, Missouri.

Ed A. Brower is following his trade of carriage and sign painter in California.

Sam Borum and his brother, Will, are both engaged in business at Nashville.

Stephen and Benjamin Jenkins are actively engaged at Nashville.

Thomas McKee is working at his trade of miller in Vernon, Texas.

Will McKee is engaged in business in Vernon, Texas.

Gentry Thompson is in the cabinet making business at Vernon, Texas.

Ras McKee is with the Lindsey Hat Company at Nashville, Tennessee.

Rufus M. Fields is in the insurance business in Nashville.

William McCorkle, a former attorney in our town, is now a preacher of the Gospel in Virginia.

Thomas Brantley is teaching in the State of Illinois.

January 2, 1890
(Another chapter on the Lebanon girls who have married and gone far, far away)

Miss Kate Anderson married Reverend Alonzo Pearson about one year ago. Mr. Pearson is a graduate of the Theological Department of Cumberland University and is now the popular pastor of the First Cumberland Presbyterian Church at St. Joseph, Missouri.

Miss Annie Burney married Reverend R. W. Binkley, who for nine years was pastor of the Cumberland Presbyterian Church at Oxford, Mississippi, but is now pastor of the Cumberland Presbyterian Church at Franklin, Kentucky.

Miss Alice Poindexter is now Mrs. Poindexter, having married her cousin, Robert Poindexter, a prominent planter and real estate agent at Shreveport, Louisiana.

Miss Emmett Thompson is now Mrs. John J. McClelland. Mr. McClelland is a graduate of the Law School of Cumberland University and is a rising young lawyer of West Point, Mississippi.

Miss Bettie Stokes married George Waters, formerly of this county, but now a prominent business man of Nashville. He is a member of the firm of W. L. Waters & Son and is manager of their immense foundry and machine shops at Nashville.

Miss Ella Green married Mr. W. C. Caldwell of Trenton, Tennessee, who was a graduate of the University Law School. Mr. Caldwell is one of the Supreme Judges of this State.

Miss Mollie Pennebaker married Mr. Frazer Edmondson of Memphis, who is a rising young lawyer of that city. He is also a graduate of Cumberland University Law School.

Miss Kate Bostick married Mr. E. R. Pennebaker. They resided in Lebanon for a long time, but Mr. Pennebaker is now a prominent grocery merchant at Nashville and is doing well.

Miss Ruby Riddle married Mr. Henry Coles of Nashville. He is the son of Col. E. W. Coles who is well-known over the state as a capitalist. Mr. Coles is a young banker.

Miss Mattie Green is the wife of Reagan Houston, who is an

alumnus of the Law School and is now a prominent young attorney of San Antonio, Texas.

Miss Carrie Thompson is now Mrs. Judge Roseborough of Belton, Texas. Mr. Roseborough received his legal training here and is a lawyer of first class ability.

Miss Mary Bostick married Honorable S. F. Wilson of Gallatin. Mr. Wilson is one of the most prominent lawyers of the State and was a few years ago a strong candidate for governor.

Miss Alice Pennebaker married Mr. Ed Campbell while that gentleman was in Lebanon attending the Law School. Mr. Campbell is now a young lawyer with bright prospects and makes his home in Lawrence, Kansas.

Miss Pauline Woolard was married last summer to Mr. W. J. Spire of Nashville. Mr. Spire is a prominent queensware merchant of Nashville.

Mr. Harry Buckman of Jacksonville, Florida had the good fortune to win the heart and hand of Miss Sallie Allison. Mr. Buckman is a lawyer and enjoys the distinction of having a large practice.

Miss Maggie Riddle married Mr. Robert Chester who is a lawyer. They reside at Jackson, Tennessee.

Camperton,
January 17 1890
    Since our last report death has visited our happy community and taken away one of our oldest and best men, Mr. Armistead Lain. The departed leaves many relatives and friends to mourn his death. They may rest assured that they have the sympathy of the entire community.

May 22, 1890
(The census enumerators have at last been selected, and while a score of hearts have been made happy because the lightning struck round about them, many scores have been made sad. They are 21 in number for this county, and their names with the district are as follows:

1.	John K. Stroud	14.	R. M. Johnson
2.	W. G. Woollard	15.	S. C. Knight
3.	G. W. Simpson	16.	L. M. Neal
4.	J. B. Tolliver	17.	J. A. Cox
5.	A. B. Woollard	18.	A. P. Williams
6.	F. P. Brockett	19.	A. P. Williams
7.	J. F. Baker	20.	W. A. Hobbs
8.	J. F. Baker	21.	S. F. Hancock
9.	J. F. Baker	22.	W. Z. Neal
10.	George Beckwith	23.	A. W. Spickard
11.	Marcus Hudson	24.	T. N. Rice
12.	J. M. Luck	25.	J. H. Osment
13.	R. M. Johnson		

August 21, 1890

LEBANON DEMOCRAT EXCERPTS

THE CENSUS

(An Enumerator Gives Some Of His Experiences)

Leaving Mount Air to the left we traveled in a northeasterly direction, until another day's work had been completed. Stopping at this farmhouse and then another, the information was generally given by the kind lady of the house, while the husband and father of the family was toiling in the fields and almost melting under the rays of one of June's warmest and sunniest days.

It was during the time of harvesting and haying, and as the old proverb says, "Make hay while the sun shines," they were certainly striving to do so. They had the sunshine as the writer can testify, and the wheat shocks and hay cocks were rapidly going up on the right and left in many fields and meadows passed by the writer. Occasionally, a fellow would be seen following his plow, and in answer to my summons would stop his jaded, perspiring animal while we would place ourselves under the nearest tree, and make a record of his part of the wealth and population of the 7th District. After getting through, the question was generally asked me, "How is the 'lection' gwine in your part of the county?" "Mightily mixed," said I. "Both men are popular and have a strong following in my country."

His answer to a similar question on my part would almost invariably tell me who he was for. If for Britton, he was going to sweep the country; or for Harkreader, as a matter of course, he would hardly miss a vote.

Men with but few exceptions tell those things like they want them, or in other words, like they think ought to be. The wish with them is generally father to the thought expressed.

As before stated, the man of the house was rarely at home, only at night or during the time for his noon meal. Frequently, on going into a house we would be surrounded by a half dozen or more children who expected to see the wares and trinkets of the pack peddler, when the documents of our work were opened and unpacked for business. Many mothers having that number of children would have to bring in the old family Bible, in order to give the correct ages of their children. Others with the same number, or even more, could readily give all the dates required without having to refer to any record whatever.

I found several colored mothers with a numerous household, who could give the ages of their children as readily as any white mothers, and that too without calling into requisition the old time and well-worn family Bible.

No trouble whatever was experienced by the writer in obtaining ages from blushing maidens, or in finding out the ages of those who are so commonly denominated as old maids.

But few of the latter class were found as the girls of my districts are so attractive in manner and person that only those who remain so from choice and found upon that list.

One lady I could mention, living in Smith County, positively refused to report her age to the enumerator. No kind of argument or persuasion could induce her to do so.

Another knight of the quill, failing to get the same information from a lady said, "Well, I guess you are about sixty, so I will just enter you at that age." The ruse had the desired effect-- she was very quick to correct him. You may put one down under age, but never would they submit to being recorded a few years older than in truth they are.

It has ever seemed strange to me why anyone should even dislike or refuse to tell their age. Nostrums or dye-stuffs of various kinds may keep back gray hairs, but nothing has ever yet been devised to keep back furrows, wrinkles, and bending, tottering forms.
But I must desist again.

OBSERVER

Barton's Creek
May 16, 1891
A candy breaking was given at the residence of Mr. M. Pass, March 11th. A host of youngsters attended the party and among them were: J. W. Hudson and Miss Cora Jarrett; M. W. Johnson and Miss Dovie Ligon; Wes Ligon and Miss Dovie Tomlin; P. R. Lane and Miss Nannie Ligon; T. F. Eddins and Miss Dovie Williams. They gathered about sundown and left at sunrise.

Mount View
March 17, 1895
Mr. John Rogers was married on the 20th to one of Mount View's fair belles, Miss Rossia Ligon, daughter of Mr. Charles W. G. Ligon. Elder J. E. B. Ridley, officiating. The wedding was a very quiet affair, no invitations were sent. We wish them the climax of happiness.

Marble Hill
March 7, 1896
Miss Jennie Patterson, daughter of Z. S. Patterson died at her home March 3rd and was buried near her home the following day. The bereaved parents have the sympathy of the entire community, and we also hate the loss of a good girl, but such things must be, and we have to bear them the best we can.

Union
April 25, 1896
Esq. Berry Vanhook of Tucker's Gap and his beautiful

and accomplished daughter, Carrie, spent the day with Mr.
E. C. Clemmons last Sunday.

Barton's Creek
July 5, 1896
       Professor J. B. Ligon, perhaps, thought if he would
frighten the chinch bugs and give them a warning of their
future danger they might become alarmed and escape for
their lives. So the other morning Mr. Ligon went out into his field, stomped on the ground, gave a yell, and
said, "I'll swear, if you bugs don't leave here and quit
killing my corn and millet, I'll kill the last fetched
one of you, b'gosh."

Barton's Creek
January 16, 1899
       W. T. Johnson, who has been visiting his father and
relatives, has returned to his home at Sylvan, Texas.
His father, M. Johnson, accompanied him home to stay only
a short while we hope.

Tick College
April 2, 1899
       There is a new schoolhouse being erected at this
place, situated on the old Franklin Road, southwest of
Lebanon which will be a great benefit to this neighborhood. It will be completed soon. When finished, we will
have singings, preaching, and all religious services
except Roman Catholics and Mormons.

OATHS OF LOYALTY

July 14, 1865
    Stephen Robinson makes oath that his sons, John H. Robinson and Leonard Robinson, have served as soldiers in the Army of the United States and have been honorably discharged.

July 14, 1865
    John H. Robinson makes oath that M. Tally and W. W. Tally are citizens of Wilson County and publicly known to be unconditional Union men and have been from the commencement of the rebellion until the present time.

July 24, 1865
    David M. Lain makes oath that he is a citizen of Wilson County and has arrived at the age of twenty-one years since the 4th March 1865 and that he has never been engaged in armed rebellion against the authority of the United States.

March 3, 1866
    F. T. Ligon makes oath that John Hunt is a citizen of Wilson County, twenty-one years of age, and is publicly known to have entertained unconditional Union sentiments from the outbreak of the rebellion until the present time.

March 3, 1866
    John B. Snow makes oath that he is a citizen of Wilson County, twenty-one years of age, and that he is a loyal citizen of the United States, and that he is a loyal citizen of this county six months, and to the best of my information he was formerly a citizen of another state.

March 3, 1866
    W. W. Whitesides makes oath that George W. Brown is a loyal citizen of the United States, that he is twenty-one years of age, that he has been a citizen of Wilson County for more than six months, that he was formerly a citizen of another state.

March 15, 1866
    A. J. Hall makes oath that David S. Holt and James W. Carruy are citizens of Wilson County, twenty-one years of age, and that he was a member of the 4th Tennessee Mounted Infantry, USA (Colonel Blackbund) from which he has been honorably discharged.

March 2, 1866
    David S. Holt makes oath that Martin Rohelia is a citizen of Wilson County, twenty-one years of age and that he was a member of the 5th Tennessee Cavalry, USA (Colonel Stokes) from which he has been honorably discharged.

March 2, 1866
    George Treiber makes oath that John Kolbe is a citizen of Wilson County, twenty-one years of age, and is publicly known to have entertained unconditional Union senti-

ments from the outbreak of the rebellion until the present time.

March 3, 1866

R. N. Moxley makes oath that J. W. Moxley is a citizen of Wilson County and has arrived at the age of twenty-
one years since 4th day of March 1865. He has never been
engaged in armed rebellion against the United States.

March 3, 1866

P. S. McBride makes oath that he is a citizen of
Wilson County and has arrived at the age of twenty-one
years since 4th day of March 1865 and that he has never
been engaged in armed rebellion against the United States.

March 3, 1866

L. D. Harrison makes oath that William Yandell, Isaac
Harrison, Thomas Telford, W. H. Brown, Thomas Peach, M.
L. Peach, Jesse N. Smith, Christopher Smith, and A. J.
Harrison are citizens of Wilson County, went to the
election ground to vote for Governor of the State and
members to the General Assembly on the 4th day of March
1865. He went with them and the election was broken up
and they were prevented from voting. He is well-satisfied they all would have voted if the election has been
holden. They had all taken the oath of allegiance and
were true friends to the Government of the United States.

March 2, 1866

William Williams makes oath that Eli Sullivan is a
citizen of this county and has been for more than six
months and publicly known to have unconditional Union
sentiments.

March 2, 1866

J. B. McHenry makes oath that John Hill, Thomas Davis
and Job Drennan were soldiers in the Federal service and
were honorably discharged from the Service. They are
citizens of Wilson County.

March 2, 1866

J. B. McHenry makes oath that Granville McPeak and
Henderson McPeak are citizens and always been loyal citizens, have never taken up arms against the United States
voluntarily.

February 25, 1866

We, H. L. Lannom and William Howard, entitled to vote
under the pursuance of the law, and have certificates,
being sworn, depose, and say that William C. Burk is and
has always been loyal to the United States and altho he
went into the Confederate Army for a time, he was forced
to do so by a contempt officer.

February 25, 1866

William Howard makes oath that Polk Hackney is a
citizen of Wilson County and has arrived at the age of
twenty-one years since the 4th of March 1865. He has
never taken up arms against the Government of the United

States.

February 25, 1866
    John Shorter makes oath that Robert Shorter is a
citizen of Wilson County, has arrived at twenty-one years
of age since the 4th day of March 1865, and that he has
never been engaged in armed rebellion against the United
States.

February 26, 1866
    E. E. Jones makes oath that E. H. Hearn is a citizen
of Wilson County, twenty-one years of age, and is publicly known to have entertained unconditional Union sentiments from the outbreak of the rebellion until the present
time.

February 24, 1866
    A. Woolard makes oath that his son, Z. J. Woolard,
is a citizen, has arrived at the age of twenty-one years,
and that he has never engaged in armed rebellion against
the United States.

February 24, 1866
    William Howard makes oath that T. W. Edwards, Stephen
Arnold, and Thomas Williams were publicly known to have
entertained unconditional Union sentiments and were
Union men during the rebellion.

February 26, 1866
    D. F. Whitlock makes oath that his brother, Isaac D.
Whitlock is a citizen of Wilson County, has arrived at
the age of twenty-one since 4th March 1865 and that he
has never taken up arms against the United States.

February 26, 1866
    A. Woolard makes oath that J. J. Winter is a young
man, citizen of Wilson County, has arrived at the age of
twenty-one years since 4th March 1865 and has never engaged in armed rebellion against the United States.

March 1, 1866
    J. J. Price makes oath that George Griffin, Frank
Bryant, and Walker Brice are citizens of Wilson County,
twenty-one years of age, and are known publicly to have
entertained unconditional Union sentiments.

February 19, 1866
    William Graves makes oath that his son, George
Graves, is a citizen of Wilson County, has arrived at the
age of twenty-one years, and has never been engaged in
armed rebellion against the United States.

February 22, 1866
    E. H. James makes oath that his son, R. J. James, is
a citizen of Wilson County, has arrived at the age of
twenty-one years, and has never been engaged in armed
rebellion against the United States.

February 22, 1866
    P. F. Ligon makes oath that to the best of his know-

ledge and belief Pat Caraway is a citizen of Wilson County, arrived at the age of twenty-one years since the 4th March 1865, and that he has not been engaged in armed rebellion against the United States.

February 26, 1866

T. J. Williams makes oath that Boyd Smith was present and voted in the election 4th March 1865 for members of the Legislature.

William M. Knight, a citizen of Wilson County, makes oath that he is acquainted with Herman G. Bennett and has been from infancy, that he was in his neighborhood, that he has never been in armed rebellion against the United States, and that he has arrived at the age of twenty-one years.

February 17, 1866

W. H. Baird and P. B. Caraway make oath that they are citizens of Wilson County, that they have never been engaged in armed rebellion against the United States, and that they each have arrived at the age of twenty-one years.

J. W. Edwards makes oath that he is personally acquainted with Thomas L. Edwards and Jacob Alsup and has been from their childhood, and also with David R. Vaughter, that they are all citizens of Wilson County, and from his knowledge of them they have been twenty-one years since the 4th March 1865. He believes and thinks well-satisfied that they have never taken up arms against the United States.

He further states that Thomas Elliott is a citizen of Wilson County, has been publicly known to be a Union man during the rebellion against the United States. Thomas L. Edwards will not be twenty-one years of age until the 2nd day of March next. He also includes George McPeak as a young man in the same condition.

B. D. Moore makes oath that J. Moore is a citizen of Wilson County, has never taken up arms against the United States, think arrived to age of twenty-one years last December.

E. E. Warner makes oath that L. Warner is a citizen, that he served during the War most of the time with the Federal Army.

February 27, 1866

J. H. Turnblin makes oath that Dr. J. H. Dukes is a citizen of Wilson County and publicly known to have entertained unconditional Union sentiments from the outbreak of the rebellion until the present time.

March 1, 1866

A. J. Hall makes oath that H. G. Sharp is twenty-one years of age, is a loyal citizen of the United States, and has been a citizen of this county more than six months and that he was to the best of my information formerly a citizen of another state.

J. H. Lain and F. L. Ligon make oath that they are citizens of Wilson County, that they have entertained unconditional Union sentiments from the outbreak, that they have known each other, and each state for the other that they are publicly known to be Union men.

August 16, 1866

W. K. McClellan makes oath that C. W. Jenkins is publicly known to be an unconditional Union Man.

August 23, 1866

J. L. Davis makes oath that he has arrived at the age of twenty-one years since the 4th day of March 1865, and that he has never been engaged in armed rebellion against the United States.

March 1, 1866

R. B. Hare, being sworn, makes oath that R. E. Kennedy is publicly known to have entertained unconditional Union sentiments, that he is a citizen of the United States, and has resided in this county more than six months.

March 6, 1866

Peyton Ligon makes oath that P. Walker is a citizen of the United States, has resided in this county more than six months, that he has entertained unconditional Union sentiments, and has been publicly known to be a Union man. That W. F. Lain, also a citizen of this county, has arrived at the age of twenty-one years since the 4th of March 1865, and has never been engaged in armed rebellion voluntarily against the United States.

Jordan Stokes makes oath that H. G. Johns has been a loyal Union man all the time. He is unquestionably entitled to vote.

P. H. Vivrett makes oath that N. P. Williams has been a citizen of Wilson County, and has been loyal all the war.

John Phillips makes oath that he voted in the election on the 22nd February 1865.

August 1, 1865

C. Palmer makes oath that I. Bush was present and voted in the election held in this county on 4th March 1865.

August 1, 1865

H. L. Mathews and J. H. Rhodes say that are well-acquainted with Richardson Adkins and that he is known in his neighborhood to have been a Union man all the war.

August 2, 1865

A. Thompson makes oath that he was present and that he saw Jacob Tate vote at the election held in this State 4th March 1865.

OATHS OF LOYALTY

B. Brockman makes oath that G. W. Noaks went to the election to vote, and the election was not held. He would have voted. He is known to be a Union man.

March 3, 1866

J. J. Price makes oath that B. W. Jones, H. C. Jewell, William Hester, Albert Hester, John Ozment, James Hester, and Joseph Fletcher are citizens of Wilson County, twenty-one years of age, and are publicly known to have entertained unconditional Union sentiments from the outbreak of the rebellion down to the present time.

John Ramey makes oath that he saw Etheldred Bass, Sr. going home from the election held in the 16th District on the 22nd of February 1865. He and him say he voted and has seen his name on the poll books.

P. P. Killey makes oath that John R. Ballew was late a citizen of North Carolina, but has been a citizen of Wilson County for more than six months and of the State more than twelve months. He is loyal to the United States Government.

August 3, 1865

John B. Thompson makes oath that he is a citizen of Wilson County, that he has arrived at the age of twenty-one years since the 4th March 1865, and that he has never engaged in armed rebellion against the United States Government.

August 15, 1865

P. C. Brooks makes oath that he is a citizen of Wilson County, has arrived at the age of twenty-one years since the 4th day of March, and has never taken up arms against the United States Government.

August 22, 1865

William Clemmons makes oath that he was present and saw his son, Etheldred Clemmons, Jr., vote the 4th March 1865 for Governor and members of the General Assembly.

August 22, 1865

Jonathan Williams makes oath that Jeremiah Bell voted in the election held in this State 4th March 1865.

August 2, 1865

G. W. Wallace makes oath that Ceary Wallace and G. W. Espy are citizens of the County and voted in the election held in this State on the 4th day of March 1865.

August 2, 1865

S. B. F. C. Barr makes oath that he was present and saw D. G. Jackson vote at the election held in this State on 22nd February 1865.

August 2, 1865

J. G. Thomas makes oath that John H. Thomas, J. F. Thomas, and W. T. Burton, late of the State of Kentucky, have been citizens of this county more than six months and are loyal citizens to the Government of the United

States.

August 2, 1865
William Knight makes oath that he was present and saw Elisha E. Warren and John A. Lannom vote in the election held in this State on 22nd February 1865.

August 2, 1865
L. J. Chapman makes oath that his brother, T. B. Chapman, voted in the election held in this State on the 4th March 1865.

July 27, 1865
John H. Rakes makes oath that H. W. Picketts, a citizen of Wilson County, was present and voted at the election held in the 15th District on 22nd February 1865 to ratify the amendments proposed to the Constitution.

July 28, 1865
Marshal Carter makes oath that Benjamin Young was present and voted in this county on the 4th day of March 1865.

July 25, 1865
John Holland makes oath that his son, Thomas Holland, has arrived at the age of twenty-one years since 4th March 1865, that he has never been engaged in armed rebellion against the Government of the United States.

July 25, 1865
R. H. Thompson, Clerk of election, makes oath that P. L. Clemmons and W. L. Bennett voted at the election held 22nd February 1865.

July 25, 1865
John B. Vivrett makes oath that he was a judge at the election held in the 2nd District 4th March 1865 and that Marcus R. Eagan voted in said election.

July 25, 1865
David R. Roberts makes oath that J. W. Roberts and William D. Runnels voted in the election held the 4th March 1865 for Governor of this State.

July 25, 1865
Thomas J. Bell makes oath that John W. Ward, E. A. Barber are citizens of Wilson County and are loyal citizens of the United States.

August 1, 1865
D. M. McKnight makes oath that Richard Mount is an unconditional Union man and has been all the War "to the best of my information and belief. I am his near neighbor."

July 25, 1865
R. H. Thompson makes oath that John Coleman was at the election on the 4th March 1865 and did not vote because he said he was too young. "I believe from information from himself and from the family that he is now twenty-one years of age and has never engaged in armed

rebellion against the Government of the United States.

July 25, 1865

Rufus L. Watson makes oath that he was at the election 4th March 1865 for Governor and that Isham L. Watson, Rufus L. Watson, and Edward K. Watson were present and voted in said election.

July 27, 1865

James McMillen makes oath that Charley McMillen voted at the 13th District of Wilson County at the election held March 4, 1865 to elect a Governor.

John A. Ozment makes oath that he was one of the judges of the election held in the 18th District on the 4th March 1865 and declared that Joseph Thompson, A. N. Thompson, J. L. Thompson, E. A. Thompson, R. H. Thompson, and James B. Thompson voted at said election and are citizens of Wilson County.

James B. Thompson makes oath that William Bennett voted at the election held the 4th March 1865 for Governor and members of the General Assembly.

H. A. Goodall makes oath that J. F. Goodall voted at the election held in this State on 22nd February 1865, that he is a citizen of Wilson County.

July 21, 1865

J. K. Blair makes oath that William B. Jennings voted in the 2nd District in Wilson County on the 4th March 1865 for Governor of the State and members of the General Assembly, that he stood by him and saw him give in his ticket.

Isaiah B. David, known to be a Union man from the commencement of the rebellion, makes oath that J. C. Coble, Moses Fite, Henry Heatly, Allen Wilson, John Keaton, Isham Keaton, and William B. Burk have been Union men all the time.

July 24, 1865

William Harris made oath that G. W. Page, a citizen of Wilson County, is publicly known to entertain unconditional Union sentiments from the outbreak of the rebellion to the present time.

July 26, 1865

J. H. Shannon made oath that his son Alex Shannon has arrived at the age of twenty-one years since the 4th day of March 1865, and that he never has been engaged in armed rebellion against the Government of the United States.

July 27, 1865

J. C. Mann makes oath that his son, T. F. Mann, has arrived at the age of twenty-one years since the 4th day of March 1865, and that he never has been engaged in armed rebellion against the Government of the United States.

July 31, 1865

A. B. Whitlock makes oath that he and his father, John Whitlock, and George Hays were present and voted in the election held in this county on 4th day of March 1865 and are citizens of Wilson County.

August 1, 1865

James A. Derment makes oath that he is a citizen of Wilson County, that he has arrived at the age of twenty-one years since the 4th day of March 1865, and that he has never been engaged in armed rebellion against the Government of the United States.

July 19, 1865

Giles H. Glenn makes oath that Giles H. Glenn, Jr. and James Coe are citizens of Wilson County and voted in the election held on the 4th March 1865 for Governor and members of the General Assembly.

B. G. Warren made oath that C. B. Warren has entertained unconditional Union sentiments from the outbreak of the rebellion down to the present time.

July 22, 1865

John Seatt makes oath that Anderson Seatt is a citizen of Wilson County, that he was present and saw him vote in Lebanon on the 4th March 1865 for Governor and members of the General Assembly.

OBITUARIES

ROSALINE L. LIGON
Wife Of R. L. Ligon, Died In Wilson County,
Tenn., March 5, 1855

Mrs. Ligon was born in Halifax County, Virginia,
near Brook-Neal, March 8th, 1820, and was married to
Richard L. Ligon on the 17th of December, 1835. She was
the mother of ten children, eight of whom she left with
her disconsolate husband to mourn her early death; but
they mourn not as those who have no hope. Although her
summons was hasty (having been sick but four days), she
met her fate with the calmness and resignation which
nothing but the Christian's hope can inspire.

The writer has never witnessed a more solemn and
deeply interesting scene than was exhibited when it was
announced to her that she could live but a few hours.
She called her husband, then her children, and then her
servants around her bed-- exhorted them all to seek the
Lord, prepare for death, and try to meet her in heaven;
she then bid each one an affectionate farewell.

She was entirely resigned to her heavenly Father's
will, relying alone on the merits of a crucified and
risen Saviour, she could say "not my will but Thine be
done."

Thus passed from earth to heaven, one greatly beloved, not only in her family but throughout the neighborhood in which she lived. She was charitable and kind to
the poor; quiet and peaceable in her neighborhood; and
her delight was in the sanctuary of the Lord. She professed religion in Virginia, but from some circumstance
she did not unite with the church at the time. Shortly
afterwards her husband moved to Tennessee and settled in
Wilson County, near the Baptist Church, on Barton's Creek,
with which she worshipped and intended to unite by bap-
tism, but from some peculiar circumstances she never received the ordinance; but she was, nevertheless regarded
as a sister beloved by all the members of the church.

May her early and triumphant death be the means of
leading her bereaved husband to that Saviour in whom she
trusted, and through whom she triumphed over the fear of
death.

BIRTHS AND DEATHS

Ann P. Ligon was born March 22, 1837.

Araminta J. H. Ligon was born September 29, 1838.

Charles W. G. Ligon was born April 13, 1840.

Amanda M. Ligon was born January 6, 1842, and was
killed on the 29th of December, 1845, by falling out of
a wagon and one of the wheels running over her.

Piddy Ligon was born February 22, 1844, and died

August 26, 1846.

    Elizabeth C. Ligon was born February 6, 1846.

    Richard R. Ligon was born November 1, 1847.

    Argalus L. Ligon was born September 6, 1849.

    Virginia H. Ligon was born March 31, 1850.

    Lafayette Ligon was born January 25, 1853.

FAMILY RECORD
Lebanon, Tennessee

    James M. Johnson born August 30, 1827; married to Elizabeth S. Bettis, September 15, 1847; died April 16, 1908.

    Elizabeth S. Bettis, wife of James M. Johnson, born November 17, 1829; died November 3, 1880.

    Thompson H. Johnson born December 22, 1849; married to Ella Moore, December 23, 1872.

    William A. Johnson born February 1, 1852; married to Mary J. Johns, January 28, 1873 and to Emma Johns, December 27, 1877.

    John M. Johnson born April 6, 1854; married to Mary W. Vanhook, December 22, 1874.

    Sallie E. Johnson born July 30, 1856; died March 30, 1882.

    James H. Johnson born January 19, 1859; died February 11, 1860.

    Nannie N. Johnson born December 12, 1860, married to J. B. Ligon, January 14, 1879.

    Joseph W. Johnson born September 13, 1865; married to Lula G. Rice, November 14, 1886.

    Zorah D. Johnson born April 17, 1867; married to John Dougherty, November 9, 1885.

    Mitchell W. Johnson born July 18, 1870; died December 21, 1947; married August 20, 1891 to Nora Dovie Ligon born March 8, 1869; died February 11, 1955.

Nashville Daily Union
January 24, 1865

    A brutal murder occurred in Wilson County, four miles northeast of Lebanon, last week, one of the most shocking it has ever been our lot to record. On Wednesday night last, the residence of Dr. James D. White, one of the most respectable citizens of the county, was entered by a negro man, armed with an axe. Having approached the bed where the Doctor and his wife were sleeping, he struck her a blow with the axe. The Doctor, aroused, sprang from the bed, seized his gun, and fired at the ruffian,

but, unfortunately, missed his aim. The negro then
turned on him, struck him several times with the axe
leaving him insensible. He then attempted to murder Dr.
White's son, a small boy, wounding him severely. Having
done this hellish work, the negro, seeing Mrs. White was
still alive, demanded of her all the money in the house.
She handed over a pocket-book containing $300, which he
took, but, saying that was not all they had, struck her
again, with the axe.

Mrs. White died of her wounds, and was buried Friday
morning. Dr. White has been insensible since he was
stricken down, and there are little hopes of his recovery.
His son may get well.

One of the Doctor's own negroes is supposed to be
guilty of the deed, as he was missing the next morning
and has not since been heard of.

Captain Waters, of Col. Stokes' Cavalry, has under-
taken to investigate the affair. He is a gentleman of
great enterprise and energy, and we trust will secure the
murderer.

Lebanon Democrat
May 29, 1890

Mrs. Bettie Newby, wife of Mr. Zack Newby, was born
in Wilson County, Tennessee and died in Leeville, Tennessee
April 14, 1890.

She professed religion and joined the M. E. Church
South at the age of 14 years in which she lived a faithful member until her death.

She was ever a faithful wife and a kind and affectionate mother, for her children loved her dearly. She
was a kind, good neighbor, for none knew her but to love
her.

Her religion beamed in her countenance and showed in
her smiles and in her works. She was a devoted wife,
ready to bear any burden, or endure any hardships. May
the memory of her peaceful death ever rest on the deeply
bereaved hearts now in their lonely home.

Her remains were laid to rest in Cedar Grove Cemetery in Lebanon, Tennessee in the presence of her friends,
April 15, 1890. The community deeply sympathize with the
family in their sad bereavement.

Lebanon Democrat
August 7, 1890

Bailey Phillips was a noble type of the olden time
gentleman. His birth dated back to the first of the present century, and the light of day was first viewed by
him in the grand old state which has ever boasted of being the mother of both states and statesmen. He was a
strong link in the chain that binds us to the land of

OBITUARIES

Pocahontas and the celebrated John Smith, whose life she
rescued from the murderous club of an infuriated father.
Uncle Bailey enjoyed the love and confidence of a large
circle of both relatives and friends. His was a glorious
old age, and the sunset of his life was as clear and
cloudless as any we have ever known. Peace to his sleep-
ing dust. To our venerable father and absent friends,
we speak the gentle good bye, yet we hope to meet again
where no tears are shed nor farewells spoken.

Lebanon, Tennessee
August 10, 1927

Charles W. G. Ligon, aged 87, Confederate veteran
and highly respected farmer died at his home on the
Franklin Road this week following an illness of several
months.

Mr. Ligon was a native of Brookneal, Virginia moving
to this county when a boy. He was one of the best known
farmers and stock raisers in the county. He served in
Company H, Seventh Tennessee Infantry in the Confederate
Army.

Funeral services were conducted from the home with
interment in the nearby Ligon Cemetery. The Rev. J. C.
Stewart of Watertown conducted the funeral services.

Mr. Ligon is survived by his sister, Mrs. Jennie
Vanhook of Lebanon; a half brother, Booker Ligon of
Lebanon; and the following sons: R. Lee Ligon, Ed
Ligon, Armsted Hannibal "Wes" Ligon, C. Richard Ligon,
and Argalus Emory "Day" Ligon, all of Lebanon; and one
daughter, Mrs. Mitchell W. (Dovie) Johnson of Lebanon.

Abernathy, Charles 84
Adams, Harris 52
Adams, Sarah D. 40
Adams, William W. 11,85
Adamson, Simon 37,54,81
Adamson, Simon P. 54
Adamson, William 54
Adkins, Richardson 117
Adkinson, Amanda A. 63
Adkinson, John J. 63
Adkinson, Matilda 63
Adkinson, Rebecca 63
Alexander, B. T. 52
Alexander, Benjamin 39
Alexander, Ezekiel 39
Alexander, George G. 40
Alexander, Isaac 25
Alexander, J. 86
Alexander, Jane 20
Alexander, Joe L. 98
Alexander, John N. 40
Alexander, Joseph L. 40
Alexander, N. G. 55
Alexander, Nelson G. 86
Alexander, Thomas B. 39
Alexander, W. S. 48
Alexander, William 7
Alexander, William L. 7
Allen, Archibald 27
Allen, Dick 107
Allen, George 66
Allen, Grant 6
Allen, J. H. 91
Allen, James 58
Allen, John 29,35
Allen, John H. 91
Allen, Joseph W. 90
Allen, Larkin 5
Allen, Lavina 104
Allen, Sarah 66
Allison, Andrew 90
Allison, Sallie 109
Alsup, A. B. 65
Alsup, A. H. 41
Alsup, Asaph 59
Alsup, C. B. 65
Alsup, Callie 41
Alsup, Dicy 41
Alsup, H. C. 65
Alsup, Indiana 65
Alsup, Isabella 41
Alsup, Jacob 116
Alsup, Nelson 6,41
Alsup, Samuel 3
Alsup, Sarah 65
Alsup, Sarah M. 42
Alsup, Susan 41
Alsup, W. G. 65
Alsup, William 32,65
Anderson, Alexander 98
Anderson, Araminta A. 54
Anderson, Berry 80
Anderson, Col. 30
Anderson, Dr. 90
Anderson, Eliza J. 27
Anderson, Francis 27
Anderson, J. M. 58,61
Anderson, James 26
Anderson, John 32
Anderson, Kate 108
Anderson, L. T. 42
Anderson, Martha H. 66
Anderson, Mary A. 44,59
Anderson, Mary D. 58
Anderson, P. 44
Anderson, Patrick 27
Anderson, Patrick H. 44
Anderson, Paulding 81,90
Anderson, R. H. 59
Anderson, Samuel 27
Anderson, Samuel C. 77
Anderson, T. C. 71
Anderson, William 86
Anderson, William B. 42

Andrews, John 37
Andrews, Mary D. 103
Andrews, W. H. 103
Archer, Josiah 8
Armistead, Fannie 102
Armstrong, G. L. 65
Armstrong, J. M. 39
Armstrong, James M. 37
Armstrong, John W. 104
Armstrong, T. W. 20
Arnold, John 90
Arnold, Stephen 115
Aston, Alexander 89
Aust, Frederick 31,32
Aust, James 77
Aust, Sarah 77
Aust, Tennessee 77
Aust, Thomas B. 31,77
Aust, William H. 77
Avery, George 86
Ayres, James 46
Ayres, Margaret 47

Babbitt 21
Bachus, Sarah 62
Bagwell, Allen 25
Bailey, B. S. 62
Barry, Jordan 62
Barry, Tennie 62
Barry, William P. 62
Bartlett, Benjamin F. 84
Barton, James W. 35
Barton, Jane 44
Barton, R. R. 54
Barton, Stephen 35
Barton, W. J. 44
Barton, William 99
Basket, Unity 17
Baskins, Robert M. 81
Baskins, William 23
Bass, Amzi 14
Bass, Archemack 52
Bass, D. J. 68
Bass, Dolphan 52
Bass, Dreddin 3
Bass, Elizabeth 14
Bass, Emily 64
Bass, Etheldred 72
Bass, Etheldred, Sr. 118
Bass, Ezekiel 42,52
Bass, H. L. 42
Bass, Harty P. 52
Bass, Henry 53
Bass, J. D. 81
Bass, Jo 17,80
Bass, John 45,52
Bass, L. H. 61
Bass, Mary 51
Bass, Nancy 3,52
Bass, Nancy J. 53
Bass, Oragon 17
Bass, Orren 29
Bass, Rachel F. 52
Bass, Richard 64
Bass, Sarah 52
Bass, Sion 29
Bass, Susan 29,45
Bass, Warren 53
Bass, Washington 53
Bass, William 45,83
Bates, James 106
Bates, John 43
Baxter, H. A. 76
Beadle, Joel 72
Beadle, Susan 72
Beadles, Abram A. 34
Beadles, Millison H. 34
Beard, John 93,94,95,98
Beard, Leonard 83
Beard, Richard 61
Beasley, Ephraim 88
Beasley, Gabriel 7

Bailey, C. H. 78
Bailey, Cassandra 62
Bailey, Jennett 19
Bailey, Jonathan 62
Bailey, William 41
Baird, A. W. 61
Baird, Annie 72
Baird, B. 66
Baird, David 35
Baird, Elizabeth 61,66
Baird, Elizabeth F. 63
Baird, Emeline 72
Baird, Fannie 43,53
Baird, J. B. 63,105
Baird, James H. 72
Baird, John H. 53
Baird, Kate 72
Baird, Martha 73
Baird, Mollie 72
Baird, P. C. 41
Baird, Rufus 63
Baird, S. E. 104
Baird, Samuel 72
Baird, Sarah 72
Baird, Terza 72
Baird, W. C. 73
Baird, W. H. 41,116
Baird, Zebulon 1
Baker, Emily 12
Baker, Harriet 70
Baker, J. F. 109
Baker, John E. 42
Baker, R. H. 92
Baker, Thomas 27
Baker, Webb 12
Ballew, John R. 118
Banks, J. J. 47
Barbee, J. S. 89
Barbee, Jane 62
Barbee, O. D., Sr. 89
Barbee, Thomas 85
Barber, E. A. 119
Barclay, Benjamin 63
Barclay, Joseph 88
Barnett, Elizabeth E. 74
Barr, Martisha 76
Barr, S. B. 118
Barrett, Betty 84
Barrett, J. A. 84
Barron, W. H. 91
Barrow, Cullen P. 59
Barrow, Henrietta 59
Barrow, James J. 59
Barrow, Mary A. 59
Barrow, William M. 59
Beasley, Thornton 85,92
Beaumont, Penelopy W. 68
Beckwith, George 109
Bedford, Abraham 17
Bedford, E. A. 54
Belcher, Littleberry 33
Belcher, S. E. 41
Bell, Benjamin L. 71
Bell, Emma 70
Bell, Emma T. 102
Bell, Harding 71
Bell, Isaac 71
Bell, James 24
Bell, John 102
Bell, John E. 19,20
Bell, Joseph G. 100
Bell, Lotty 71
Bell, Martha H. 71
Bell, Mary E. 103
Bell, Mary F. 71
Bell, Mary P. 100
Bell, Nancy 6
Bell, Samuel C. 75
Bell, Samuel W. 101
Bell, T. J. 103
Bell, Thomas J. 71,119
Bell, Wiley W. 11
Bell, William A. 101
Bell, William L. 71

Bennett, Herman G. 116
Bennett, Ideson 39
Bennett, John M. 86
Bennett, W. L. 119
Bennett, William 39,120
Benson, P. P. 40
Bentley, J. F. 59
Bentley, James M. 59
Benton, Benjamin 7
Benton, Franklin 7
Benton, Hugh 7
Benton, Jackson 7
Benton, Lewis 7
Berry, E. 89
Berry, Jesse 31
Berry, John M. 76
Berry, Joseph 30,87
Berry, Rebecca 76
Bersford, Joyce 44
Bett, Jeremiah 34
Bett, Mary D. 34
Bettes, A. C. 49
Bettes, J. D. 54
Bettes, J. W. 38
Bettes, John 27
Bettes, John W. 35
Bettes, Martha E. 38
Bettes, Winefred 77
Bettes, Wyatt 3
Bettis, Elizabeth S. 123
Betty, W. F. 80
Bilbro, William 82
Billings, Henry 26
Binkley, R. W. 108
Birgett, Luvina 77
Black, Alexander 106
Black, Hugh 21
Black, Lawson 37
Blackbund, Colonel 113
Blair, Betty 74
Blair, J. K. 120
Blair, James J. 68
Blair, Martha 75
Blalock, Annie L. 42
Blalock, Felix H. 42
Blalock, James M. 42
Blalock, Margaret M. 42
Bligh, Alex 9
Bloodworth, Jack 45
Bloodworth, Smith 38
Bloodworth, William 38
Bloodworth, Wilson 38
Blythe, G. Y. 80
Blythe, J. Y. 48,71
Boddie, George W. 75
Bodine, Nancy 14
Bodine, Thomas W. 14
Bogle, Jannett 21
Bond, Asaph 38
Bond, Elizabeth 55,56
Bond, Elizabeth S. 67
Bond, G. W. 56
Bond, Harvey H. 67
Bond, Jane 57
Bond, Jerry 56
Bond, John 33,99
Bond, Louiza J. 67
Bond, Martha 50
Bond, Martha A. 55
Bond, Mary 38
Bond, Mary F. 67
Bond, Sarah 67
Bond, W. C. 50
Bone, John 88
Bone, Mack 90
Bone, Martha 42
Bonner, John 2,3,25,38
Bonner, John, Sr. 88
Booker, Andrew 79
Booker, John 86
Boon, W. B. 75
Boone, John 89
Borum, Richard 27
Borum, Sam 107

Borum, Will 107
Bostick, Kate 74,108
Bostick, Martha 74
Bostick, Mary 109
Bostick, Mary S. 74
Bostick, T. H. 48
Bowden, Ann A. 38
Bowden, James C. 38
Bowers, Caroline P. 37
Bowers, Jane 47,60
Bowers, John 60
Boyd, Synthia 49
Boyd, William R. 48
Boze, Mrs. 12
Boze, Nancy 12
Bradberry, Charles 30
Bradberry, Nancy 30
Bradbury, Reuben 1
Braden, J. 80
Bradford, Eli M. 95
Bradley, Jonas 27,81
Bradley, Thomas 30
Bradley, William 43
Bradshaw, J. M. 80
Bradshaw, Lavisa 34
Bradshaw, S. J. 84
Bradshaw, Samuel 84
Bradshaw, Thomas 34
Bradshaw, Thomas, Jr. 83
Bradshaw, W. L. 84
Bradshaw, William 9
Bradshaw, Willis 34
Brantley, Etheldred 8
Brantley, Thomas 108
Brantley, Walter 106
Brashears, Jane 6
Brett, A. 47
Brett, B. B. 68
Brett, Hardy 47
Brevard, Alfred A. 6
Brevard, Clarissa H. 6
Brevard, Cynthia D. 6
Brevard, Cyrus W. 6
Brevard, Hannah L. 6
Brevard, Hugh 7
Brevard, Jane M. 6
Brevard, John C. 6
Brevard, John, Sr. 6,7
Brevard, Nancy 6
Brevard, Polly 7
Brevard, William 7
Briant, Cinthia 37
Brice, Walker 115
Bridge, Alexander 41
Bridges, Brinkley 21
Bridges, James A. 15
Bridges, Nancy 54,59
Bridges, Sampson 25
Brien, J. C. 99
Briggs, B. F. 45
Brinkley, Mark 9
Britt, Benjamin B. 87
Brockett, F. P. 109
Brockman, B. 118
Brooks, P. C. 118
Brower, Ed A. 107
Brown, Albert 70
Brown, B. C. 97,98
Brown, Dolly A. 104
Brown, Edny 103
Brown, G. W. 70
Brown, George 52
Brown, J. E. 70
Brown, Jackson 1
Brown, Jane 41,70,102
Brown, John 85
Brown, John C. 70
Brown, John L. 92
Brown, Jonas 6
Brown, Leander 70
Brown, Margaret 42
Brown, Martha 101
Brown, Mary 53
Brown, Molly A. 101

Brown, Nancy 70
Brown, R. 94
Brown, Rebecca 44
Brown, Susan 70
Brown, Thomas 5,7
Brown, W. H. 114
Brown, William 70
Bruce, Charles 31,74
Bruce, L. 103
Bryan, John W. 83
Bryan, Nelson J. 83
Bryan, T. J. 80
Bryan, William M. 83
Bryant, Frank 115
Bryant, Harriet A. 34
Bryant, James 39
Bryant, James K. 54
Bryant, John H. 76
Bryant, Mary A. 54
Bryant, Samuel 34
Buchanan, Ann 40
Buchanan, John 82
Bucher, David 51
Bucher, Henry 51
Bucher, Sophrona 51
Buckman, Harry 109
Bucy, Martha 54
Bucy, William E. 54
Bullard, George H. 88
Burchett, Mary 50
Burdine, Euphenia E. 59
Burdine, Flora 59
Burdine, J. B. 50
Burdine, John B. 59
Burdine, Laura L. 59
Burdine, Martha J. 59
Burdine, Mary D. 59
Burdine, Mary E. 59
Burdine, Nathan B. 59
Burdine, Thomas J. 59
Burk, Thomas 33
Burk, William B. 120
Burk, William C. 114
Burke, Alice 40
Burke, Arnold 6
Burke, James 41
Burke, Louiza 41
Burke, William H. 41
Burks, Thomas 31
Burney, Annie 108
Burns, Brantley 33
Burns, John C. 73
Burns, Reverend 104
Burros, Harriet 17
Burton, Bob 106
Burton, C. C. 46
Burton, John 106
Burton, Robert M. 8,32
Burton, W. T. 118
Bush, I. 117
Butler, William 30
Byrn, Ransom H. 28,33

Cabbott, Fred 106
Caldwell, W. C. 108
Calhoun, Carrie 102
Calhoun, Carrie M. 103
Calhoun, Ewing G. 103
Calhoun, Frank 102
Calhoun, Julea 102
Calhoun, Lilla M. 103
Calhoun, Mattie 102
Calhoun, Mattie S. 104
Calhoun, May 104
Calhoun, P. B. 102
Calhoun, P. G. 102
Calhoun, Thomas 89,100
Callaway, Josephine 60
Campbell, Catherine 47
Campbell, David 82
Campbell, David H. 47
Campbell, Ed 109

Campbell, Fannie A. 44
Campbell, Governor 47
Campbell, Hugh 86
Campbell, James 31
Campbell, John 47
Campbell, John A. 44
Campbell, Joseph A. 44
Campbell, Lemuel R. 44
Campbell, M. H. 44
Campbell, Margaret H. 44,47
Campbell, Mary A. 44
Campbell, Susan 64
Campbell, W. H. 45
Campbell, William 9,86
Campbell, William B. 44,47
Cannon, Joshua 34
Cantrell, Bailey 106
Caplenor, Julia A. 101
Caplenor, Lee 81
Caraway, Merrit 38
Caraway, Nancy 63
Caraway, P. B. 116
Caraway, Pat 116
Caraway, Sophia 38
Carlin, William, Jr. 30
Carral, Misha 25
Carroll, Mishack 26
Carruy, James W. 113
Carter, Alonzo 102
Carter, Charles G. 62
Carter, Charles T. 102
Carter, Emily 101
Carter, Etta 102,104
Carter, James 1
Carter, John J. 87
Carter, Julia 48
Carter, July B. 103
Carter, L. T. 103
Carter, Lenny 18
Carter, Leora 103
Carter, Leroy 28
Carter, Marshal 119
Carter, Martha 103
Carter, Mary 48,79,89,102
Carter, P. R. 103
Carter, Ruth 103
Carter, Solomon 95,96
Carter, William 7
Carter, William H. 15,81,89,
    102
Cartmell, H. M. 74
Cartmell, Henry H. 74
Cartmell, Isabella 74
Cartmell, James S. 40,74
Cartmell, Margaret 73
Cartmell, Mary E. 74
Cartmell, N. 41
Cartmell, Sarah 41
Cartmell, Sophia 74
Cartmell, W. M. 74,75
Cartmell, William H. 74
Cartright, Benajah 25
Cartwright, Edward 85
Cartwright, Matthew 85
Cartwright, Will 106
Cartwright, William 50
Caruth, James 65
Caruth, Mary C. 65
Caruthers, R. L. 61
Caruthers, Robert 86
Caruthers, Robert L. 71,90
Carver, Archibald 40,67
Carver, David H. 53
Carver, Eunice 67
Carver, Henry 48
Carver, Isaac 78
Carver, James 48
Carver, James H. 53
Carver, John W. 42
Carver, Lucy A. 67
Carver, Martha C. 42
Carver, Martha E. 67
Carver, Martha J. 53
Carver, Mary J. 67

Carver, Nicey E. 53
Carver, P. M. 53
Carver, Pemelia C. 67
Carver, Pleasant J. 67
Carver, Pleasant P. 67
Carver, Rhoda A. 67
Carver, Samuel 67
Carver, Samuel L. 67
Carver, Sarah E. 53
Carver, Trephena A. 53
Carver, Trephrena 48
Carver, William H. 53
Cason, Ann M. 43
Cason, Casandria 54
Cason, Favor 43
Cason, Indianna 43
Cason, James H. 54
Cason, Jeremiah F. 43
Cason, John M. 43
Cason, Joseph M. 43
Cason, Rebecca N. 43
Castleman, J. L. 53
Castleman, John L. 70
Castleman, R. B. 49,83,105
Castleman, Sarah J. 70
Catherall, Charles 8
Cauthon, J. H. 95
Cauthon, John H. 95
Cawthon, Amanda E. 78
Cawthon, D. C. 78
Cawthon, Eliza W. 40
Cawthon, J. N. 94
Cawthon, J. P. 46,48,58
Cawthon, John R. 40
Cawthon, Parthena W. 40
Chamberlain, Samuel 24
Chambers, John 37
Chambers, Lewis 27,40
Chambers, Thomas 85
Chambers, Wilson 79
Chandler, A. L. 79
Chandler, Ardena F. 74
Chandler, E. C. 74
Chandler, J. K. 79
Chandler, Jordan 67,72
Chandler, Mary C. 61
Chandler, William 23
Chapman, Allaphair H. 63
Chapman, L. J. 119
Chapman, T. B. 53,63,76,119
Chappell, Humphrey 21,22
Chappell, William 28
Chapple, Humphrey 3
Chastain, J. S. 89
Chester, Robert 109
Chumney, Pleasant 11
Clark, David 48
Clark, John 72
Clark, John A. 92
Clark, Louiza J. 72
Clark, Rufus 88
Clark, Thomas 1
Clark, W. P. 99
Clarke, Joseph 58
Clay, Carlos G. 76
Clay, Edward 26
Clay, Elizabeth 75,77
Clay, Green 104
Clay, John W. 70
Clay, Mitchell 76
Clemmons, E. A. 83
Clemmons, E. C. 112
Clemmons, E. D. 76
Clemmons, Elizabeth L. 67
Clemmons, Emily A. 67
Clemmons, Etheldred 44
Clemmons, Etheldred, Jr. 118
Clemmons, J. H. 76
Clemmons, James 82
Clemmons, James L. 83
Clemmons, Jeptha 46
Clemmons, Leland F. 67
Clemmons, Martha 43
Clemmons, Mary F. 67

Clemmons, Nancy G. 54
Clemmons, P. L. 119
Clemmons, Presley L. 67
Clemmons, W. C. 42
Clemmons, William 49,118
Clemmons, William L. 57
Clemmons, William S. 69
Clendening, William 9
Clopton, John A. 41,42
Cloyd, Ezekiel 27,89
Cloyd, John 27
Cluck, B. S. 81
Cluck, J. L. 45
Cobb, Olyada 101
Coble, J. C. 120
Cock, Elizabeth 27
Cock, Jarratt 29
Cock, John 27
Cock, Joseph 28
Cock, Martha 29
Coe, I. A. 83
Coe, Isaiah 70
Coe, James 121
Cofield, Wallis 88
Cole, E. W. 77
Cole, Robert 33
Cole, Sarah B. 11
Cole, William H. 77
Coleman, John 119
Coleman, Mary J. 64
Coleman, Robert 64
Coleman, Sally 58
Coleman, Thomas 74
Coles, E. W. 108
Coles, G. W. 75
Coles, Henry 108
Coles, Robert 91
Coles, Samuel 43
Collier, B. P. 79
Collier, Florie 83,84
Collier, J. P. 83,84
Collier, M. D. 79
Collier, Mary P. 63
Colquet, William 104
Comer, Freeland 87
Comer, S. R. 105
Comin, Matt W. 55
Compton, James 51
Conatsy, L. Dow 103
Conyer, William 22
Conyers, Thomas 88
Cook, Ann E. 74,75
Cook, Betsy 47
Cook, Clark 61
Cook, D., Jr. 61
Cook, Eliza J. 75
Cook, Elizabeth 60
Cook, Elvira 74
Cook, George 61
Cook, Green 74
Cook, Green B. 74,86
Cook, Jesse 5,39
Cook, L. N. 38,50,70
Cook, Lemuel N. 86
Cook, Mary A. 39
Cooksey, J. B. 38
Coonrod, Nicholas 89
Cooper, Benjamin B. 8
Cooper, Mary 101
Copeland, Elizabeth 57
Copeland, Samuel 81
Coppage, Harriel 53
Coram, Martha J. 53
Corder, Martha A. 57
Corder, Patsy 30,32
Corder, Robert A. 57
Corder, William G. 57
Corley, Elisha 34
Corley, Maggie 103
Corley, May 103
Corley, Virgy 103
Corley, William 15,16,34
Corum, J. D. 76
Couch, Martha 12

Couch, W. J. 99
Cowan, Albert 105
Cowen, James 28
Cowger, Adam 5,31
Cox, Henry R. 43
Cox, J. A. 109
Cox, Robert 91
Cox, Thomas 32
Craddock, Matilda 11
Craddock, R. W. 73
Craddock, Richard 31
Craddock, Richard C. 31
Craddock, Robert 31
Craddock, Suckey 31
Craig, Crawford M. 11
Crawford, Edmund 90
Crawford, J. W. 62
Crayton, Jane 3
Creel, Elijah 78
Crittenden, John J. 34
Crittenden, Pryor 5
Crowell, Mary E. 101
Crudup, John 46,58
Crump, W. R. 98
Crunk, Nancy 34
Crutcher, Carter 22
Crutchfield, Elizabeth B. 35
Cummings, Charles W. 32
Cummings, George D. 6
Cummings, Isabella 41
Cummings, Isbel 41
Cunningham, Betty 102
Cunningham, James 22
Cunningham, John 73
Cunningham, Nancy 102
Cunningham, Sam 104
Cunningham, Sarah 102
Cunningham, Susanna R. 101
Curd, Ed 70
Curd, John N. 58
Curd, Susan 58
Currey, Eli 95
Currey, Elijah 95,96,98
Currey, James H. 75
Currey, M. M. 94
Currey, Moses M. 75,93,95
Currey, Peggy 75

Dallis, Robert 28
Dandridge, Mary 41
Daniel, Christopher 25
David, Isaiah B. 58,120
Davidson, F. F. 103
Davidson, S. T. 103
Davis, A. R. 38
Davis, Anderson T. 73
Davis, Anna 55
Davis, Arthur L. 30
Davis, B. H. 78
Davis, Benjamin 55
Davis, Benjamin H. 71
Davis, Cain 19
Davis, E. A. 53
Davis, Emma M. 52
Davis, Franklin 102
Davis, G. W. 64
Davis, Harvy 52
Davis, I. 79
Davis, Isaac 64
Davis, Isaac T. 64
Davis, J. E. 55
Davis, J. L. 117
Davis, James E. 52
Davis, James W. 52
Davis, Jesse T. 79
Davis, John 83
Davis, John M. 80
Davis, John R. 89
Davis, L. H. 64
Davis, Lara J. 64
Davis, Lucinda F. 76

Davis, Lue 79
Davis, Martha D. 75
Davis, Mary 77
Davis, Mary E. 52
Davis, Mary R. 64
Davis, Mary T. 73
Davis, Nancy 64
Davis, Octavia A. 76
Davis, Rachel 64
Davis, Robert C. 7
Davis, Samuel 52
Davis, Samuel, Jr. 53
Davis, Samuel W. 89
Davis, Thomas 114
Davis, Thomas C. 3
Davis, William 80
Dawson, David 21
Dawson, Freelan 101
Dawson, Martha 101,104
Dawson, W. A. 39
Day, Ella 75
Day, Samuel J. 75
Day, Sarah J. 75
Day, Thomas A. 75
Debow, Ann 66
Debow, Bird 66
Debow, Eula L. 76
Debow, H. C. 76
Debow, Hugh C. 66
Debow, John 66,76
Debow, Mary A. 66
Delay, Thomas 26
Dement, Jane 47
Denton, Henry 80
Derment, James A. 121
Dew, Ann 58
Dew, Matthew 32
Dew, William C. 47
Dias, Lewis 104
Dickason, J. H. 62
Dickens 101
Dickens, Bell 103
Dickens, Eddy 103
Dickens, Ellen 102
Dickens, Gertina 103
Dickens, Jodie 104
Dickens, Jodie W. 103
Dickens, Martha E. 102
Dickens, Paul 103
Dickens, Sireany E. 103
Dies, Mrs. 103
Dies, Samuel 71
Dikes, J. M. 75
Dill, Catherine 70
Dill, J. W. 64
Dill, John 70,85
Dill, William 27,85
Dillard, A. J. 35
Dillard, Dempsey 91
Dillard, Edward 21,22
Dillard, Frances R. 91
Dillard, George 21
Dillard, William 21
Dillon, C. R. 46
Dismukes, J. F. 46
Dodd, David 51
Dodd, Mark 51
Dodd, Samuel 26
Dodd, William 51
Dodson, Julia 42
Donaldson, Rachel 66
Donnell, A. E. 56
Donnell, Catherine 47
Donnell, F. M. 56
Donnell, F. R. 91
Donnell, George 92
Donnell, James A. 62
Donnell, Jane F. 42
Donnell, Jany 62
Donnell, Josiah 67,91
Donnell, Margaret 38
Donnell, Mary 70
Donnell, Mary E. 41
Donnell, Nancy 67

Donnell, R. B. 38
Donnell, S. M. 47
Donnell, Samuel 93,98
Donnell, Samuel C. 47
Donnell, Syllava 62
Donnell, William, Sr. 88
Donoho, Bettie 72,73
Donoho, Ed 49
Donoho, Henry M. 73
Donoho, Mary 72,73
Doss, James P. 66
Dotson, Elizabeth 58
Dotson, William 58
Dougherty, John 123
Douglass, Burchett 31
Douglass, Martha H. 48,75
Drake, Brittain 35
Drake, Edmund B. 27,35
Drake, Elijah B. 35
Drake, James C. 31
Drake, Reuben 80
Drennan, D. C. 65
Drennan, J. D. 65
Drennan, James 43,91,93
Drennan, Job 114
Drennan, John 1,65
Drennan, Mary 70
Drennan, Thomas J. 43
Duffy, Al G. 106
Duke, A. D. 34
Duke, Alfred 39
Duke, Darthula 37
Duke, Jane 41
Duke, John 37
Duke, Nancy 34
Duke, Samuel 37
Duke, Sion 37
Dukes, Alford 83
Dukes, J. H. 116
Dunn, Catherine 50
Dunn, Elizabeth 30
Dunn, Hannah C. 40
Dunn, William 30
Dyer, Fanny 30
Dyer, William 30

Eagan, Amon 49
Eagan, Judey 49
Eagan, M. R. 50
Eagan, Marous R. 119
Eagan, Milberry 49
Earheart, Absolom 47
Earheart, Jacob 35
Eason, Ann 48
Eason, Eli E. 23
Eason, Elizabeth J. 34
Eason, Ira E. 23,30,32
Eason, James F. 48
Eason, James K. 32
Eason, Lavicy F. 48
Eason, Lewis W. 48
Eason, Samuel E. 34
Eason, Sarah A. 71
Eatherly, Alexander F. 52
Eatherly, Bird 19
Eatherly, Ervin 63
Eatherly, Ewing M. 52
Eatherly, Frances A. 52
Eatherly, Harriet 63
Eatherly, James 63
Eatherly, Jane 63
Eatherly, John B. 63
Eatherly, John R. 5
Eatherly, Jonathan 5,51
Eatherly, Lucinda E. 63
Eatherly, Mary 63
Eatherly, Matthew 64
Eatherly, Rebecca 63
Eatherly, Rebecca A. 63
Eatherly, Rufus 52
Eatherly, Tabitha B. 20
Eatherly, Thompson 52

Eatherly, William 63
Eatherly, William J. 52
Eatherly, Yewell 63
Eddins, T. F. 111
Eddins, William 50
Edmondson, Frazer 108
Edwards, Eaton 29
Edwards, J. W. 39,116
Edwards, John 41
Edwards, Stokes 31
Edwards, T. W. 115
Edwards, Thomas 81
Edwards, Thomas L. 116
Edwards, Thomas M. 84
Edwards, William 3
Elliott, Thomas 116
Ellis, Ann 101
Ellis, Anneth R. 100
Ellis, Elizabeth 49
Ellis, John B. 101,104
Ellis, Moses 49,91
Enoch, David 22
Epps, James 8
Eskew, Alfred 57
Eskew, C. P. 59
Eskew, John C. 71
Eskew, Martha C. 61
Eskew, William 43
Espy, G. W. 118
Estes, Henderson 76
Estes, Lucy 64
Estes, Martha 6
Estes, Matthew 63
Estes, Nancy M. 46
Estes, Robert 64
Estes, Robert E. 46
Estes, Thomas H. 64
Estes, W. J. 46
Estes, W. L. 46
Evans, George A. 26,35
Evans, Polk 17
Evans, Thursey A. 35
Ewing, S. H. 45

Fakes, Ann E. 68
Fakes, Ella 72
Fakes, J. M., Jr. 91
Fakes, John M. 91
Fakes, Mary 68,72
Fakes, Sally 68
Fakes, W. O. 91
Falconer, E. P. 9
Falconer, Edward P. 7
Farris, Lydia T. 102
Ferrel, William 102
Ferrell, B. 104
Ferrell, H. J. 52
Ferrell, William W. 5
Ferrill, Mary A. 100
Field, Mary 38
Fields, Catherine 30
Fields, David 30,31
Fields, John 30,31,80,105
Fields, Nancy 80
Fields, Rachel 30,31
Fields, Redden 30
Fields, Richard 30
Fields, Rufus M. 108
Figures, Matthew 27
Finley, Bettie 58
Finley, Ike 107
Finley, Jesse J. 9
Finley, O. G. 58
Finley, Obe 107
Finley, W. M., Jr. 107
Fisher, John 40
Fisher, Levi 40
Fisher, Phebe 55
Fisher, Philip 55
Fisher, Richard W. 40
Fisher, Sarah A. 15
Fisher, Susan 40

Fite, Albert 56
Fite, Caroline 64
Fite, Daniel 58,79
Fite, Edmond L. 58
Fite, Edwin C. 56,57,75
Fite, Helen A. 58
Fite, Henry A. 58
Fite, J. L. 65,75
Fite, J. W. 57
Fite, Jacob 56,57
Fite, Jacob C. 56
Fite, James 56
Fite, John 56
Fite, John H. 58
Fite, Joseph 86
Fite, L. D. 64
Fite, Lemuel 64
Fite, Leonard 64,86
Fite, Leonard B. 56,57
Fite, Margaret J. 58
Fite, Martha 75
Fite, Martha E. 58
Fite, Mary V. 58
Fite, Matilda 56
Fite, Moses 120
Fite, Moses H. 58
Fite, Samuel M. 57
Fite, Thomas D. 64
Fite, Thomas M. 58
Fite, William 58
Fletcher, Joseph 118
Foley, Fanny 102,104
Fonville, Mary B. 71
Fonville, William L. 71
Forbis, Nancy C. 54
Forbis, Willis 28
Ford, J. J. 41
Forrester, William 107
Foster, Alexander 88,101
Foster, Andrew 89
Foster, David 93,98
Foster, Franklin 27
Foster, James 54
Foster, Mary T. 102
Foster, Nancy 54
Foster, R. 94
Foster, Robert 54
Foust, Betsy 68
Fowler, Jasper 39
Franklin, J. W. 81
Frazier, James 85,88
Freeman, Abediah 88
Freeman, Darrel 68,86
Freeman, Ida 58
Freeman, James C. 76
Freeman, Nancy 58
Freeman, Sarah 57
Fullerton, John T. 29
Fullerton, Nathaniel 26
Fullerton, Robert 8
Fullerton, Sally 29
Fuqua, Alice 101
Fuqua, Elizabeth 102
Fuqua, James H. 102
Fuqua, Jane A. 100
Fuston, James 9

Gaimwell, Mary S. 101
Gaines, C. W. 43
Gaines, Gideon G. 48
Gambill, Washington 20
Gann, Elizabeth W. 100, 102
Gann, Ludie 104
Gann, Lusana F. 101
Gann, Robert 100,102
Gannon, Harvey 80
Gardner, Morgan 86
Garner, John 86
Garrett, Nelly 37
Garrison, Elizabeth 30
Garrison, John 30

Gates, Amanda M. 63
Gates, Elizabeth 25
Gatton, Elizabeth 40
Gee, Allen A. 80
Geer, Pleasant 74
George, Manervy E. 54
George, Rebecca 82
George, Thomas 1
George, Vester 78
Gibson, Aaron 38
Gibson, Aaron B. 38
Gibson, Elizabeth 38
Gibson, Hugh 25
Gibson, Ira B. 74
Gibson, Isaac E. 74
Gibson, Joseph S. 8
Gibson, Margaret L. 38
Gibson, Martha A. 38
Gibson, Martha J. 58
Gibson, Ruth J. 38
Gibson, Thomas 58
Gibson, Thomas J. 38
Gibson, Thomas W. 74
Gill, William 86
Gillespie, Mickey 68
Gilliam, Edmund 42
Gleaves, Absolum 33
Gleaves, Annie 84
Gleaves, Benjamin 46
Gleaves, Guy T. 46
Gleaves, J. W. 46
Gleaves, Jesse 46
Gleaves, Jessie H. 84
Gleaves, John 46
Gleaves, John T. 46
Gleaves, Julia A. 46
Gleaves, Mickey A. 46
Gleaves, T. H. 88
Gleaves, Tavel 46,67
Glenn, Daniel 40
Glenn, Giles G. 38
Glenn, Giles H. 6,40,121
Glenn, Giles H., Jr. 121
Gleves, John L. 52
Godfrey, James 34
Golden, J. L. 53
Goldston, Eli 71
Goldstone, W. B. 44
Golladay, Isaac 88,90
Golladay, Sam 67
Goodall, Frances M. 35
Goodall, H. A. 45,70,120
Goodall, Harrison A. 35
Goodall, J. F. 120
Goodall, J. T. 45
Goodall, John T., Jr. 70
Goodall, Parks, 5,35
Goodall, William 7
Goodbar, Henry 17
Goodman, Mary 11
Goodwin, Allen 31
Goodwin, Boswell 29
Goodwin, Jesse A. 29
Goodwin, Mary 7
Goodwin, William J. 7
Goosen, B. A. 38
Gordon, Catherine C. 44
Gordon, Col. 80
Gosset, Abraham 27
Gosset, John 27
Grandstaff, Benjamin 19
Grandstaff, John 84
Grandstaff, Mary 51
Graves, Benjamin 46
Graves, Bernice 37
Graves, E. 37
Graves, Elizabeth A. 69
Graves, George 115
Graves, James M. 69
Graves, John 37
Graves, John E. 37
Graves, Lester 37
Graves, Makajah 37
Graves, Nancy 22

Graves, Puss 37
Graves, Reuben 74
Graves, Rice 74
Graves, Richard D. 37
Graves, William 115
Graves, William H. 41
Graves, Williamson S. 37
Green, Bettie 74
Green, Col. 32
Green, E. A. 38
Green, Eli R. 64
Green, Elizabeth 53
Green, Ella 108
Green, Emarilda E. 54
Green, Isaac 82
Green, J. H. 38
Green, John 58
Green, John A. 38
Green, L. A. 56
Green, L. B. 77
Green, Lavisa 44
Green, Mattie 108
Green, N. M. 99
Green, Nathan 38,40,48,74
Green, Orville 47
Green, Polly 76
Green, Robert 38
Green, Thomas S. 31,88
Green, W. A. 76
Green, William 21,38
Greer, Arch A. 107
Gregg, J. P. 80
Gregg, Shadrack 3,23
Gribble, Cling 106
Griffin, George 115
Grigg, Lue P. 78
Grigg, Susan E. 70,78
Grimmett, Jacob 67,90
Crisham, Thomas 22
Grissim, Bertha 104
Grissim, C. 103
Grissim, H. W. 89
Grissim, Hamlet 104
Grissim, J. Huby 103
Grissim, James G. 104
Grissim, Jennie 104
Grissim, Leula G. 103
Grissim, Mary E. 103
Grissim, Robert D. 103
Grissim, W. Hamlet 103
Grissom, Young 70
Grogan, Constantine 45
Guill, Bennett 33
Guill, J. H. 53
Guill, Josiah 33
Guill, Judieth 33
Gundall, William B. 84
Guthrie, James 88
Gwynn, A. 95
Gwynn, Andrew 47
Gwynn, Esther 47,77
Gwynn, H. R. 68

Haas, James 85
Hackney, Polk 114
Hagar, Beverly D. 71
Hagarty, Elizabeth 59
Hagerty, Jane 78
Hagerty, Miley 78
Hale, C. W. 71
Hale, Edgar 71
Hale, Emily 64
Hale, J. R. 71
Hale, Jeremiah 25
Hale, Jeremiah M. 27
Hale, John H. 71
Hale, Lina 71
Hale, Parilee 71
Hale, Stella 71
Hale, W. J. 71
Haley, J. B. 84,87
Haley, Willard 107
Haley, William 80

Hall, A. J. 113,116
Hall, Drury 78
Hall, J. 92
Hall, William 49
Halliman, William 3
Hallum, Morris 25
Hallum, Nancy 77
Hamblen, William D. 54
Hamblin, Eliza 72
Hamblin, Pamelia 72
Hamblin, W. F. 72
Hamblin, William D. 70
Hamelton, D. D. 37
Hamelton, James 37,38
Hamelton, S. C. 37
Hamer, William 84
Hamilton, Frusannah 76
Hamilton, James 55,62,63,
    77
Hamilton, John W. 43
Hamilton, Rebecca 49
Hamilton, Robert 1
Hamilton, Susanna 43
Hamlet, Mary 92
Hamlet, Samuel 92
Hamlett, Mary 85
Hamlett, Samuel 85
Hammons, Andrew J. 54
Hammons, George W. 54
Hammons, James L. 54
Hammons, John 54
Hammons, Matthew 54
Hancock, Allen 79
Hancock, D. T. 70
Hancock, David T. 63
Hancock, Dawson 3,85
Hancock, Frances A. 63
Hancock, Francis A. 70
Hancock, Harriet A. 70
Hancock, Hope 88
Hancock, J. B. 63
Hancock, J. E. 70
Hancock, James H. 63,71
Hancock, John E. 63
Hancock, L. E. 70
Hancock, Louisa E. 63
Hancock, M. A. 70
Hancock, Martha 74
Hancock, Martin 22,49,50,
    63
Hancock, Mary E. 63
Hancock, N. C. 70
Hancock, N. D. 76,78
Hancock, Nancy C. 63
Hancock, Nelson 8
Hancock, S. B. 70
Hancock, S. F. 109
Hancock, S. J. 70
Hancock, Sally J. 63
Hancock, Simon 88
Hancock, Sophia B. 63
Hancock, W. D. 76,105
Hancock, Wesley 85
Hancock, William 49,63
Hankins, Fanny 102
Hankins, M. C. 84
Hankins, Mrs. 102
Hankins, Sarah 101
Hankins, W. G. 102
Hannah, John 93
Hannah, William 93
Haralson, J. S. 44
Haralson, Polly A. 74
Haralson, Sandy 80
Hardaway, Jane 70
Harding, Johnson 86
Hardwick, Dr. 44
Hardy, Sterling 88
Hare, R. B. 117
Harkreader, John F. 75
Harlan, John 64
Harlan, R. F. 63
Harpole, Adam 33
Harpole, Jacob 5

Harrington, Elizabeth 58
Harrington, Higdon 24
Harrington, Thomas 30
Harrington, Truman 58
Harrington, William 5
Harris, A. H. 74
Harris, Alford H. 88
Harris, Arthur 28
Harris, B. W. 83
Harris, Demps 80
Harris, Eliza 19
Harris, Hannah R. 66
Harris, Harriet 62
Harris, J. P. 92
Harris, Jack 80
Harris, Jasper 79
Harris, John R. 57
Harris, Lidia A. 100
Harris, Martha 66
Harris, P. W. 66,92
Harris, Susan 103
Harris, T. R. 92
Harris, Thomas 7
Harris, W. F. 66
Harris, William 120
Harris, William, Sr. 66
Harrison, A. J. 114
Harrison, Col. 44
Harrison, Frances B. 44
Harrison, Isaac 114
Harrison, James 12
Harrison, James S. 76
Harrison, L. D. 114
Hart, Sally 62
Hartsfield, Fanny 27
Hartsfield, William 27
Harvel, Henry 23
Hass, Henry 40
Hass, James A. 40
Hass, Margaret A. 40
Hass, Sarah 40
Hass, Susannah H. 40
Hastings, D. B. 89
Hastings, F. B. 83
Hastings, Nancy 83
Hatcher, Ag 101
Hatton, Margaret 40
Hatton, Robert C. 40
Haw, James 35
Hawk, Matthew 85
Hawkins, A. W. 104
Hawkins, Eliza 45
Hawkins, Elizabeth 101
Hawkins, Elizabeth H. 56
Hawkins, William H. 56
Hayes, C. E. 98
Hayes, Jo M. 106
Haynes, Harry 107
Hays, Charles 34
Hays, Eliza H. 58
Hays, George 121
Hays, Jane B. 74
Hays, John R. 34
Hays, Joseph 34
Hays, Lavina 64
Hays, R. T. 67
Hays, Rebecca 50
Hays, Samuel 34,50
Hearn, Bettie 64,65
Hearn, E. H. 115
Hearn, Ebenezer 87
Hearn, Elizabeth 50
Hearn, G. L. 84
Hearn, George 87
Hearn, Hardy F. 64
Hearn, Jacob S. 86
Hearn, James L. 72
Hearn, James W. 35,64
Hearn, John 87
Hearn, Lucretia 83
Hearn, Martha 47
Hearn, Mary F. 35
Hearn, Milberry P. 64
Hearn, O. D. 50,64,84

Hearn, Purnel 64
Hearn, Purnell 86
Hearn, R. D. 64
Hearn, Sally 29
Hearn, Smith 70
Hearn, Stephen 85
Hearn, Stephen H. 41
Hearn, Sue A. 64
Hearn, Thomas 86
Hearn, W. P. 84
Heath, Henry 9
Heatly, Henry 120
Hedgepath, James M. 72
Hedgepath, Jeremiah M. 72
Hedgepath, John 72
Hedgepath, Margaret 72
Hedgepath, Robert F. 72
Hedgpeth, J. M. 54
Heflin, John 104
Hegarty, Dennis 9,33
Hegerty, Patrick 35
Hegerty, Patrick H. 31
Helm, Mary E. 69
Henderson, H. L. 81
Henderson, James 3
Hendrick, Robert W. 101
Henry, Sally 29
Henry, Samuel 29
Herring, Jesse 91
Herring, Mary 91
Herrod, John 1
Hester, Albert 118
Hester, James 118
Hester, William 118
Hewgley, Berdotta 59
Hewgley, John 59
Hewgley, S. W. 88
Hewgley, W. B. 37
Hibbitt, D. C. 69
Hibbitt, Eliza M. 69
Hibbitts, D. C. 68
Hibbitts, David C. 68
Hibbitts, Elizabeth 68
Hibbitts, James 68
Hibbitts, John J. 68
Hibbitts, Josiah R. 68
Hibbitts, Walter 68
Hichols, Benjamin 86
Hickerson, Mary S. 45
Hickman, Lemuel 23
Hickman, Noah 23
Hickman, Samuel L. 34
Hickman, Samuel T. 25
Hickman, Snowden 34
Hickman, Wright 77
Hight, Joseph 33
Hight, Sallie 76
Hight, Sarah 57
Hill, Braxton 6
Hill, Earl 67
Hill, F. T. 67
Hill, Harry 106
Hill, Jacob 33
Hill, John 114
Hill, Lavice 42
Hill, Nancy 55
Hill, Nancy E. 67
Hill, Samuel 31
Hill, Thomas P. 5
Hill, William 82
Hilliard, Isaac 3
Hinds, J. J. 90
Hitton, Mr. 97,98
Hobbs, Green 63
Hobbs, W. A. 81,109
Hobson, John 85
Hodge, Elizabeth 51
Hodge, Jane 51
Hodge, William 5,23
Hodge, Wilson 8
Hodges, Jesse 83
Holland, John 119
Holland, Thomas 119
Holliman, Alex 23
Holloway, A. J. 49

Holloway, Andrew J. 71
Holloway, L. 105
Holloway, Levi 49
Holloway, Levi D. 49
Holman, Annie 66
Holman, Joseph 79
Holman, Thomas L. 43
Holman, Thomas P. 66
Holman, William R. 44
Holt, B. 46
Holt, David S. 113
Holt, Lucretia 46
Holt, Martha 46
Hooker, Benjamin 23
Hooker, J. F. 62,72
Hooker, J. M. 92
Hooker, Jonathan 85
Hooker, Joshua 85
Hooker, P. C. 72
Hooker, R. W. 98
Hooker, William 90
Horn, Clarisa 56
Horn, Clarissa 55
Horn, E. P. 55,85,88
Horn, Eliza F. 63
Horn, Richard 55
Housman, Susannah 24
Houston, John 80
Houston, Reagan 108
Howard, William 114,115
Howell, Caleb 8
Howell, Joanna 77
Howell, Quincey 77
Howell, Rebecca A. 77
Howell, Thomas 77
Hubbard, Elizabeth 23
Hubbard, Mandy 62
Huchison, George 85
Huddleston, Anthony W. 84
Huddleston, Elizabeth 81
Huddleston, G. G. 51
Huddleston, George A. 32
Huddleston, J. T. 81
Huddleston, Mahala 76
Huddleston, Mahala H. 69
Huddleston, William A. 51,
  69
Hudson, Alafair 44
Hudson, Allaphair 63
Hudson, J. W. 111
Hudson, John 8
Hudson, Marcus 109
Hudson, P. P. 44,87
Hudson, Virginia 102
Huffman, Archibald 45
Huffman, Elizabeth 45
Huffman, Nancy 45
Huffman, Robert 45
Huffman, William 45
Hughes, Martin F. 71
Hughes, Robert 46
Hughes, Simpson 77
Hughey, William E. 39
Hughs, John 104
Hughs, Robert 8
Huguely, Abram 35
Hunt, A. M. 44
Hunt, Alfred M. 87
Hunt, Elijah C. 64
Hunt, George 64
Hunt, Hartwell 64
Hunt, James M. 49,50
Hunt, Jane 64
Hunt, John 113
Hunt, John C. 64
Hunt, John T. 49
Hunt, Josiah 64
Hunt, Leddy C. 50
Hunt, Maria W. 50
Hunt, Nora J. 50
Hunt, P. E. 50
Hunt, Patience 9
Hunt, Penelope E. 49
Hunt, Permelia W. 49

Hunt, Sarah H. 50
Hunt, Thomas 50
Hunt, Thomas H. 33
Hunt, William C. 64
Hunt, William D. 50
Hunter, Isaac H. 48

Impson, Isaac 22
Irby, Joseph 4,38
Ivey, A. J. 42

Jackson, Asa 57
Jackson, D. G. 118
Jackson, Henry 88
Jackson, Isham 38
Jackson, J. B. 94
Jackson, Jesse 88
Jackson, John B. 54,88,
  98
Jackson, John C. 71
Jackson, Mark 25
Jackson, Mary 88
Jackson, Mary M. 25,38
Jackson, Nancy 15
Jackson, Nancy A. 16
Jackson, Nancy L. 54
Jackson, Nannie E. 69
Jackson, Reuben 85
Jackson, S. C. 40
Jackson, Sally A. 54
Jackson, Sarah A. 74
Jackson, Thomas 86
Jackson, William H. 40
Jacoby, Edward 86
Jacobs, Edward G. 86
James, Catherine W. 40
James, Daniel 47
James, E. H. 115
James, Malinda 47
James, R. J. 115
James, Susan 62
Jarman, S. 67
Jarman, Shad 84
Jarman, Shadrack 88
Jarman, William 88
Jarmon, Easter 76
Jarmon, Frances 76
Jarmon, William 76
Jarrell, Jane 37
Jarrell, John W. 37
Jarrett, Cora 111
Jarrett, John 85,88
Jenkins, Benjamin 107
Jenkins, C. W. 117
Jenkins, David 40,41
Jenkins, Eliza 45
Jenkins, Elizabeth 41,45,49
Jenkins, John R. 45
Jenkins, Obadiah 45
Jenkins, Stephen 107
Jenkins, William B. 45
Jennings, Anderson 48,56
Jennings, Clem 65
Jennings, G. W. 44
Jennings, George 65
Jennings, George W. 53
Jennings, J. H. 48
Jennings, J. R. 90
Jennings, James H. 65,68
Jennings, Jesse 65
Jennings, Louisa M. 65
Jennings, Malinda 48
Jennings, Polly 62
Jennings, Rial C. 7
Jennings, Robert 27
Jennings, Samuel 48
Jennings, Susan 52
Jennings, Temperance 65
Jennings, William 62
Jennings, William B. 52,120
Jewell, A. M. 46
Jewell, H. C. 118

Jewell, James T. 46
Johns, Bluford 69
Johns, C. L. 99
Johns, Emma 123
Johns, H. G. 39,117
Johns, Mary J. 123
Johns, William 69
Johns, William M. 37
Johnson, A. 101
Johnson, A. E. 99
Johnson, Calvary 52
Johnson, Carrie C. 86
Johnson, Carwell 34
Johnson, Clem 34
Johnson, Dovie 125
Johnson, E. Davidson 55
Johnson, Elizabeth 54,72
Johnson, Frances M. 101
Johnson, Gregory 22
Johnson, H. R. 91
Johnson, Harry 102
Johnson, Henry F. 7,35
Johnson, J. C. 71
Johnson, J. H. 74
Johnson, J. M. 77
Johnson, J. R. 91
Johnson, James 22,67,102
Johnson, James H. 7,35,
  38,123
Johnson, James M. 123
Johnson, James R. 7
Johnson, James S. 104
Johnson, Jeremiah 8,34
Johnson, Joe 80
Johnson, John 54,88
Johnson, John H. 48
Johnson, John M. 123
Johnson, John R. 6
Johnson, Joseph 85,88,90
Johnson, Joseph W. 123
Johnson, Lizzie 103
Johnson, M. 112
Johnson, M. W. 111
Johnson, Martha 48,91
Johnson, Martha A. 104
Johnson, Martha H. 102
Johnson, Mary 7,103
Johnson, Mathias 77
Johnson, Mavias 101
Johnson, Mayfield 9
Johnson, Mitchell W. 123,
  125
Johnson, Nancy 102
Johnson, Nannie 104
Johnson, Nannie N. 123
Johnson, Patrick 69
Johnson, Paulding 54
Johnson, Philip 22
Johnson, R. M. 109
Johnson, Rebeca 104
Johnson, Rebecca 101
Johnson, Reuben 6,7,8
Johnson, Robertson 64
Johnson, Sallie E. 123
Johnson, Samuel 9
Johnson, Thompson H. 123
Johnson, W. A. 87
Johnson, W. B. 71
Johnson, W. T. 112
Johnson, William 8
Johnson, William A. 123
Johnson, William W. 23
Johnson, Zorah D. 123
Joiner, Martha 25
Jolly, Isham 46
Jones, Alfred 28
Jones, Allen 5,29
Jones, Ann R. 61
Jones, B. W. 118
Jones, E. E. 115
Jones, Edward 67
Jones, Elijah 69
Jones, Elizabeth 90
Jones, John 7,8,28,29

Jones, Martha 35
Jones, Mrs. 97
Jones, Needham 97
Jones, Richard 28
Jones, Thomas P. 90
Joplin, Robert 37
Joplin, Sarah 69
Juniper, Susan 17
Justice, Rachel J. 66

Keaton, Isham 120
Keaton, Jacob 33
Keaton, James 64
Keaton, John 120
Keaton, Neil 64
Keeton, Nancy 11
Kelley, Joshua 82
Kelly, D. C. 44
Kelly, Daniel 69
Kelly, John 86
Kelly, Top 69
Kemper, Adam 57,63
Kemper, James M. 57
Kemper, Jemimah 57
Kennedy, H. S. 50
Kennedy, Isaac 22
Kennedy, John S. 31
Kennedy, R. E. 117
Kerby, Ellen 64
Key, H. W. 80
Kidder, A. C. 49
Killey, P. P. 118
King, P. T. 98
King, Mary J. 47
King, Samuel 98,100
King, Susan 73
King, T. F. 81
King, William 73
Kirkpatrick, David 91
Kirkpatrick, Dr. 104
Kirkpatrick, John C. 48,65,
  91
Kirkpatrick, Robert 105
Kittrell, Isham 34
Kittrell, S. J. 34
Knight, David 31
Knight, J. L. 46
Knight, James, Jr. 81
Knight, Mahala J. 55
Knight, Robert 49
Knight, S. C. 109
Knight, Sophronia 49
Knight, Susan 57
Knight, William 30,31,119
Knight, William M. 116
Knox, B. F. 64
Knox, Bette 39
Knox, W. C. 39,62
Kolbe, John 113
Koonce, Mary 31
Koonce, Nancy 42
Koonce, Philip 31

Lacks, William 74
Lain, Armstead 3,35,109
Lain, B. F. 42
Lain, David M. 113
Lain, Drury 35
Lain, Elizabeth 8
Lain, G. B. 47
Lain, J. H. 117
Lain, James H. 53
Lain, James S. 47
Lain, Mary 71
Lain, Milton 46
Lain, Nancy 48,71
Lain, R. H. 105
Lain, Thomas B. 35,46
Lain, Tyre 48
Lain, W. F. 117
Lain, Willard 46

Lain, William P. 55
Laine, R. H. 74
Lamb, J. W. 104
Lambert, Warner 34,35
Lamoine, Will 106
Lancaster, Levi S. 5,8
Lane, J. H. 83
Lane, J. T. 80
Lane, Martha 41
Lane, Martha S. 77
Lane, P. R. 111
Lane, Purnell 42
Lane, Robert 83
Lane, Thornton 77
Lanius, J. C. 69
Lanius, P. C. 69
Lanius, Richard P. 69
Lanius, William 69
Lannom, H. L. 114
Lannom, John A. 119
Lansden, Robert W. 90
Lasater, Jacob B. 29
Lasater, Lavina 42
Lash, George 6
Laughlin, Samuel H. 30
Law, Gideon H. 93
Law, James 93
Layne, George W. 71
Leatherwood, A. M. 8
Ledbetter, Charles 88
Lee, Elizabeth 37
Lee, William L. 37
Leech, John 21
Lester, Henry D. 68
Lester, James 64
Lester, John A. 68
Lester, Joshua 68
Lewis, Cornelius N. 23
Lewis, Carol 11
Lewis, Carrol 37
Lewis, George 107
Liggan, Henry 33
Ligon, A. E. 67
Ligon, Amanda M. 122
Ligon, Ann P. 122
Ligon, Araminta J. 122
Ligon, Argalus E. 125
Ligon, Argalus L. 123
Ligon, Armsted H. 125
Ligon, Booker 125
Ligon, C. Richard 125
Ligon, Charles W. 111,122,
  125
Ligon, Day 125
Ligon, Dovie 111
Ligon, Ed 125
Ligon, Elizabeth C. 123
Ligon, F. L. 117
Ligon, F. T. 113
Ligon, J. B. 112,123
Ligon, John G. 41,82
Ligon, John H. 83
Ligon, Lafayette 123
Ligon, M. E. 67
Ligon, Martha E. 59
Ligon, Mary C. 67
Ligon, Nannie 111
Ligon, Nora D. 123
Ligon, P. F. 115
Ligon, Peyton 117
Ligon, Piddy 122
Ligon, R. L. 62,65,122
Ligon, R. Lee 125
Ligon, R. R. 62
Ligon, Richard R. 123
Ligon, Rosaline L. 122
Ligon, Rossia 111
Ligon, Virginia H. 123
Ligon, W. B. 59,67
Ligon, Wes 111,125
Lindsey, E. L. 39
Lindsey, Eli 72
Lindsey, Elizabeth 77
Lindsey, Ellen 77

Lindsey, George 77
Lindsey, H. L. 51
Lindsey, J. B. 72,91
Lindsey, James 72
Lindsey, Josiah 72
Lindsey, Lawrence 51
Lindsey, Lewis 77
Lindsey, Lucelius 72
Lindsey, Lucy 47
Lindsey, Malinda 72
Lindsey, Melan 72
Lindsley, Lewis 99
Lindsley, N. L. 62
Link, Jefferson 17
Lipscomb, P. 74,77
Livingstone, H. L. 98
Lockett, Henry J. 42
Logue, Carnes 39
Logue, Dr. 97
Logue, John 92
Logue, L. G. 39
Lowe, Margaret E. 52
Lowe, Mary E. 52
Lowe, Rosabella 52
Lowe, Sarah M. 52
Loyd, Foster 58
Loyd, Harriet 74
Loyd, Lemuel 74
Loyd, Matilda 45
Lucas, George A. 26
Luck, J. M. 109
Luck, W. W. 45
Lumpkin, John W. 21
Lyon, Elizabeth 8
Lyons, Susannah 73
Lyons, Thomas W. 52

McAdow, James 7
McBride, P. S. 114
McCaffrey, Elizabeth 56
McCaffrey, James 56
McCaffrey, John 51,56
McCaffrey, Levy 56
McCaffrey, Rebecca 51
McCaffrey, Robert 56
McCaffrey, Sary A. 56
McClain, J. S. 40
McClain, Jo 39
McClain, John A. 39
McClain, Josiah S. 74
McClain, Manerva 39,57
McClain, Martha 74
McClain, Panthia 39
McClain, Rufus 58
McClain, Rufus P. 39
McClain, William 39
McClelland, John J. 108
McClelland, W. K. 117
McConnell, Elizabeth M. 63
McCorkle, Emma J. 48
McCorkle, Henry H. 48
McCorkle, Kitty A. 48
McCorkle, Miles 48
McCorkle, William 48,108
McCullock, J. C. 39
McCullock, James 56
McCutcheon, B. R. 37
McDaniel, J. W. 84
McDearman, Anna 37
McDearman, Cynthia E. 53
McDearman, Sally A. 37
McDearman, Wilee 95,96
McDearman, Winfield 37
McDonald, Frances T. 101
McDonald, George 44
McDonald, H. G. 104
McDonald, J. C. 81
McDonald, Manerva H. 100
McDonald, W. H. 43
McDonald, William G. 100
McDonnold, B. W. 100
McFarland, Ada B. 55

McFarland, Charlotte 55
McFarland, Dicy 38
McFarland, Ira 13
McFarland, James 38,82
McFarland, James H. 55
McFarland, James P. 62
McFarland, John P. 38
McFarland, John W. 55
McFarland, M. D. 37
McFarland, Mattie E. 55
McFarland, P. 38
McGee, A. 102
McGee, Amanda 103
McGehee, Josiah 23
McGregor, Eudora 44
McGregor, Frances 53
McGregor, William 53
McHaney, William 27,31
McHenry, Elizabeth 7
McHenry, J. B. 114
McHenry, Jesse 7
McHenry, John 7
McKee, Ras 108
McKee, S. R. 73
McKee, Thomas 107
McKee, Will 107
McKinney, Ann 58
McKinney, Wesley 58
McKnight, D. M. 119
McLarin, John H. 49
McMillen, Andrew 45
McMillen, Charley 120
McMillen, Frances 45
McMillen, James 120
McMillen, Jane 45
McMillen, Jensy 45
McMillen, Joseph 45
McMillen, Lily 45
McMillen, Mary 45
McMillen, Peggy 45
McMillen, Sarah 45
McMillen, Tennessee 45
McMillen, Thomas 45
McMillen, William 45,50
McMillen, Z. 45
McMinn, Elihu 31,42
McMinn, Samuel N. 42
McMurry, Ann E. 71
McMurry, David 3,89
McMurry, Elizabeth 71
McMurry, J. M. 71
McMurry, Sarah F. 101
McNairy, John 82
McNairy, Nathaniel A. 1
McNichols, Donald 27
McNickols, John 12
McNicol, Elizabeth 12
McPeak, Ann E. 75
McPeak, Granville 114
McPeak, Henderson 114
McQuisten, George F. 85
McSpadden, T. C. 73
McSpaden, Cynthia H. 101
McSpaden, Nancy A. 100
McSpaden, Samuel T. 101
McSpaden, Thomas C. 100
McSpedden, Nancy 104
McWilliams, E. L. 98

Mabry, John W. 70
Mabry, Miranda 70
Mace, B. M. 79
Mace, George 79
Macon, S. W. 73
Maddox, Brother 99
Maddox, E. 99
Maddox, Elijah 99
Maddox, Wilson L. 30
Magness, Dicey 17
Maholland, John 87
Major, A. M. 47
Major, Elizabeth 47

Major, J. A. 39
Major, John A. 47
Major, N. M. 62
Major, W. B. 47
Major, Wilson B. 47
Malone, Ann 38,73
Malone, Jerry 38
Malone, John 39
Malone, Lemuel 38
Malone, Mary 39
Malone, Nancy 38
Malone, Robert 38,39
Malone, Tennessee 39
Mann, J. C. 120
Mann, T. F. 120
Manning, Robert 9
Marks, Bailey 72
Marks, Britton 89
Marks, Elizabeth 72
Marks, George 72
Marks, J. B. 43
Marler, R. 37
Marler, W. 37
Marlon, Elizabeth 21
Marlon, Nancy 21
Marrs, Martha 48
Marrs, R. A. 48
Marshal, Edward 104
Marshall, David 81
Marshall, E. A. 88
Marshall, James 98
Marshall, John C. 90
Marshall, Robert 90,104
Marshall, William T. 103
Martin, Amos 53
Martin, Andrew 38
Martin, Andrew B. 61,90
Martin, Caleb 53
Martin, Catherine 53
Martin, David 5
Martin, Elijah 53
Martin, Elizabeth C. 43,66
Martin, Elizabeth M. 53
Martin, Ezekiel 84
Martin, George W. 45
Martin, J. H. 105
Martin, J. M. 56,65
Martin, James 17
Martin, James B. 45
Martin, James M. 53
Martin, Jane 53
Martin, Jasper 62
Martin, Kate M. 65
Martin, M. 48
Martin, Margaret 64
Martin, Martha 11
Martin, Mary J. 43,44,64
Martin, Mary L. 44
Martin, Ned 17
Martin, O. L. 59
Martin, Ralph 43
Martin, Samuel 53
Martin, Thomas 53
Martin, Thomas C. 47
Martin, W. D. 83
Martin, William L. 39
Mason, John 32
Massey, A. A. 86
Massey, Abram 87
Massey, Ann E. 101
Massey, Mary 55
Mathews, H. L. 117
Matthews, H. C. 48,76
Matthews, Matt 84
Mattock, Wilson 30
Maxwell, J. M. 68
Maxwell, William H. 8
Maxwell, William M. 8
Medlin, Rebecca 5
Melton, Eliza 25
Melton, Samuel 25
Melven, Justina S. 100
Melven, N. 101
Melven, Walter W. 100

Melvin, Alice B. 101
Melvin, Andrew 35
Melvin, Edmund 35
Melvin, Edwin C. 101
Melvin, Joseph 35
Meredith, Eliza 56
Meredith, William B. 56
Merrell, Benjamin 25
Merritt, G. H. 105
Merritt, John 32
Midgett, Richard 85
Miers, C. A. 94
Miers, Dinnah 47
Miers, E. A. 94
Miers, G. M. 94
Miers, Morgan 47
Miers, Peter 47
Miers, Washington 47
Miers, William 47
Miligan, Jane 21
Miller, Joseph M. 45
Miller, Sarah F. 58
Miller, Wesley 19
Mires, Adam 3
Mitchel, John C. 102
Mitchel, Nancy E. 102
Mitchell, Garret G. 34
Mitchell, Harriet A. 34
Mitchell, Lucy 62
Mitchell, Martha 38
Mitchell, Partheny 11
Mitchell, Paulding 38
Mitchell, Robert 38
Mitchell, Robert R. 34
Modglin, Benton 23
Modglin, Britton 27
Modglin, James 30
Modglin, William 83
Moody, Nancy J. 20
Mooney, John 6
Mooningham, H. B. 12
Moore, Alexander 44
Moore, Alford 86
Moore, Alfred 85
Moore, Armstead 44
Moore, B. D. 98,116
Moore, Cleopatra 62
Moore, D. B. 58
Moore, Edward 88
Moore, Ella 123
Moore, J. 116
Moore, Jesse L. 90
Moore, Maria 79
Moore, Mary G. 65
Moore, Robert 44
Moore, Samuel 90
Moore, Samuel B. 44
Moore, Samuel L. 44
Moore, Susan F. 66
Moore, Thomas C. 101
Moore, Whitfield 70
Moore, William 35,85,88
Mooring, Henry 70
Mooring, William 70
Morris, Henry H. 5
Morris, Laurel 53
Morris, R. H. 53
Morris, Tempa L. 69
Morriss, Samuel 85
Mortimer, Sally 23
Morton, Hughes 35
Morton, William 35
Moseley, Elizabeth 43
Moseley, Finis 106
Moseley, J. H. 49
Moseley, James H. 50
Moseley, Jno. L. 106
Moseley, Manerva 49
Moseley, Samuel L. 51
Moseley, W. J. 50
Moser, A. H. 49,50
Moser, Berry 69
Moser, Henry, Sr. 46
Moser, J. M. 50

Moser, Nancy L. 49
Moser, Pheoba 55
Motheral, Elizabeth A. 63
Motheral, George W. 63
Motheral, Jane 75
Motheral, John R. 75
Motheral, L. J. 63
Motheral, Martha R. 63
Motheral, Robert 75
Motheral, Samuel 91
Motheral, Vandalia 63
Mottley, Joseph 38,57,70,
  86
Mottley, S. T. 57
Mount, Amos 57
Mount, Mathias 57
Mount, Richard 57,119
Mount, Richard A. 57
Mount, Robert L. 20
Mount, William 57
Moxley, J. W. 114
Moxley, Nancy L. 77
Moxley, R. N. 114
Muirhead, A. G. 80
Muirhead, John 8,31
Murphy, Mary 77
Murphy, Robert E. 77
Murry, Anny 62
Murry, James L. 42
Murry, N. 84,87
Murry, Nathaniel 72
Muse, Brother 99
Myers, Edward 85
Myers, Henry 17

Nailor, Sally 31
Neal, Bob 107
Neal, C. W. 45,58
Neal, F. M. 107
Neal, G. A. 39
Neal, George 39
Neal, James 59
Neal, L. M. 109
Neal, Nancy 48
Neal, Robert C. 45
Neal, Sam 107
Neal, W. Z. 109
Neal, Will 107
Nelson, Jane 51
Nettles, Burrel G. 9
Nettles, William 26
New, Bettie 79
New, Betty 82
New, Martin 79,84
New, Martin V. 82
New, William 87
Newby, Bettie 124
Newby, Zack 124
Nicholas, Benjamin 85
Nichols, John W. 22
Nickens, Andrew 6
Nickens, Archibald 5
Nickens, John 5
Noaks, G. W. 118
Noble, E. 92
Nokes, George W. 87
Nolin, Mary 37
Nolin, William H. 37
Norman, Annie P. 65
Norman, H. T. 65
Norman, Hannah 23
Norman, Joseph 23
Norman, Matilda C. 65
Norman, Sallie H. 65
Norman, Thomas 40,65,92,106
Norris, J. William 104
North, Eliza 104
Nowlin, Mary 30

Oakley, George 40
Oakley, George M. 98
Oakley, John 50
Oakley, Nathan 47
O'Bryan, John 7
Odum, Frances 63
Odum, John 63
Odum, Wesley 17
Ogle, G. A. 99
Oldham, C. H. 65
Oldham, George 84
Oldham, James 80,102
Oldham, John S. 101
Oldham, Nancy 102
Oldham, Nancy D. 100
Oldham, Richard, Jr. 101
Oldham, Richard, Sr. 100
Oldham, Samuel 101
Oldham, Susan 102
Oldham, William 84
O'Neal, Asa 64,70
O'Neal, G. W. 64
Organ, Madison 9
Organ, Samuel F. 101
Organ, Woodford 8
Osborn, Dr. 97
Osborn, T. C. 98
Osborn, Thomas 97
Osburn, Norris J. 101
Osment, C. 105
Osment, J. H. 109
Outlaw, Ellen 41
Owen, John 56,80
Owen, John H. 61
Owen, Mary A. 59
Owen, Shadrack 28
Ozment, Darkus 21
Ozment, Eli 21
Ozment, James 6
Ozment, John 118
Ozment, John A. 120

Padgett, George R. 88
Page, Ann 104
Page, G. W. 120
Page, Larkin 81
Page, Thomas 17
Page, Wesley 85,92
Palmer, C. 117
Palmer, Isaac 25
Palmer, Isham 6
Palmer, John 66,91
Palmer, Richard H. 91
Palmer, Thomas K. 6
Parham, Lewis W. 43
Parham, Martha 43
Parker, Jessie 80
Parker, Lou 19
Parnell, B. 104
Parsons, Malinda 11
Parten, Henry 42
Parten, Tempy 42
Partin, B. C. 43
Partin, Henry 43
Partin, James 7
Partlow, J. N. 62,72,75
Partlow, Rebecca 62
Partlow, Sary J. 62
Partlow, Thomas 85
Partlow, W. T. 92
Pass, M. 111
Patterson, A. J. 57
Patterson, Burrell 84
Patterson, Jennie 111
Patterson, John F. 30
Patterson, John L. 39
Patterson, Lewis 57,76
Patterson, Mary 31
Patterson, Polly 66
Patterson, Polly A. 57
Patterson, S. B. 66
Patterson, W. A. 81

Patterson, Z. S. 111
Patton, Elizabeth 57
Patton, J. N. 52
Patton, James N. 34
Patton, James T. 90
Patton, John 30,90
Patton, Joseph H. 90
Patton, Joseph T. 90
Patton, Lathan 28
Patton, Rebecca 28
Patton, S. D. 90
Patton, Thomas 85
Paul, B. H. 76
Paul, John W. 76
Paul, William 76
Paul, William B. 76
Payne, Alfred B. 34
Payne, Alice 72
Payne, Benjamin W. 34
Payne, Corah 72
Payne, Daniel F. 34
Payne, Douglas 72
Payne, Ellen 72
Payne, Emily 72
Payne, George W. 34
Payne, Jesse 72
Payne, Lea 72
Payne, Mar 72
Payne, Mary 72
Payne, Permelia 72
Payne, Sallie A. 72
Payne, Solurah B. 72
Peace, Jane H. 17
Peace, William H. 8
Peach, G. 97
Peach, Gassaway 88
Peach, M. L. 114
Peach, Thomas 114
Pearson, Alonzo 108
Pemberton, John 30,61
Pendleton, Lewis 92
Pennebaker, Alice 109
Pennebaker, E. R. 108
Pennebaker, Edwin R. 71
Pennebaker, Edwin R., Jr. 71
Pennebaker, Mollie 108
Penning, William B. 74
Perkins, John 9
Perriman, Joseph W. 29
Perry, Burwell 1
Peyton, B. S. 47
Peyton, Brown 106
Peyton, J. W. 88
Peyton, John W. 82
Phelps, Jesse 29
Phelps, Victoria 61
Phelps, William R. 32
Philips, Benjamin 50
Philips, David 50
Philips, Francis L. 47
Philips, Harden 50
Philips, J. W. 50
Philips, John 50,68
Philips, John S. 50
Philips, Josiah 50
Philips, L. 50
Philips, Malinda 50
Philips, Phebe 22
Philips, Rebecca 39
Philips, Thomas 68
Philips, William 50
Philips, Wilson 50
Phillips, Bailey 124
Phillips, George 80
Phillips, H. 80
Phillips, John 99,117
Phillips, Nancy P. 67
Phillips, R. T. 98
Phillips, Thomas H. 101
Phillips, William K. 55
Phipps, W. R. 26
Pickett, C. 80
Pickett, C. H. 106
Pickett, Calvin 80

Pickett, H. W. 73
Pickett, J. 80
Picketts, H. W. 119
Piland, Benjamin 23
Pitman, Lavinia A. 57
Pittman, Caroline 79
Pittman, John 79
Pittman, John J. 55
Poindexter, Alice 108
Poindexter, Robert 108
Pool, Seth P. 3
Porterfield, James 32
Porterfield, S. H. 46
Porterfield, Samuel H. 26
Posey, B. L. 53
Posey, Martha 51
Powell, D. D. 39
Powell, Edward S. 55
Powell, George F. 55
Powell, German G. 55
Powell, John 87
Powell, John M. 55,74
Powell, Martha E. 55
Powell, Price P. 55
Powell, Robert D. 55
Powell, Ruth A. 55
Powell, Sally H. 55
Powell, Sarah J. 55
Powell, Silas T. 55
Powell, William 87
Powell, William A. 39
Powell, William T. 55
Poyner, John O. 34
Preston, S. S. 70
Price, Berry 7
Price, J. J. 115,118
Price, Jesse P. 80
Price, Jessie R. 80
Price, John 68
Price, John W. 49,68
Price, Kinney 57
Price, Matilda E. 40
Price, Milly 57
Price, Sallie 68
Price, Solomon 79
Price, W. W. 61
Price, Walter 106
Price, Will 106
Price, William 68
Pride, Isabella 12
Pritchett, Benjamin 40
Prichett, George 40
Prichett, Sophrona 40
Proctor, David 61
Proctor, J. A. 75
Proctor, Nancy 75
Pross, Daniel 85
Provine, Alexander 23
Provine, John 94,95
Proyer, M. 103
Pruett, Lucy 62
Pryor, John 5
Puckett, A. A. 38
Puckett, Benjamin 86
Puckett, Coleman 45
Puckett, Elizabeth 48
Puckett, J. G. 46
Puckett, John 5
Puckett, Thomas A. 97
Pursley, William B. 87
Putman, J. W. 45
Putman, W. L. 38

Quarles, D. W. 63
Quarles, William 26
Quesenbury, R. H. 62

Rachley, Allen 22,23
Ragland, H. 50
Ragling, John 32

Rains, John 84
Rains, Nancy 70
Rakes, John H. 119
Ramey, John 118
Ramsey, Ann E. 74,75
Rather, Baker 3,4,37
Rather, Sarah G. 3,37
Ray, Elijah 1
Ray, Willis 21
Read, Thomas J. 3
Reece, Mary 56
Reece, Page 19
Reed, Eli 105
Reed, Green 87
Reed, L. J. 87
Reed, Lawrence 64
Reed, Margaret 34
Reed, R. D. 72
Reed, Robert 34
Reed, T. J. 103
Reeves, Jeremiah T. 26
Reeves, Martha 100,104
Reeves, Nancy D. 73
Reson, Peter 7
Rhodes, Elisha S. 29
Rhodes, Frederick L. 29
Rhodes, J. H. 117
Rhodes, Thomas 29
Rice, Edna A. 74
Rice, Esther, Jr. 95
Rice, Horace 38
Rice, Isabella 12
Rice, J. H. 92
Rice, J. S. 99
Rice, James 105
Rice, James H. 54
Rice, John S. 99
Rice, Lula G. 123
Rice, T. N. 109
Rice, Thomas 92
Rice, Thomas B. 98
Rice, William 62
Richardson, Bernard 9
Ricketts, Elizabeth 23
Ricketts, Robert 30
Ricketts, Robert H. 9
Ricketts, Samuel A. 82
Riddle, H. Y. 68
Riddle, Maggie 109
Riddle, Maggie H. 40
Riddle, Ruby 108
Ridley, J. E. 111
Rieff, John 85
Rigan, Samuel 8
Right, Benjamin 56
Right, Fanny 56
Right, Rebecca 56
Risen, Mary A. 47
Rison, James 60
Rison, Mary A. 60
Roach, Elizabeth H. 35
Roach, J. J. 95
Roach, James A. 35
Roach, John 95
Roach, John N. 93
Roach, Margaret M. 40
Roach, Mary J. 42
Robb, Jane 69
Robb, Margaret E. 69
Robb, William 69
Robbin, Cora 54
Robbin, Elnora 54
Robbin, Susan 54
Roberts, David R. 119
Robertson, Fountain 33
Robertson, John H. 51
Robertson, L. L. 39
Robertson, Lewis W. 40
Robertson, Perk 41
Robertson, W. G. 51
Robins, Susan 72
Robinson, Edward 86
Robinson, James W. 48
Robinson, John H. 113

Robinson, Leonard 113
Robinson, Stephen 48,113
Rodgers, Monroe 102
Rodgers, Sallie 102
Rogers, Alfred B. 71
Rogers, Catherine F. 71
Rogers, Christopher C. 63,71
Rogers, Eliza J. 61
Rogers, Frances E. 71
Rogers, Henry 71
Rogers, Henry A. 61
Rogers, Henry J. 71
Rogers, Houston L. 61
Rogers, James M. 61
Rogers, Jane 71
Rogers, John 111
Rogers, John A. 71
Rogers, John C. 61
Rogers, Louiza 61
Rogers, Maggie L. 61
Rogers, Robert 7,12
Rogers, Sarah J. 43,68
Rogers, Viola 61
Rogers, William J. 61,71
Rohelia, Martin 113
Roland, J. A. 76
Roland, Jenny 76
Roland, Wilee 13
Roseborough, Judge 109
Ross, Allen 57,85,86
Ross, E. T. 57
Ross, Fountain P. 57
Ross, Henry P. 57
Ross, James G. 57
Ross, John W. 57
Ross, Margaret 57
Ross, Mitchell 57
Ross, Sarah 57
Ross, William A. 57
Rotramel, David 9
Roulston, James G. 7
Rucker, Elizabeth 72
Rucker, J. H. 72
Rucker, James P. 72
Rucker, S. B. 72
Rucks, Margaret 17
Rucks, Sally D. 55
Rucks, Willie 81
Runnels, William D. 119
Rushing, W. A. 80
Russell, Bob 107
Russell, C. C. 98
Russell, E. R. 85
Russell, Evaline 37
Russell, F. M. 69
Russell, Sarah J. 74
Rutland, Blake 83
Rutledge, Nancy 70
Ruyle, Aaron 86

Saddler, Anders 105
Saddler, Frank 105
Sadler, Eliza A. 40
Sadler, Mary F. 40
Sanders, Andrew 54
Sanders, Charles H. 78
Sanders, D. L. 58
Sanders, Esther 54
Sanders, F. J. 78
Sanders, J. C. 20
Sanders, John 32
Sanders, Joseph 54
Sanders, Julias 31
Sanders, Lettisha 58
Sanders, Parthena 31
Sanders, Polly 29
Sanders, R. C. 58
Sanders, Sally 54
Sanders, Susan B. 78
Sanders, William R. 78
Sands, William 22
Sanford, James 11
Scales, C. B. 44

Scales, David C. 68
Scales, Mary H. 47
Scobey, A. E. 87
Scobey, J. B. 67
Scobey, James E. 41
Scobey, R. C. 87
Scoby, James M. 45
Scoby, Robert C. 45
Scott, Amanda 57
Scott, Dorcas R. 56
Scott, James 8,28
Scott, Leander 56,57
Seatt, Anderson 121
Seatt, Harrison 29
Seatt, Herrod 29
Seatt, Jane 29
Seatt, Jarratt 29
Seatt, John 121
Seatt, Margaret 29
Seatt, Nancy 29
Seatt, Sally 29
Seatt, Timothy 29
Seay, Charley 80
Seay, Daniel 35,86
Seay, Jo 77
Seay, John 87
Seay, John, Sr. 86
Seay, Page 80
Seay, Thomas 84
Seay, W. W. 62
Seay, William 86
Sellars, Betty A. 70
Settle, Caldonia 17,18
Settle, Leroy B. 35
Sewell, James 71
Shannon, A. 54
Shannon, Alex 120
Shannon, C. F. 54
Shannon, Clementy 54
Shannon, E. K. 54
Shannon, Etheldred J. 43
Shannon, George W. 44
Shannon, Henry J. 43
Shannon, Isabella 54
Shannon, J. H. 54,120
Shannon, James 43,90
Shannon, John 80
Shannon, William R. 44
Sharp, H. C. 116
Sharp, John G. 74
Sharp, Sarah E. 74
Sharp, William D. 74
Shaw, Caroline 41
Shaw, Elizabeth 43
Shaw, Hicksey 46
Shaw, James 2,3,24
Shearin, Wood S. 34
Shears, James 12
Shelton, James 68
Shelton, V. L. 47
Shepherd, John F. 101
Sherrell, Samuel W. 26
Sherrill, A. J. 80
Sherrill, Archibald 90
Sherrill, Eliza 52
Sherrill, James W. 92
Sherrill, Jane C. 61
Sherrill, L. W. 52
Sherrill, William 90
Ship, John A. 101
Ship, Julia 101,103
Ship, Lavinia A. 102
Ship, Luvenia 104
Ship, M. 102
Ship, Samuel 103
Ship, Venie 102
Shipp, Eliza 102
Shipp, J. A. 89
Shipp, John 103
Shores, Jonathan 6
Shores, Philip 6
Shorter, Delia 66
Shorter, H. C. 66
Shorter, John 72,115

Shorter, Robert 115
Shreeve, J. W. 74,77
Shryer, Mary I. 63
Shuston, Benjamin F. 15
Simmons, W. A. 65,67
Simpson, G. W. 109
Simpson, John L. 48
Simpson, John T. 76
Simpson, Pius 29
Sims, Diretha A. 64
Sims, Eugenia 64
Sims, Frances 45
Sims, J. G. 48
Sims, M. L. 35
Sims, Nancy 64
Sims, Sally 64
Sims, Sally A. 64
Sims, Susan 64
Sinclair, Eli 95,96
Skeen, Eda 65
Skein, John 88
Slaughter, Isham 57
Smart, John 3,21
Smart, Phillip 82
Smith, A. W. 98
Smith, Abraham 24
Smith, Boyd 116
Smith, C. C. 52
Smith, Christopher 114
Smith, David B. 9
Smith, E. L. 48
Smith, E. S. 57
Smith, Edward 87
Smith, Edward P. 103
Smith, Elizabeth 62,68,69,
   89
Smith, Elmira J. 66
Smith, George F. 90
Smith, George K. 90
Smith, Gilla 11
Smith, Harvey 92
Smith, Henry 21
Smith, Isaac 42,64
Smith, J. C. 49
Smith, J. J. 68
Smith, J. W. 70
Smith, James M. 66
Smith, Jesse N. 114
Smith, John 21
Smith, John H. 83
Smith, John J. 49
Smith, John W. 66
Smith, Josiah 69
Smith, L. D. 75
Smith, L. W. 91
Smith, Martha N. 28
Smith, Mary E. 63
Smith, Maxwell 63
Smith, Presley 102
Smith, Robert 93
Smith, Samuel B. 68
Smith, Samuel H. 68
Smith, Sarah 17,78
Smith, Sarah A. 69
Smith, Saul 89
Smith, Susan E. 71
Smith, Thomas 1
Smith, Thomas F. 89
Smith, Thomas J. 34,66
Smith, W. D. 52
Smith, William B. 63
Smith, William H. 90
Smithwick, Mildred S. 75
Smithwick, Samuel 45
Sneed, Major 32
Snow, John B. 53,113
Snow, Josey M. 53
Snow, Lilla D. 53
Snow, Martha A. 53
Somers, James 22
Spears, William 86
Sperry, Elizabeth 25
Sperry, Samuel 61
Sperry, Thomas 25

Spickard, A. W. 109
Spire, W. J. 109
Spradley, Calvin 9
Spradley, Tabner 31
Spradley, William 6
Spradlin, Lorinda F. 71
Spradlin, Obediah 1
Spring, Samuel 86
Springs, Abner 86
Springs, Jefferson 55
Springs, William 55
Stamps, John 1
Standley, Mary 26
Steed, S. F. 82
Steel, James 88
Steel, William 9
Steele, Gary 35
Steele, William 89
Stevenson, Benjamin F. 83
Stevenson, Elizabeth 83
Stevenson, Isaac N. 38
Stewart, A. C. 107
Stewart, J. C. 125
Stewart, John 9
Stewart, Louiza 49
Stewart, Sarah F. 54
Stokes, Bettie 108
Stokes, Colonel 113,124
Stokes, Jordan 106,117
Stokes, Walter 106
Stone, A. B. 92
Stone, Henry S. 103,104
Stone, Newbern P. 6,8
Stone, Reuben 22
Stone, Susan 45
Stratton, Ed 107
Stratton, S. G. 67
Stratton, Thomas J. 69,73,
  80
Straughn, Rockerlany 60
Straughn, Roxalany 47
Stroud, John K. 109
Stroud, T. B. 59
Stuart, John 17
Sudarth, Mattie 104
Suddarth, Alice 102
Suddarth, Anderson K. 103
Suddarth, Clarra J. 103
Suddarth, Eliza 103
Suddarth, Hattie 102
Suddarth, Robert D. 103
Suddeth, Lula 101
Suddeth, W. H. 104
Suddeth, W. W. 104
Sugg, Aquilla 23
Sugg, Cullin E. 91
Sugg, Elizabeth H. 91
Sullivan, A. S. 72
Sullivan, Almeda B. 77
Sullivan, Ambros 72
Sullivan, Benjamin 63
Sullivan, Eli 114
Sullivan, J. N. 72
Sullivan, Malvina F. 51
Sullivan, Martha J. 77
Sullivan, Mary 63,72
Sullivan, Mary P. 77
Sullivan, Mary R. 63
Sullivan, Sylvania 51
Summerhill, Frank 72
Swain, Annie F. 65
Swain, Solomon 43
Swan, George L. 86
Swann, James G. 45
Sweatt, Robert 83
Sweatt, Robert P. 41
Swindell, Joel 34
Swindell, Thomas A. 34
Swingley, Fannie 79
Sypert, Betsy 58
Sypert, H. 60
Sypert, John C. 47,55,60
Sypert, Lawrence 31,58
Sypert, Mathew W. 60

Sypert, R. B. 80
Sypert, Thomas 60
Sypert, Thomas, Jr. 60
Sypert, William 7
Sypert, William C. 47,58
Sypert, William L. 60

Talley, Archebald 43
Talley, D. G. 43
Talley, Martin 33
Talley, Spencer W. 27,32
Tally, Elizabeth 22
Tally, J. T. 45
Tally, James 25
Tally, M. 113
Tally, Spencer W. 28
Tally, W. W. 113
Tally, William W. 32
Tapp, John S. 88,90
Tarpley, S. O. 49
Tarver, Adaline 50
Tarver, Almeda 50
Tarver, B. J. 41,47,50
Tarver, Benjamin 5
Tarver, Benjamin J. 59,74
Tarver, Burrell 50
Tarver, Jane 50
Tarver, John 50
Tarver, John B. 59
Tarver, Lucinda 58
Tarver, Lucy 59
Tarver, Malissa 50
Tarver, Matilda 50
Tarver, Robert 50
Tarver, Silas 59
Tate, A. J. 37
Tate, Jacob 117
Tate, Polly 40
Tate, Robert S. 90
Tate, Z. 37
Tatom, Barnard 1
Tatum, W. B. 44
Taylor, Caleb 85
Taylor, Catherine F. 71
Taylor, E. A. 41
Taylor, Felix H. 62
Taylor, Fountain G. 87
Taylor, J. C. 72
Taylor, John 1
Taylor, John D. 87
Taylor, Joshua, Sr. 84
Taylor, Joshua V. 84
Taylor, Luiza A. 75
Taylor, Manuel 85
Taylor, Matilda 37
Taylor, Memiel 92
Taylor, Polly 71
Taylor, Samuel D. 87
Taylor, Thomas H. 73
Telford, H. 94,97
Telford, Hugh 91,92,93
Telford, James 63
Telford, John 26,35
Telford, L. E. 94
Telford, Mary W. 94
Telford, Roxy 63
Telford, Sarah 35
Telford, T. F. 94
Telford, Thomas 91,94,95,
  114
Telford, William H. 35
Temples, Joseph 9
Terrill, William 82
Terry, Eliza J. 71
Thaxton, William 32
Thomas, Harrison 56
Thomas, Henry 26
Thomas, J. F. 118
Thomas, J. G. 118
Thomas, John G. 26,49
Thomas, John H. 118
Thompson, A. 117

Thompson, A. J. 37
Thompson, A. N. 120
Thompson, Andrew 40,92,106
Thompson, Anna 51
Thompson, Carrie 109
Thompson, E. A. 120
Thompson, E. L. 41
Thompson, E. S., Jr. 92
Thompson, Elizabeth 57
Thompson, Emma 61
Thompson, Emmett 108
Thompson, G. W. 89,91
Thompson, Gentry 108
Thompson, J. L. 106,120
Thompson, James B. 120
Thompson, James L. 72
Thompson, Joe K. 92
Thompson, John B. 118
Thompson, John N. 92
Thompson, Joseph 92,120
Thompson, Lillard 80,90
Thompson, M. J. 61
Thompson, Mary 73
Thompson, Mary F. 61
Thompson, Mary W. 72
Thompson, Milas 92
Thompson, Milly 40
Thompson, Osborn 52
Thompson, P. 46,91
Thompson, Peter 41,76
Thompson, R. H. 92,119,120
Thompson, Rachel 74
Thompson, Samantha C. 52
Thompson, W. D. 59
Thompson, William 15
Thompson, William G. 65
Thornton, E. H. 81
Thornton, Seth 8
Thrower, Elizabeth 12
Tiller, Mary 51
Tiller, Mason 51
Tiller, Virginia 51
Tims, Cynthia 29
Tippett, John 25
Tippitt, John C. 7
Tippitt, Richard 17
Tipton, James 21
Tipton, Joshua 92
Tisdale, Piety 29
Tittle, Samuel 23
Todd, Juliette H. 67
Todd, W. F. 47,67
Todd, William F. 67
Tolliver, J. B. 109
Tolliver, Z. 74
Tomblin, William 5
Tomlin, Dovie 111
Tomlinson, Irvin 50
Tomlinson, James 68
Tomlinson, Vilena E. 101
Tomlinson, William 44
Tompkins, E. H. 50
Tompkins, Edmund H. 50
Tompkins, James L. 50
Tompkins, James S. 83
Tompkins, Samuel W. 50
Tompson, Dr. 44
Townsend, Richard 33
Towson, Elizabeth B. 37
Tracy, Thomas 86
Treiber, George 113
Tribble, Isaiah 30
Tribble, John 62
Trinum, Jack 106
Trout, John 22
Truett, Henry 76
Tucker, Elizabeth 53
Tucker, Mary 65
Tuggle, Thomas 37
Tuggle, Tom 69
Tumblin, William 8
Turnblin, J. H. 116
Turner, Alfred M. 50
Turner, Anice 59

Turner, B. J. 80
Turner, Bettie 77
Turner, Cinderella 62
Turner, E. A. 59,61
Turner, Elizabeth A. 50
Turner, J. W. 61
Turner, James 81
Turner, Joel P. 61
Turner, John 17
Turner, L. L. 61
Turner, Marion H. 61
Turner, Martha 47
Turner, Rufus W. 61,77
Turner, T. M. 61
Turner, Thomas 61
Turnham, Thomas 21

Ubanks, Thomas 32
Underwood, Lucinda 17

Vanhook, Berry 112
Vanhook, Carrie 112
Vanhook, Jennie 125
Vanhook, Mary W. 123
Vanhoozer, Amanda 65
Vanhoozer, Ardena 65
Vanhoozer, Arenda 65
Vanhoozer, Delila 65
Vanhoozer, F. 52
Vanhoozer, Gentry L. 65
Vanhoozer, L. J. 52
Vanhoozer, Lambert 39,57
Vanhoozer, Lavinia 65
Vanhoozer, Mary A. 57
Vanhoozer, Nancy E. 52
Vanhoozer, Rutherford G. 65
Vanhoozer, Valentine 65
Vanhoozer, William R. 65
Vant, Elijah 86
Vantrease, Catherine 59
Vantrease, Elizabeth A. 65
Vantrease, Ezekiel 59
Vantrease, J. J. 65
Vantrease, Jackson 59
Vantrease, Jacob 59
Vantrease, John 59
Vantrease, Nicholas 59,66
Vantrease, William 41,59
Vaughan, Abraham 27
Vaughan, Anna H. 65
Vaughan, Edward D. 65
Vaughan, H. L. 65
Vaughan, Hundley L. 89
Vaughan, James 75
Vaughan, James T. 65
Vaughan, John D. 65
Vaughan, M. L. 65
Vaughan, Mary W. 65
Vaughan, Sarah A. 65
Vaughan, Talleyrand L. 65
Vaughan, William W. 65
Vaughter, David R. 116
Vick, A. W. 80
Vick, Alex W. 71
Vick, Alexander 47
Visey, John 52
Visey, Martha 52
Visey, Richard R. 52
Visey, Sargant P. 52
Visey, Valnius L. 52
Visey, Virginia A. 52
Visey, William H. 52
Vivrett, E. B. 57
Vivrett, Indiana 57
Vivrett, J. B. 39,42
Vivrett, J. D. 53,54
Vivrett, John B. 5,119
Vivrett, Larry 9
Vivrett, Micajah 46
Vivrett, P. H. 46,117
Vivrett, Thomas 45,53

Vivrett, William B. 5
Vowell, James 27

Wade, Martha A. 71
Wade, William H. 71
Walker, Alfred 8
Walker, Delianna 54
Walker, Dug 79
Walker, Elizabeth J. 34
Walker, H. L. 98
Walker, J. W. 81
Walker, John 38
Walker, Marcus 80
Walker, P. 117
Walker, Pierce 34
Walker, Solomon 25
Walker, Syllava 62
Wallace, Catherine E. 69
Wallace, Ceary 118
Wallace, G. W. 118
Wallace, James 57
Wallace, James F. 57,70
Wallace, Louiza 57
Walsh, Brunette R. 64
Walsh, M. L. 64
Wammack, Elijah 39
Wammack, Frances P. 17
Wammack, L. D. 39
Wammack, Martha 17
Wammack, Richard 3
Ward, Fountainella 59
Ward, James 33
Ward, John W. 119
Warmack, Hester J. 19
Warner, E. E. 116
Warner, L. 116
Warren, Ann 11
Warren, B. G. 48,121
Warren, Benjamin 49
Warren, Booth 25
Warren, C. B. 121
Warren, Elisha E. 119
Warren, Emma J. 103,104
Warren, H. 101
Warren, Lindley 11
Warren, T. B. 104
Warren, W. G. 49
Warren, William G. 104
Warren, William L. 85
Washington, Gilbert G. 3
Waters, Captain 124
Waters, Edgar 77
Waters, George 108
Waters, James 73
Waters, Sarah 51
Waters, W. L. 53,108
Watkins, Jane H. 101
Watkins, Mary S. 101
Watkins, Moses 101
Watkins, Nancy 73
Watkins, Robert S. 101
Watkins, Thomas 73
Watson, Edward K. 120
Watson, Isham L. 120
Watson, Rufus L. 7,120
Watson, W. T. 106
Watson, William 83
Weatherly, Diretha A. 20
Webb, Mary P. 68
Webb, Micha 9
Webb, Ross 85
Webster, William 89
West, Elizabeth 8
Wharton, Betty 40
Wharton, Caroline C. 40
Wharton, Joseph 79
Wharton, Joseph P. 40
Wharton, Lea 51
Wharton, Mary 40
Wharton, Robert H. 40
Wheeler, George F. 88
Whitaker, Mark 86

White, Edward A. 88,90
White, Frank L. 67
White, George 88
White, J. B. 38
White, James D. 67,123
White, James W. 42
White, Jennie B. 67
White, John 84
White, John L. 26
White, John W. 42
White, Lorenzo 67
White, Lucy S. 68
White, Mary A. 43
White, Nellie R. 67
White, Sallie 84
White, Sue S. 67
White, Susan 42
Whitehead, Annie J. 66
Whitehead, Marion 66
Whitescarver, R. M. 59
Whitesides, F. 76
Whitesides, W. W. 113
Whitlock, A. B. 51,121
Whitlock, D. F. 115
Whitlock, Isaac D. 115
Whitlock, John 121
Whitlock, Martha J. 46
Whitlock, Robert F. 42
Whitlock, Stanhope 51
Whitlock, T. W. 46
Whitlock, Thomas K. 42
Whitsett, D. A. 62
Whitsett, John B. 62
Whitsett, M. R. 62
Whitsett, William H. 62
Whitson, Will 107
Wier, David 32
Wier, Delafayette 32
Wier, Dudley 32
Wier, George 32
Wier, Greenberry 32
Wier, James 32
Wier, John 29,32
Wier, Loving 32
Wier, Robert 28,32
Wier, Sally 32
Wier, Thomas 32
Wilburn, W. P. 99
Wilburn, Wommack 99
Wiley, David L. 56
Wilkerson, William 32
Wilkinson, J. F. 45
Willard, Beverly 17
Willard, James 21
Williams, A. L. 61
Williams, A. P. 109
Williams, Amanda 51
Williams, Aquilla 51
Williams, Benjamin 53
Williams, Columbus 20
Williams, Dovie 111
Williams, Elijah 5,53
Williams, Elisha 53
Williams, Francina 66
Williams, George 58
Williams, Howel J. 35
Williams, Howell W. 61
Williams, Hyram 53
Williams, Isabella 53
Williams, J. H. 42
Williams, Jeremiah 5
Williams, John 53
Williams, John W. 53
Williams, Jonathan 118
Williams, M. H. 61
Williams, Margaret A. 35
Williams, Mary 64
Williams, Mary F. 53
Williams, N. P. 117
Williams, Nancy 102
Williams, Nathan 29
Williams, Polly 27
Williams, R. N. 61
Williams, Rebecca 39

Williams, Robert 5
Williams, Sarah 53,61
Williams, Sidney 61
Williams, T. J. 116
Williams, Thomas 115
Williams, W. W. 61
Williams, William 84,114
Williams, William J. 53
Williamson, Chaney 80
Williamson, George 61
Williamson, Hiram 80
Williamson, James 85
Williamson, John 12
Williamson, John M. 61
Williamson, Martha 11,40
Williamson, P. G. 89
Williamson, P. K. 61
Williamson, Perlina A. 34
Williamson, Richard 80
Williamson, Sarah 11
Williamson, Sarah A. 61
Williamson, T. E. 61
Williamson, Thomas 34
Williamson, Thomas E. 56
Williamson, William 11,61
Willis, Jane 64
Willis, Thomas 82
Wilson, Allen 120
Wilson, E. 82
Wilson, Frederick 1
Wilson, James 1
Wilson, Joseph 1
Wilson, Joseph L. 27,30
Wilson, Martha 1
Wilson, S. F. 109
Wilson, Victoria 79,82
Wilson, W. E. 79
Wilson, Wash 79
Wilson, William 98
Winchester, James 89
Winford, B. W. 63,77
Winham, Matilda 22
Winston, Anthony 28
Winston, Caesar 80
Winston, Isaac 84
Winston, John J. 90
Winston, William 28
Winter, J. J. 115
Winters, Andrew J. 65
Winters, Julia A. 94
Wiseman, Sallie 78
Wiseman, Sarah 71
Witt, Margaret E. 75
Womack, E. R. 89
Womack, J. S. 80
Womack, J. S. 80
Womack, M. L. 89
Wood, Albert 89
Wood, Elizabeth 40
Wood, F. P. 49
Wood, Flemming P. 49
Wood, J. F. 51
Wood, James S. 51
Wood, Mary 49
Wood, Moses 51
Wood, R. F. 92
Wood, Reuben 91,93,95
Wood, Reuben M. 93
Wood, Tabitha 52
Wood, William 92
Woodal, George 25
Woodal, Henry 25
Woodall, Samuel 25
Woodliff, Whitehead 8
Woodrum, W. L. 92
Woodrum, William 93
Woodrum, William S. 75
Woods, Mary 65
Woodward, Hezekiah 88
Woolard, A. 115
Woolard, Pauline 109
Woolard, Z. J. 115
Woolen, Joshua 81
Woolen, Leven 81

Woollard, A. B. 109
Woollard, Alfred 7
Woollard, Allison 5
Woollard, W. G. 109
Word, Julia 70
Word, Mary 44
Word, Tabitha 44
Wortham, William 28
Wray, Edney 49
Wray, Jack 49
Wray, Simpson 27
Wray, William 27
Wright, Alexander 37
Wright, Benjamin 56
Wright, E. M. 89
Wright, Elizabeth 75
Wright, Fanny 56
Wright, Hollis 88
Wright, J. P. 55
Wright, James P. 70,75
Wright, James W. 37
Wright, John 30,31,48
Wright, Josephine 75
Wright, Josiah 59
Wright, Lemuel 59
Wright, Littleberry 75
Wright, Mary 51,59
Wright, Nancy A. 59
Wright, Rebecca 55,56
Wright, Rebecca A. 75
Wright, Samuel M. 59
Wright, Sarah J. 15,59
Wright, W. B. 38
Wynn, Joseph B. 7
Wynne, J. B. 86
Wynne, J. K. 74
Wynne, James A. 74

Yandel, James Sr. 95,96
Yandel, William 95,96
Yandell, William 114
Young, A. S. 37
Young, Abe 80
Young, Alexander 83
Young, Ann 58
Young, Benjamin 119
Young, Betsy 58
Young, Charly 102
Young, Cora 103
Young, David 47,62,83,103
Young, Doak 80
Young, Doke 68
Young, Eli 104
Young, Elizabeth 70
Young, Hannah 54
Young, James 68
Young, Joseph D., Sr. 66
Young, Joseph, Jr. 39
Young, Louis 80
Young, Margaret B. 73
Young, Marshall 106
Young, Mary A. 101
Young, R. L. 89
Young, Sallie 68
Young, Stacy 57
Young, T. L. 103
Young, Thomas 101
Young, William 21,47,54
Youree, Patrick 33

Zachary, R. B. 56
Zackery, Isabella J. 41
Zackery, J. A. 41
Zackery, Lavina 41
Zackery, R. B. 41

www.ingramcontent.com/pod-product-compliance
Lightning Source LLC
Chambersburg PA
CBHW021831020426
42334CB00014B/581